CITY UNDER SIEGE

CITY UNDER SIEGE

Richmond in the Civil War

Mike Wright

Cooper Square Press

First Cooper Square Edition 2002 **03-04**
03-04BT12.23

This Cooper Square Press paperback edition of *City under Siege* is an unabridged republication of the edition first published in Lanham, Maryland in 1995, with the addition of nineteen textual emendations. It is reprinted by arrangement with the author.

Published by Cooper Square Press
A Member of the Rowman & Littlefield Publishing Group
150 Fifth Avenue, Suite 817
New York, New York 10011
www.coopersquarepress.com

Distributed by National Book Network

Library of Congress Cataloging-in-Publication Data Available.

ISBN: 0-8154-1220-7 (pbk.: alk. paper)

♾™ The paper used in this publication meets the minimum requirements of American National Standard for Information Sciences—Permanence of Paper for Printed Library Materials, ANSI/NISO Z39.48–1992.
Manufactured in the United States of America.

For Lin

It was the garden of the golden apples,
A long garden between a railway and a road,
In the sow's rooting where the hen scratches
We dipped our hands into the pockets of
  God.

Patrick Kavanagh, "The Long Garden,"
from *Tarry Flynn*

Because I love the South, I rejoice in the failure of the Confederacy. Conceive of this Union divided into two separate and independent sovereignties! [Still] I recognize and pay loving tribute to the virtues of the leaders of the secession. . .and to the immortal courage of the soldiers of the Confederacy.

Woodrow Wilson while a law student
at the University of Virginia in 1880

Contents

Acknowledgments

I am greatly indebted to many people for their help in the preparation of this narrative. Friends and relatives read much of the text and offered criticism and corrections. Any errors are mine. Marc and Mary Ann Wright took time from wedding plans and college graduation to aid in my research. Chris Wright, a self-proclaimed redneck whose biggest regret is that he was born in the North, is encouragement enough to anyone to write about the South. As good, hospitable Southerners and friends, Butch and Susie Cook opened their Richmond home to me several times during my research. In fact, much of this narrative was written while sitting on a chair they gave me. In addition to being good friends, Susie is a great cook (pun intended).

To various librarians around the country, I give my thanks. Many, including Joanna Wright, formerly of the Wheeling, Illinois library, went out of their way to find microfilm copies of newspapers from Richmond under siege. Employees at the Virginia Historical Society, the Virginia State Library, the Valentine Museum, and the Museum of the Confederacy, all in Richmond, were generous in their time and efforts. The Chicago Historical Society staff helped me find what's left of Libby Prison; I thank you. Special thanks to Corrine Hudgins of the Museum of the Confederacy.

Parts of this book appeared earlier, edited as narration in "The Great Campaigns of the Civil War," produced by Questar Video of Chicago; my thanks to Questar's Albert Nader for his enthusiasm and support. Portions also appeared in *greatly different form in America's Civil War*.

And, above all, I thank that group that has honored me with companionship for more than three decades, beginning in the dark ages of high school and continuing through colleges and families and careers. Among the things I appreciate most are your friendship, encouragement, and support: to the Virginians at Duck!

Introduction

The Civil War was an ordeal for the American people—a challenge for the North, a disaster for the South. And for Richmond, Virginia, the Civil War was a turning point in its life as a city. Richmond was the capital of the Confederacy for nearly four years. For most of that time it was ringed by enemy troops, its people were held hostage, its world hung by the threads of railroad lines. For nearly four years, Richmond was a city under siege.

Three million Americans fought in the Civil War, as most people call it, or as others name it, the War Between the States, the War of Secession, the War for Southern Independence, even The Late Unpleasantness. The author's grandmother referred to it simply as "The War." In 1894, when the U.S. Government began publishing the massive *Official Records of the Union and Confederate Armies*, the name given the conflict was "War of the Rebellion." Calling it The Civil War is so simple it seems incorrect; it was a most uncivil, Civil War.

More than 600,000 died, many through disease and infection. Hundreds of thousands more were wounded. When the sounds of cannon and musket died out, left behind were the echoes of peg legs and crutches, limping across the land.

No matter on which side he served, the average soldier was five feet, eight-and-a-half inches tall, weighed 143 pounds, and was twenty-five years old; most enlisted at eighteen. Many were younger, as young as nine. It has been estimated that more than 100,000 Union soldiers were younger than fifteen. About 40 percent of Union Army soldiers were twenty-one years old or younger. As usual, the Civil War was a young man's war, gullible youth sent to battle by angry old men.

The soldiers' chances of dying in combat were one in sixty-five, one in ten of being wounded, and of dying of disease, one in thirteen.

Though this book is primarily about Richmond, we will make occasional forays into battles with which Richmonders and other Virginians were involved—Antietam and Gettysburg, for example—and with what we'll refer to as the War In the West—Chickamauga and Atlanta among them. But Richmond was the center of the Confederacy, and life there depended on the war, both east and west.

L. P. Hartley, in *The Go-Between*, wrote, "The past is a foreign country; they do things differently there." But did those who lived in Richmond under siege live in a different land? Are they just like us, nearly a century-and-a-half later, fighting and struggling for life?

These are their words, their thoughts. These are their diaries, their memories, and letters. This book is life as they saw it.

1

Prologue of Spring

Virginia winters mean cold rains and sleet-covered streets, morning snow and afternoon sludge. Summers are sweaty hot with not nearly enough breeze. There is no fall; the weather goes from September to winter. Spring is the time for life in Richmond—flowers and budding trees, sparkling skies and warm breezes. Still, it can fool you; spring in Richmond can be sunny one moment, gray the next. The wind never quite decides whether to set trees gently waving or to rattle windows with ice and rain, whether to cover the ground with dogwood petals or with snowflakes. There is a wonder to Richmond in spring, a smell of flower stalls and old bricks, of growth and maturity. It's in the air as it comes off the James River. If winter was harsh, in spring the James roars past you, under bridges and over rapids, often flooding streets and shops. Spring can also bring drought, letting young children hop from rock to rock as the river trickles its way to the Atlantic Ocean.

3

Spring gives Richmond folks time to talk and reflect, no longer shuddering in the damp cold of winter, not yet sweltering in the steamy heat of summer. Spring is gentle to Richmond. It's a dreaming season, a time to remember. Richmonders do that a lot, you know—dream and remember.

Walk Monument Avenue and see Lee and Jackson and Stuart ride again to the bugles' call. Often Richmonders dream back to those riders' own times, times when their city was the capital of a new nation and the most sought-after bit of land in the world.

Often these days you see posters and T-shirts and postcards: Forget, Hell! And you wonder if this means Richmonders won't forget their lost cause. Or "Please forget the hell in which Richmond existed for four years in the mid-nineteenth century."

* * *

This spring of 1861 is the last gentle season the city will know for a while. The ladies are still dressed in dark winter woolens but walk about without heavy coats; the wise among them carry shawls in case the weather suddenly changes, for they know it will do just that, change at a moment's notice. Men step cautiously over the Fan District's cobblestones, wary on these cold mornings of ice- and mud-filled crevices, always ready to jump out of the way of teamsters hurrying by with wagonloads of tobacco, or riders carrying messages to the state secession convention now meeting not far away.

Flowers push through their mulch of pine leaves, long leaf pines, carpets of pines, sweet pungent pines. Pines that will provide cool shade in the too-soon summer or, when cut and burned, fiery heat in the winter that's long off, pines that will give pitch for tar and boards for homes and furniture. Pines that most certainly will provide material for coffins in the coming war—so many coffins that Richmond will almost run out of pines. So many coffins that morticians won't be able to keep up with the demand.

At the Tredegar Iron Works, slaves at hire and whites at wages work side by side to turn out steel for Virginia's railroads, pots for North Carolina's cooks, and filigree material for Georgia's blacksmiths. And also iron for cannon and steel for rifles and bayonets. Tredegar is the main source of cannon for the Southern armies—more than 1,100 cannon over the course of the war, plus mines, torpedoes, and other war machinery. All of this will influence the choice of Richmond as the Confederate Capital.

Everywhere, from Shockoe Slip to Capitol Hill, crowds of people gather in small groups to share beguiling truths and dreadful rumors about the governments. Governments, plural, for Richmond is a city between two countries—one that its past generations had helped found, another its present generation wants to put in place.

And war, everywhere is talk of war. If war is to come, its people know Richmond will be right in the middle of it.

Robert E. Lee hasn't yet made up his mind whether to join any Confederate army that might include Virginia, but he has already decided not to remain in the U.S. army if Virginia secedes:

> Secession is nothing but revolution. . . . Still, a union that can be maintained by swords and bayonets, and in which strife and civil war are to take the place of brotherly love and kindness, has no charm for me. If the Union is dissolved, the government disrupted, I shall return to my native state and share the miseries of my people. Save in her defense, I will draw my sword no more.[1]

Now it is spring, nearly three months since the Charleston *Mercury*'s headline, "The Union Is Dissolved." All 169 members of the South Carolina legislature approved the ordinance dissolving "the union now subsisting between South Carolina and other States."[2] Following were Mississippi, Florida, Alabama, Georgia, Louisiana, and Texas. Just last month, on February 4th, delegates from those seven states met in Montgomery, Alabama, and organized the Confederacy. There isn't much difference between the constitution of the new nation they hope to form and that of the old nation they hope to leave. But it is a states rights' constitution that allows slavery and limits the powers of the president.[3] Each state will "act in its sovereign and independent character," the new Confederate States Constitution declares.

"The man and the hour have met!" William L. Yancy proclaimed in introducing the new nation's new president on February 16. And Jefferson Davis accepted the call. Davis had hoped to receive a commission in the Confederate army, but the Confederate Congress voted him to a higher office:

> The time for compromise has now passed. . . . The South is determined to maintain her position, and make all who oppose her smell Southern powder and feel Southern steel.[4]

The band then plays "Dixie," a minstrel song written by a Northerner (some say by two northern blacks). The only thing that is left is for Virginia to join in.

So March drifts in with petal-soft winds, and spring comes to Richmond, and whispers grow to shouts. The Mother of States is abandoning her Northern children—a convention to outline that abandonment is meeting here now in Richmond. The official convention is secret, meeting behind closed doors. But a Spontaneous People's Convention meets openly at

Metropolitan Hall, a doorkeeper carrying a drawn sword to keep order. There isn't any disorder but a lot of oratory. Leading off is a grandson of Patrick Henry, followed by a grandson of Thomas Jefferson. Overnight, someone replaces the American flag flying over the capitol with the Bonnie Blue flag of the Confederacy. Virginia Governor "Honest John" (named so during his tenure as a U.S. Congressman) Letcher still sees the state as being part of the United States and orders the Bonnie Blue flag of the Confederacy replaced by the blue flag of Virginia.

Debate continues in the convention.

First, however, a thorn in the Confederacy's side must be removed: Fort Sumter. Six days after South Carolina voted to leave the union, Union army Major Robert Anderson quietly, secretly, transferred his command from Fort Moultrie to Fort Sumter. Instantly, he became the North's hero, the "one true man" in the United States, wrote Leverett Saltonstall of Boston.[5] The question then became what to do about the thorn? One thing both sides knew, the fort could not last long without reinforcements, both men and material.

President James Buchanan knew this and approved a plan. On January 9, 1861, the *Star of the West* arrived at Charleston harbor, loaded with supplies for Fort Sumter. Shore batteries lined her up in their sights, and shots were fired. The *Star*'s captain decided in favor of discretion and against valor. He turned and sailed away. Then followed moments of agreement and weeks of stalemate.

Richmonders grab newspapers off presses and read with concern the accounts of Fort Sumter and Major Anderson. They know their summer will depend on Charleston's spring. Virginia still wavers on the side of the Union. It will take a show of arms for the Old Dominion to join the new Confederacy. The curtain on that show is about to be raised.

So convention delegates meet now to decide, not whether, but when Virginia will leave. Robert Young Conrad of Winchester writes his family:

> Feby 27th
> We are yet engaged in what now seems an endless de-
> bate upon the comee [committee]. . . . Although we
> have been here only two weeks, the charges are so
> enormous, that I had this morning a hotel bill of $70
> and $80. . . .
> The convention is going on with equal pace. . . .[W]e,
> with locked doors, are debating closely, word by word,
> our resolutions. . . .[6]

> March 2nd 1861
> What work we have done is not yet apparent nor will
> it be until the comee [committee] shall report.[7]

> Mar 13th 61
> In Convention today, ex pres. Tyler made a very
> spirited commencement of his reply to [President
> Abraham] Lincoln's two-day speech. The old man's
> strength however gave out and left him. . .and we
> adjourned. . . .
> We are now trying to agree upon proposed constitu-
> tional amendments—other subjects yet untouched I
> see no chance of beholding the Blue Ridge for more
> than a fortnight yet. We hear that the northern people
> will give anything we ask. . . . But Lincoln & his crew
> have his way. . . .
> Your letters are a great comfort from home.[8]

The Confederacy agrees not to attack Fort Sumter so long as the Union doesn't try to reinforce it. But time is running out and so are Major Anderson's supplies. He wires Washington that he has enough to last only until mid-April.

Monday, March 4: James Buchanan leaves office and Abraham Lincoln take over. Buchanan leaves to his successor the question of what to do about Major Anderson and Fort Sumter, and Lincoln acts rapidly. Two days after his inauguration, President Lincoln sends South Carolina Governor Francis Pickens a message:

> [A]n attempt will be made to supply Fort Sumter with provisions only. . . . [If the attempt] be not resisted, no effort to throw men, arms, or ammunition will be made, without further notice [except] in case of an attack on the Fort.[9]

The message isn't entirely truthful. While the warning is being issued, another plan is being readied. Supply ships, protected by Union warships under the command of Gustavus V. Fox, will sail to the bar at Charleston harbor, transfer men and supplies to smaller boats, and head for Fort Sumter in the dark.

From the Richmond secession convention, Robert Young Conrad gave his version of the Fort Sumter situation:

> Mr. Lincoln has not only compelled Anderson to defend Sumpter [sic] and thrown strong reinforcements into Fort Pickins [sic], but he has (in reply to our committee, which has just returned) developed a determined polity which, if backed by the northern people, must, in time bring on a ruinous war.[10]

Jefferson Davis has his own plan for Fort Sumter: attack the fort before the Union navy can reinforce it. Shortly before dawn on April 12th, cadets from The Citadel, South Carolina's military academy, fire on Fort Sumter. Pierre Gustave Toutant Beauregard, the son of a wealthy Creole planter, is in charge of the bombardment. He studied artillery at West Point. His teacher was Major Robert Anderson, and at Fort Sumter,

Beauregard showed his former teacher just how much he had learned.

It is five days later now, and months of bickering, late nights and long speeches come to an end here in Richmond. "The convention has passed an 'ordinance of secession,'" Robert Young Conrad writes:

> The shouts in the street now reach our ears, even up here, and we shall have the wildest rejoicing here during the rest of this day and night.[11]

The rejoicing continues for several days. Conrad may not be alone in his opposition to secession, but he appears to be in the minority, at least right after the deed was done:

> Last night we had a grand illumination of this city with a long and brilliant procession. . .through the streets, in honor of the secession of Virginia. I walked the streets [and] heard one man say "it would be more appropriate if they were rejoicing for peace instead of war"—the only echo I heard of my own feelings—everybody else appearing in high glee.[12]

Conrad is tired (the convention debated the issue for several months), disappointed (he is uncertain of secession), and lonely: "Will some one of you write to me every day until I get back?"[13]

Others will grow equally tired, disappointed, and lonely; it is the way of war. A war to determine, as Abraham Lincoln will later put it, "whether that nation, or any nation so conceived, can long endure" finally is under way. Virginia has left the Union it had helped found.

2

Revolution or Rebellion?

For years, it was clear to many on both sides of a nonexistent border that Richmond and the South were different from, say, New York and the North. "We are not one people," the New York *Tribune* declared in 1855:

> We are two peoples. We are a people of Freedom and a people of Slavery. Between the two, conflict is inevitable.[1]

And so, "The Southern Marseillaise" became a favorite Richmond tune:

> Sons of the South, awake to glory!
> Hark! hark! what myriads bid you rise.
> Your children, wives and grandsires hoary,
> Beyond their tears and hear their cries.

11

It ended:

> To arms! to arms! ye brave
> Th' avenging sword unsheathe!

"The secession of a state is an act of revolution," declared Senator Alfred Iverson of Georgia.[2]

Many others agreed. Jefferson Davis, however, was not among them; he didn't like the term "revolution," as applied to secession. The South left the Union, he said, "to *save* ourselves from revolution."[3]

Revolution or rebellion, the emotion wasn't new to Richmond. After all, Virginia and Richmond were leaders in the fight to free America from Great Britain and form a new government.

Once gained, that freedom from Britain wasn't taken lightly, and union was held sacred. The year was 1812; the cause was New England's condemnation of what was then known as "Mr. Madison's War":

> No man, no association of men, no state or set of states *has a right to withdraw itself* from the Union of its own accord. [Only] the same power which knit us together, can. . .unknit. . .this illustrious Union, . . . [It] has been cemented by the blood of our fore-fathers. [T]he pride of America and the wonder of the world must not be tamely sacrificed to the heated brains or the aspiring hearts of a few malcontents. The Union must be saved.[4]

It was another time, another era, another war—forty-seven years earlier. The writer, Thomas Ritchie, editor of the Richmond *Enquirer*, referred to delegates to the 1812 Hartford Convention who wished, he wrote, "to dash to pieces the holy ark of the Union of our country." Times changed, causes changed.

* * *

Then, as now, Richmonders gloried in their past. Their city was an outpost of the Jamestown colony in the 1600s, had been Virginia's capital since 1779, and for years was the largest city in the largest state in the United States. The Jefferson-designed, classically inspired, columned capitol stands proudly on one of Richmond's seven hills. Sunday churchgoers at St. John's sit in pews that still echo Patrick Henry's cry for liberty or death. Not far away is Varina, where John Rolfe and Pocahontas lived and loved.

South, along the James River, are the "College Lands," site of the first chartered college in the United States, predecessor to the College of William and Mary—building halted, instruction forgotten in the massacre of 1622. Farther south stand plantation homes of Virginia's early gentry: Shirley, with its own king—"King" Carter; Westover, home to generations of Byrds; Berkeley, birthplace of a signer of the Declaration of Independence, a president of the United States, the first thanksgiving, and bourbon whiskey—plantations that were summer homes to many who served in Virginia's General Assembly in Richmond.

It is a city with a proud past and an equally proud present. The decade before the American Civil War was one of tremendous growth in Richmond. Its population jumped nearly 48 percent, from 27,000 to 39,910, according to the U.S. census of 1860. And commerce was growing. For example, Richmond was the nation's leading port of entry for South American coffee beans. In turn, large quantities of flour were shipped south. Half of the tobacco grown in Virginia and North Carolina was marketed in Richmond. It was said to be the "wealthiest city of its size in America and perhaps the world."

Coal mines in nearby Chesterfield County boomed in the 1860s; workers were brought in from all over the world—Scotland, Ireland, Wales. New forms of transportation were needed to carry the coal. Mulepower along the James River and the Kanawha Canal was giving way to the power of iron horses. The Richmond, Fredericksburg & Potomac Railroad headed northward, and by 1836, the first twenty miles had been completed. There was no stopping this new mode of travel and transportation, but Richmond and the South in general were far behind the North in railroads. Having more cities built along navigable rivers than did the North, the South depended more on ships and less on trains. Still, tracks were being laid, and rail lines were being built rapidly.

There were forecasts of unprecedented growth in the city, and Richmond's economy was expected to shoot upwards. Instead, shots of another, much deadlier, variety became a reality.

Richmond obviously was prosperous on the eve of the Civil War, but just as obviously it had problems. It was a city on the brink, but whether the brink of greatness or of distress, was uncertain.

Like many other Southern cities in 1861, Richmond was concerned about its black population. Most blacks were slaves; it was still debated whether free blacks should even be allowed to remain in the state. The majority of Southern whites, however, did not own, and never had owned, slaves; by one estimate, only 37 percent of Southerners held slaves. Many who did debated whether to free them. Always they waffled, always they fell back on the myth of cost. There's the financial consideration, they told themselves, and put off any final decision on the issue. Even some blacks who owned slaves (instances in New Orleans come to mind) hesitated over abolition.

The question also worried some visitors. Charles Dickens visited Richmond in the 1840s. He stayed at the Exchange Hotel and was feted grandly. Richmond was proud of its guest, and if one were to judge only from his initial response, Dickens enjoyed his stay there. When he returned to England, however, Dickens wrote a blistering attack of the city. He was revolted by the institution of slavery; he noted "gloom and dejection" in the city and an air of "ruin and decay," an air of darkness "not of skin but of mind, which meets the stranger's eyes at every turn."

Richmond lacked many things in common with most other major cities. It had no public schools in the modern sense; its white students were sent to other cities, even to other countries, for education. Richmond's black residents were largely illiterate. It's estimated that only 80 percent of the South's white population was literate; 95 percent of New England's white adult population could read and write.[5] Despite its proximity to the nation's first attempt at higher education, the nearest colleges were down river in Williamsburg or over the mountains in Charlottesville.

* * *

On May 29, 1861, Virginia Governor John Letcher welcomed to the city the Honorable Jefferson Davis, President and Commander-in-Chief of the Confederate States of America. "The National Ruler [has come to] the Metropolis," Letcher claimed.

Davis wasn't the only new resident of Richmond. His arrival was preceded by that of 3,000 Confederate troops stationed in and around the city. In modern terms, that would be as if we suddenly added twenty thousand people to Richmond's current population. The relatively small but bustling town was no more, and the past would return only as memory.

Howell Cobb, the first president of the Confederate Congress, had told an Atlanta audience why the capital must be moved to Richmond:

> Her soil will, perhaps, be the battle ground of this struggle. Her enemies are gathered around her to force her into subjection to their foul dictates. We felt it was [Richmond's] duty to be the seat of war. We wanted to let Virginia know that whatever threats or dangers were presented to her, filled our hearts with sympathy for her, which we are willing to exhibit, to show that there was not a man in the Confederacy who was afraid to be at his post in Virginia.[6]

One month before Cobb's prediction, former author and newspaper editor-turned-civil-servant John Beauchamp Jones began a diary he was to keep during Richmond's four-year siege. Jones had been a successful writer, an early-day Louis L'Amour or Zane Grey, writing tales of the old West. He approved of slavery yet opposed secession. Himself a native of Baltimore, Jones turned to his wife's South during the war. He wrote in his diary a very strange passage. It's part dream, part imagination, and was perhaps written in fear:

> We have a flaming comet in the sky. It comes unannounced, and takes a northwestern course. I saw a great black ball moving in the heavens, and it obscured the moon. The stars were in motion visibly, and for a time afforded the only light. Then a brilliant halo illuminated the zenith like the quick-shooting irradiations of the aurora borealis. And men ran in

different directions, uttering cries of agony. As I gazed
upon the fading and dissolving moon, I thought of the
war brought upon us, and the end of the United
States government.[7]

It is perhaps too easy to read this as Jones's subconscious pre-
cognition (or conscious post-cognition, since he edited his diary
after the war) of a South that would rise, shine brightly, and
then fall, with men running "in different directions, uttering
cries of agony." Too easy, perhaps, but perhaps not unjustified.

3

Every House a House of Mourning

A little more than a month after Virginia seceded from the United States of America, the Congress of the Confederate States of America met in Richmond. It was May 21, 1861, and Richmond became the capital of its own world: the Confederacy.[1] The city immediately began to change, altering just as drastically the lives of those who called Richmond home. "The changes wrought in the appearance of Richmond," one of those residents wrote, "can only be understood by those who daily witnessed the stirring scenes which were occurring."[2] Sallie A. Brock Putnam was a lifelong resident of Richmond, a teenager at war's beginning. Her memoirs, originally ascribed to "A Richmond Lady," were published in 1867. She added to her description of the changes, "One excitement had not had time to subside before a fresh cause presented itself." Sometimes, it

18

might be imagined, Richmonders wished that excitement *would* subside.

The U.S. government and the Northern press were preoccupied with an "on-to-Richmond" attitude that threatened the Union war effort by tying up troops needed elsewhere.[3] The attitude also emotionally and physically affected Richmond. Life grew more difficult as prices rose, food shortages became frequent, and the city grew more crowded almost daily.

Almost before they knew it, Richmonders were under siege, and it didn't take long to feel the effects of war. "In a few months," Mrs. Putnam wrote, "the usual routine of social life in Richmond had undergone a complete change." While men rushed off to war (or at least rushed off to join the military—that's sometimes very different), women of the city were busy with the "scraping and carding of lint, the rolling of bandages, and the manufacture of cartridges and many other things unnecessary to mention." Soon, she added, it was "a very rare occurrence to meet a young man of the usual age for military duty in the garb of a civilian."[4]

July 1861, and Richmond was the staging point from which the Confederate army sent out troops to stop Virginia's enemy. Most troops headed north to lines and soon to battles, as Union forces moved in an attempt to take Richmond. Already, the Confederacy had joined the Union in determining that Richmond's defenses would be a decisive point in deciding whether the new nation would survive.

As the Southern states withdrew from the Republic to form the Confederacy, the U.S. military found itself in a peculiar position. Many Southerners were wearing Yankee blue uniforms. Then, as now, a large part of the officer's corps of the U.S. army and navy was from the South, and when war came, many of those same officers went with the land of their birth. Both Jefferson Davis and Robert E. Lee graduated from the military academy at West Point and served in the Union

army. Later, Davis was a U.S. senator and served as secretary
of war under President Franklin Pierce. Lee had been superintendent at West Point, led U.S. troops in the Mexican War and
against John Brown at Harpers Ferry. His last U.S. army post
was Fort Mason, Texas. He was Colonel Lee then, fifty-three
years old, and in command of the 2nd U.S. Cavalry. In late
January 1861, he wrote his wife:

> As far as I can judge by the [news]papers, we are
> between a state of anarchy and civil war. May God
> avert from us both. . . . I fear that mankind will not
> for years be sufficiently Christianized to bear the
> absence of restraint and force. . . . I must try and be
> patient and await the end, for I can do nothing to
> hasten or retard it.[5]

When he quit the U.S. army to join his home state of Virginia,
the federal government confiscated Lee's home, Arlington, and
planted a graveyard—Arlington National Cemetery—in its front
yard to make certain he would never live there again. Long
after Lee's death, the U.S. government compensated his heirs
for seizing Arlington: $150,000.

In April 1861, before his home state seceded, James
Ewell Brown "Jeb" Stuart was a lieutenant in the U.S. army,
serving in Kansas. An old friend and relative, John Esten
Cooke, wrote to Stuart, trying to persuade him to join Virginia
and the South:

> Remain with the Lincoln humbug and political farce
> government, you [cannot]. He's a foreign despotism to
> you and to me. I'll fight against it if the time for
> fighting comes. I, with hundreds more, bound our-
> selves the other day by reaching agreement to resist
> by force of arms that government and the government
> of Virginia too, and stop the Federal guns.[6]

Stuart agreed and resigned his Federal commission a few days later. Cooke became Confederate Major General Stuart's ordnance officer and later wrote about both Stuart and General Lee.

Many Southern military men living in the North joined the Confederacy, but few Northerners living in the South joined the Union in the coming fight. When war grew imminent, the regular army of the United States had only about 16,000 men under arms.[7] Of these, according to prewar estimates published in the Richmond *Dispatch*, more than 13,500 were stationed in forts locked within the Confederacy.[8] As recruiting, and later conscription, went on, Southern farm boys used to shooting to provide food for the table found themselves facing city-bred and immigrant youths who were less likely to be familiar with firearms. The U. S. Sanitary Commission reported that 47 percent of Union soldiers were farmers or farm workers. A separate study showed 61 percent of Confederate soldiers were farmers or planters.

The twenty-three states of the North counted some 22 million people. The South had barely more than 9 million, about 3.5 million of whom were black slaves. It is estimated that the South had only 1.1 million white males between the ages of fifteen and forty, compared to the North's 4 million males eligible for military duty.[9]

Although the numbers of both men and material favored the North, some factors favored the South, even if only temporarily. The North faced the handicap of having to take the war to the South; all the South had to do was bar the door and hold on. Richmond's fighting spirit gave the South an early advantage. After all, the South was defending hearth and home, defending its desires for independence and freedom (white independence, white freedom), and the Confederacy was fighting off the invasion of an unwanted oppressor. It worked for a while; but even so, life in Richmond grew desperate.

For the moment, at least, it was no contest. Richmond is at the head of the navigable waters of the James River, about 110 miles from Washington. Between the two capital cities lies the town of Manassas. It was there that the first important battle of the war occurred: the First Battle of Manassas, Bull Run, as the Yankees called it. It was July 21, 1861. Neither army was well trained, neither corps of officers was used to handling large groups of men. It was a scene of confusion.

The Confederate flags caused confusion. In addition to unit and state colors, the "Bonnie Blue Flag" flew. Troops also carried the Rebel "Stars and Bars." At times it was mistaken for the American flag, sometimes confusing troops of both sides: who was friend, who was foe?

And uniforms. At Manassas there may have been as many differently colored uniforms as there were regiments. The Confederacy really never seemed to settle on one uniform design, but the First Battle of Manassas was ridiculous, given the almost parti-color of the South: gray, blue, "butternut brown," not to mention the Souaves with their blue jackets and red pantaloons. Or the 79th New York, a unit made up of Scottish highlanders; they wore kilted dress uniforms. The 33rd Virginia of General Thomas J. Jackson's Brigade wore blue uniforms. When this group attacked Union artillery that was shelling the Confederate lines, Union forces thought the Southern troops were part of their own infantry that had come to their support, and they held their fire. The Virginians opened fire and wiped out the Union artillery.

What had begun as a picnic for many residents of Washington, D.C., ended in, as it was called, "the great skedaddle" of Union soldiers anxious to get out of the battle.

Dr. Hunter Holmes McGuire was the chief surgeon with the Jackson Brigade at Manassas Junction. On July 24, 1861, he wrote his father, Hugh Holmes McGuire, in Winchester,

Virginia. At the top of his first page is Dr. McGuire's hand-drawn sketch of the troop emplacements in the battle:

I've no doubt you have heard all sorts of reports in regard to our fight last Sunday, and many wrong ones, so I have stolen an hour to let you know something about it. I've made a very poor draft of the position of our men and the enemy and send it, though I know you will understand little of it.

When the battle first commenced, the Georgia, Alabama and some South Carolina troops occupied the position of the 1st Brigade, they were badly cut up but fought well and hard and held the position for two hours, exposed to a heavy fire. Here Col. Burton was killed, while carrying the colours and leading a charge. Here too the 6th Alabama regiment lost nearly half their men and all their officers. At last the Carolinians ran, then Georgia fell back thru the remnants of Alabama. Beauregard rode rapidly along the lines and rallied them, but not until they had nearly reached the Court House road, and the enemy had gotten beyond the pine bushes in full pursuit. Here the Louisiana Regiments charged them with the bayonet and they turned and ran, as they always did afterwards at a charge by men acting under orders.

Ned brought poor [word unreadable] back from the field to me late in the day and as I lifted him from the horse he died. I did not see where he was shot. I only looked to see that he was dead as I was *very very* busy. I have amputated [word unreadable]'s arm, will send him home tomorrow. . . .

Our loss I do not know but suppose it to be about 2500 killed and wounded. Probably 1/3 of these killed. That of the enemy it is impossible to reckon but it was immense somewhere between 5000 and 10,000. The field was covered with the dead men for miles

along the road they were laying. The moon was full
the night of the battle and a more awful sight I have
never witnessed as I went among the dead and wounded of both sides.[10]

Eugene Blackford was a major with the 5th Alabama Voluntary
Infantry at Manassas. He, like Dr. McGuire, wrote his father
with news of the battle:

[T]he field was literally covered with bodies. . . .
For five miles before reaching [the battlefield] I saw
men limping off, more or less wounded. We met
wagon loads of bodies coming off to Manassas, where
they are now piled in heaps.[11]

It was at Manassas that Union troops first heard the Rebel yell,
a wail that must is as much felt as heard; it cannot adequately
be portrayed with words. However, one Northern veteran later
tried his pen at a description:

There is nothing like it on this side of the infernal re-
gion. The peculiar corkscrew sensation that it sends
down your backbone [during battle] can never be told.
You have to feel it.[12]

There is a theory held by some modern anthropologists that the
Civil War was actually another war between England and
Scotland, removed over the Atlantic. The reasoning goes that
many Southerners, then as now, traced their ancestry to
Scottish immigration via, for example, North Carolina's Cape
Fear River. If that is so, then perhaps the Rebel yell can trace
its ancestry to the similar yell screamed by Scots as they ran
into battle against the hated *sassenach*, the English.

McGuire and Blackford were at the battle and saw its blood and gore, but there were others not there who saw only glory.

> The plain, broken and wooded, bounded on all sides, as far as the eye could reach by the azure lines of the Blue Ridge [Mountains], was gay with bright uniforms, the parti-colored flags, the glistening armor of the soldiers.[13]

That was Sallie Putnam, safely in Richmond. Not being in the battle made it easier to think in terms of "gay" uniforms, "parti-colored flags." Thoughts of death came later.

The South had its first victory and its first hero, General Thomas J. "Stonewall" Jackson, West Point class of 1846 and a professor of military tactics at Virginia Military Institute. The South also had its first deaths, including General Bernard E. Bee, who gave Jackson his sobriquet that same day of battle.

* * *

As Richmond soon learned, where soldiers go and where war exists, death and injury reside nearby. On July 29, 1861, J. B. Jones wrote, "To-day quite a number of our wounded men on crutches, and with arms in splints, made their appearance in the streets and created a sensation."[14] Prophetically, he added, "A year hence, and we shall be accustomed to such spectacles."

When news of the Confederate victory reached Richmond, a 100-gun salute was fired from the Virginia state capitol grounds. Crowds gathered, guns were fired, and speeches were delivered.

Sallie Putnam obviously didn't know about the capitol grounds salute. Richmond, she said, took news of the battle calmly—perhaps too calmly for a romantic young girl:

> There were no bonfires kindled, no bells rung, no cannon fired, none of the parades which the event might have been expected to call forth.[15]

Beneath it all, John Jones saw a fervor unmatched by the North: "Never was there such a patriotic *people* as ours."[16]

The people of Richmond had laid "their blood. . .upon the altar of their country with enthusiasm," he added.

Soon, they would lay their wealth on that same altar.

The War in the West

I

Fort Donelson

Six days after the Manassas skedaddle, Lincoln found a new general. He turned to George McClellan, giving the "Young Napoleon" command of the Army of the Potomac. "Little Mac," as he was also called, recruited, trained, and made plans—he was good at that. But mainly, he paraded around Washington's Willard Hotel—something else he did well.

While McClellan paraded, Lincoln worked. He designed the three-point Anaconda Plan (named after a South American snake) to divide and conquer the South: blockade and strangle the east coast, capture Richmond, and take control of the Mississippi River, the river Native American Indians called "the Father of Waters." The war in the west quickly became a war of rivers.

First, the giant Missouri River comes from the new northwest, from North Dakota, through the plains of Nebraska, across Sac and Iowa and Fox Indian Country. From the North, in Minnesota, the Mississippi winds over the land of the Sauk and Sioux, skirts Wisconsin and Illinois and takes mud from the modern towns of Clinton and Moline, gathering with it the waters of the smaller Rock and Illinois Rivers.

The Missouri's flow is east from Kansas City to St. Louis, then the two giants meet. Once joined, they wash the towns of Kaskaskia and Shawneeland and wait for more of the Father's children.

From the east in Pennsylvania comes the sometimes raging Ohio River, falling past towns like Moundsville and Vienna and Newell Run, winding and winding by Aberdeen and Ripley. Touching Cincinnati along the way, and Rising Sun, Louisville, New Boston, Evansville. Together, then, the rivers pick up the flow from the Wabash and charge past Uniontown, Shawneetown, Paducah, and Metropolis. Finally, they join the waiting Mississippi at a town called Cairo.

The Big Muddy is complete now. It unites the nation's northwest and midwest and east. The Father of Waters has gathered in all his children but divides the nation in two.

Downstream, between two other rivers, Lincoln's Anaconda began to twist and turn, ready to strike.

To the new west of Kentucky, Tennessee, and northern Georgia, Lincoln assigned to the garrison at Cairo, Illinois, a little-known, and not particularly well-thought-of, officer named Ulysses S. Grant.

He was thirty-nine when he took command. When he enrolled at West point in 1839, he was just seventeen, stood five-feet-one-inch tall and weighed only 117 pounds. By the time the war between the North and South began, Grant had shot up to five-feet-seven but remained slight. He had blue eyes with light-brown hair and beard, close-cut and short; he was lightly freckled. He was noted for being practical, not neat.

Even the circumstances of his name were messy. He was born *Hiram* Ulysses Grant, but a family friend who saw to his appointment at West Point changed all that. By the time

Congressman Thomas Hamer got around to writing in Grant's name, the young cadet-to-be had come to call himself Ulysses H. Grant (a switch of first and middle names). Democrat Hamer could not remember the "Hiram" but knew he had to give his appointee a middle name, so he added Grant's mother's maiden name, Simpson.[1] Grant found he'd been enrolled that way but, at the time, made no effort to change it. He never got around to correcting the error, and by the time he graduated from West Point, he was firmly and forever Ulysses S. Grant.

So far in his life, Grant hadn't done much except fail. After West Point, he fought well in Mexico. But then he grew depressed and began drinking, and he had to resign his commission. Grant tried farming, and failed at that. He tried selling real estate, and failed at that, too.[2] He once owned a slave but freed the individual, William Jones, preferring not to sell him, although the Grants were desperate for money at the time.

Once, he waited for two days outside General McClellan's office, hoping to get a wartime commission, but McClellan was too busy to see him, so Grant went home.[3] He was there in June of 1861, working at the family harness shop in Galena, Illinois, when that state's governor commissioned him a colonel of volunteers. By August, he had earned a promotion to brigadier general.

Book-writing, academic-minded, bug-eyed Major General Henry Wager Halleck was commander of the Union Army of the Missouri and Grant's commanding officer. His men called him "Old Brains." He grew jealous of Grant.

* * *

The Confederacy controlled the Mississippi River as far north
as Memphis, threatening St. Louis. To aid their attack, the
North built gunboats, flat-bottomed, wide-beamed, and shallow-
draft. Two and a-half inches of iron armor, sloping up like a
casement, protected the gunboats' crews. Such a craft resembled nothing so much as a turtle, so they were nicknamed
"Pook's turtles," after their builder, Samuel Pook. They were
loaded with cannon and mortars.[4]

To strengthen its control of the rivers, the Confederate
army built Forts Henry and Donelson in Tennessee.

In February 1862, nine months after Manassas, Grant
headed south from Cairo with boatloads of troops. Fort Henry
was half submerged by the flooding Tennessee River, so it
didn't take much for the Rebels to abandon it. A quick
bombardment by Federal gunboats, and the Confederate army
scrambled over to the stronger Fort Donelson.

Grant telegraphed General Halleck, announcing his
victory at Fort Henry and promising he'd take Fort Donelson
by February 8.[5] He'd take it, all right, but not by the eighth.

Including Fort Donelson, the Rebels had only 75,000
men stretched from Kentucky to Virginia. That's a lot of land
but not a lot of troops to guard it.

But this widespread army had something else. It had the
South's highest ranking field officer as its commander: Albert
Sydney Johnston. He stood six-feet-one-inch tall and weighed
two-hundred pounds, a dynamic presence. Like many other
Confederate generals, he was a West Point graduate. He was
also something of a politician and for two years he'd been
Secretary of War for the Republic of Texas. He was back in a
Federal uniform when Lincoln offered him a high command,
but Johnston was a personal friend of Jefferson Davis and
declined Lincoln's offer. He left his post in California, dodging
Union patrols and Indian raids along the way to return to his
native Texas and the Confederacy.[6]

After he lost Fort Henry, Johnston made two major mistakes. First, he split his army into two parts, a move that weakened both halves. And, second, he left in command of Fort Donelson the Confederacy's two worst generals, John B. Floyd and Gideon J. Pillow.[7]

Floyd had been secretary of war under President James Buchanan. He quit when Buchanan wouldn't give up Fort Sumter and was afraid that if he were captured wearing a Confederate uniform he'd be hanged for treason. He was also under indictment in Washington, charged with embezzling public funds and shipping army munitions to the Confederacy.[8]

Pillow was opinionated, self-important, inept, and cantankerous. Grant knew him from the war in Mexico and welcomed him as an opponent.[9]

Their third in command was Simon Bolivar Buckner, the best of the three Confederate generals at Fort Donelson. He and Grant had been friends since their days at West Point. And when Grant was broke, Buckner loaned his old friend money.[10]

Friday, February 14 was warm, almost spring-like, and the troops threw aside their blankets. By the next day, they wished they had them back. A sudden winter storm sent temperatures falling to a shivering twelve degrees. That morning, the Confederate commanders made a daring decision: Don't wait for the Union to march on the fort. Attack! It was so unexpected it succeeded. A quick push south, and Federal troops fell back. By noon, the Rebels had an escape route in sight, the road to Nashville.[11]

But Floyd and Pillow stopped fighting and began arguing over tactics. Their decision was the strangest tactic of all; they marched their troops back inside the fort.[12] Grant had been at a council of war on a river boat, and when he returned, he quickly repaired the damages to his lines, slamming shut the Confederates' door to freedom.

Floyd and Pillow sent separate messages to Johnston, each claiming he'd won a great victory, but even they didn't believe it. They were outnumbered, and Grant had them surrounded; so, that night, rather than be taken prisoner (or suffer the onerousness of surrender, they abandoned Fort Donelson and slipped across the Cumberland River. Nathan Bedford Forrest also didn't like the idea of either dying or surrendering, and he took his cavalry troops out of the fort, across an icy creek too deep for the infantry to follow. It was up to Buckner to surrender.

Just after dawn on the 16th Buckner asked Grant for terms. He hoped his old friend would be lenient. But Grant saw a difference between a peacetime friend and a wartime enemy and answered, "no terms except unconditional and immediate surrender." It was a term new to Buckner, but he had a pretty good idea what it meant.

So it was Monday morning, and Buckner was in his headquarters, having a breakfast of corn bread and coffee with another old friend, Union Major General Lewis Wallace. After the war, Wallace would serve on the court-martial of Lincoln's assassins. He would turn deeply religious and become a famous author, mainly for his novel *Ben Hur*.

Grant stormed into the tavern, and he wasn't much for "old times and coffee" until he took care of business. Commandeering Buckner's headquarters, he accepted Buckner's surrender.

Then the two got to gossiping about General Pillow. Grant remembered Pillow from the Mexican war and hadn't been impressed. Buckner said that Pillow had left Fort Donelson during the night, adding, "[H]e thought you'd rather get hold of him than any other man in the Southern Confederacy," but Pillow's reputation was known to Grant:

If I had got him, I'd let him go again. He will do us
more good commanding you fellows.[13]

Both Pillow and Floyd were removed from command without
a court of inquiry.

Grant ordered his friend and benefactor Buckner sent
off as a prisoner of war. First, however, Grant offered him his
purse, in case his old friend needed money. The debt was paid.
The next time Grant and Buckner would meet would be less
than two weeks before Grant's death of throat cancer in 1885.

With Fort Donelson, the North had its first major
victory. It had 12,000 Confederate prisoners on its hands and a
general who knew how to win: "Unconditional Surrender
Grant."

Richmond newspapers put a different (if strange and
self-serving) spin on the Union victory. Losing Forts Henry and
Donelson "were for our own good!" Such days of adversity

> prove the worth of men and nations. . . . We must go
> to the work with greater earnestness than we have yet
> shown.[14]

Temporary Richmond resident Mary Chesnut simply said:

> Fort Donelson has fallen. . . . It is prisoners for them
> that we cannot spare. Or prisoners for us that we may
> not be able to feed.[15]

Three weeks after the defeat at Fort Donelson, the South
suffered another setback when it lost all of Missouri in a battle
fought in neighboring Arkansas, near the town of Pea Ridge.
Former congressman-turned-soldier Brigadier General Samuel
R. Curtis was in command of the Union Army in southwestern
Missouri. He had orders to drive the rebels from the state.
When Curtis marched with fewer than 12,000 men into the

Confederate stronghold of Springfield, the state guard under former Missouri Governor Sterling Price retreated into the Boston Mountains of Arkansas, south of Fayetteville.

General Benjamin McCulloch joined forces with Price. McCulloch had more military experience, but Price was placed under him, a fact that galled Price. Price also hated the horrors of war inflicted on civilians by military troops, realizing, however, that many of these horrors came from his own soldiers. He led troops of Franz Sigel's German regiments,which had a deserved reputation for persistent foraging when they were out of touch with their own supply lines. Curtis wrote his brother that the sight of burned homes and barns was "sickening," adding, "which for the sake of humanity I could pray were effaced from the record of events." The misery left by his solders, Curtis believed, should cause "all. . .forever more earnestly [to] employ Heaven to deliver us from 'war, pestilence, and famine.'"[16]

Into this fracas, Jefferson Davis sent for Major General Earl Van Dorn, and, on March 4th, Van Dorn pushed his 17,000-man force north, toward Curtis. It was one of the few instances in which the Confederates went into a major battle with notably larger numbers. Curtis fell back to Pea Ridge, Arkansas, where he dug in. But Van Dorn chose not to attack Curtis head-on and led his troops on a flanking attack to cut off Union supplies. He would then attack Rebel troops from the rear. But a Northern scout, "Wild Bill" Hickock, detected the move and, when Van Dorn began his attack on the seventh, he found Curtis wasn't surprised but, rather, was sitting and waiting for him.

With Van Dorn were a large contingent of Native Americans from the Five Civilized Nations in Indian Territory. They hoped that, if the South won the war, Native Americans could regain what white settlers had taken from them.

Chief John Ross of the Cherokees had, at first, favored neutrality. But soon he gave in to pro-Confederacy tribesmen, mainly Stand Watie, whose formal name was Degadoga. On his own, Watie raised first a company, then a regiment. Watie was first a colonel, then a general.

At Pea Ridge, his troops distinguished themselves. With guns and tomahawks, they fought alongside the 9th Texas Cavalry. Their bows and arrows panicked Union artillery troops. That was the first day; on the second, it was the rebels' turn to run, and Watie's troops held their position until the last possible moment.[17]

Confederate troops were running short of ammunition, and the Union Army stood between the rebels and their supplies. The two armies concentrated around Elkhorn Tavern.

Seven-thousand Federal troops under German-American Franz Sigel swept forward—an almost textbook charge—and the Confederate defense quickly turned into a rout. Van Dorn's men scattered so fast, so widely, it took the rebel leader almost two weeks to pull them together again. David Ash was with Company B of the 37th Illinois Volunteer Infantry when he wrote home:

Dearest Eliza
The [minié] balls flew thick and fast. They cut the brush around my head, but fortunately none hit me. We all fell back a few rods and loaded and went up on to them again. We fired into them again and they returned the fire. There were four regiments of them at that time and only two of us. They had a good many Indians. . . .
There was a buckshot hit me in the shoulder, just merely going through my clothes, and made a little red spot.

The morning of the 8th, we were rallied out before
sun-up and went about a mile and formed a line of
battle along a fence.

Five regiments then formed a line and commenced to
advance on them. . . . [W]e stopped some of them in
the brush for good, they were thick laying dead as
they fell. There was quite a lot of them killed. There
was a flag taken. It was a beautiful one. . . .

[The Confederates] wound a great many more in
proportion to what they kill than we do, for their guns
are not so good—they have a great many shotguns
and small rifles. Their surgeons don't have many of
our balls to pick out, for they generally go through.

Albert Hilliard was laying alongside of me when he
was shot, says he, "Oh Dave, I am shot." It was the
hardest thing I have done for some time to call the
roll the first time after the battle, so many of our boys
wounded and one killed. But Eliza, I don't know
whether it is over yet or not.[18]

Two Confederate generals died at Pea Ridge, James M. McIn-
tosh and Ben McCulluch, in a lop-sided affair that saw the
Federals win. Missouri remained with the Union, thanks in no
small part to Sam Curtis. Curtis wrote his brother a short while
after the battle, musing about death and about the "bold rocky
mountain. . .under whose shadow so many fell." He obviously
was greatly affected by it all.

The scene is silent and sad. The vulture and the wolf
now have the dominion, and the dead friends and foes
sleep in the same lonely graves.[19]

After Pea Ridge, Albert Sidney Johnston ordered Van Dorn to
join him in Corinth, Mississippi. He arrived with about 15,000
troops, too late to take part in the Battle of Shiloh.

4

Prince John and the Little Napoleon

Enter two characters onto the Richmond stage, each different, each similar to the other. To the south, Major General John Bankhead Magruder.

Fifty years old, tall, erect, flashy, handsome, impressive despite a lisp; he was nicknamed "Prince John."[1] The Richmond *Dispatch* said he "looked every inch a King."[2] To the north was Major General George B. McClellan, "the Little Napoleon," as he came to be called. General Ulysses S. Grant later called McClellan "one of the mysteries of the war."[3] At this point, however, McClellan was the North's favorite general, certainly its most hoped-for.

Shortly after Manassas, President Lincoln decided to enforce the blockade of the South and reinforce the Union troops in Virginia, and for this he needed men. He signed into law a bill authorizing the enlistment of an additional 500,000 troops.[4] The day following Manassas, President Lincoln summoned McClellan to Washington to head up these troops, organized into the Army of the Potomac.

Armies are all alike, it seems. Hurry up and wait. After the First Battle of Manassas, it was almost nine months before Federal troops did much in the eastern theater other than sit around Washington, guarding the Willard Hotel, some critics might claim. McClellan himself frequently sent messages to his superiors saying, "All quiet along the Potomac."[5]

One thing can be said: McClellan was superb at organizing if less than successful in carrying out plans. He weeded out incompetents, instilled discipline, gave his troops pride, and in turn received their respect and admiration. General George B. McClellan, it might be said, trained one helluva army. Trouble was, he didn't use it. He also thought very highly of himself, writing his wife Ellen Marcy McClellan:

> I find myself in a strange position here: President, Cabinet, Genl. Scott & all deferring to me.
> By some strange operation of magic, I seem to have become *the* power of the land.
> You have no idea how the men brighten up when I go among them. I can see every eye glisten. . . . You never heard such yelling. . . . I was called to it. My life seems to have been unwittingly directed to this great end.[6]

Despite all the uproar and cheers of "On to Richmond," the Little Napoleon claimed he could not march on the Confederate capital because the Rebel army standing between him and his goal was too strong; actually it was less than half the size of the Army of the Potomac. McClellan wanted to flank his Southern opponent, General Joseph E. Johnston, but it was a move

Lincoln didn't like; it would have left Washington open to Confederate troops, Lincoln believed. In any event, before McClellan could march around, then head toward Richmond, Johnston fell back behind the Rappahannock River to the south.

President Lincoln was, in his usual, slow-talking, slow-writing way, quickly frustrated with McClellan. On April 9th he wrote:

> It is called the Army of the Potomac but it is only McClellan's bodyguard. . . . If McClellan is not using the army, I should like to borrow it for a while.[7]

At last, in a brilliant if belated move (one not unlike General Douglas MacArthur's Inchon landing in the 20th century Korean conflict), McClellan headed away from Washington and sailed into Hampton Roads, landing behind the enemy lines, near Fortress Monroe, Virginia. It was the start of his Peninsula Campaign. Never one to travel lightly, McClellan took with him an estimated 121,500 men, 59 batteries of artillery, 25,000 animals, 1,100 supply wagons, and tons of military goods.[8]

Facing this onslaught, General John Magruder had roughly 11,000 men dug in behind the Warwick River. "The Little Napoleon" hesitated. "Prince John" bluffed. The Confederate general marched his troops right, he marched them left, marched them up and down, always in sight—sometimes, viewed by air, from the Northern army's balloon *Intrepid*. But always Magruder's troops remained out of firing range. He placed fake cannon, later to be known as Quaker cannon, in the trenches. He had the peninsula railroad run back and forth all night long to fool the Little Napoleon into believing Southern troops by the thousands were preparing for battle.

In a colloquial phrase: Magruder faked McClellan's socks off. McClellan failed to act, and when President Lincoln complained, McClellan wrote his wife, Ellen, that if Lincoln

wanted to break through the enemy lines, "he had better come
& do it himself."[9] McClellan concluded that he could only take
the Confederate forces by siege.

While McClellan hesitated, General Joseph E. Johnston
took over the Confederate forces, uniting his army with
Magruder's. It was a hard blow for the flashy Magruder. The
man who had, almost single-handedly, held off McClellan and
his army, was now number four in command of the Peninsula's
troops, behind not only Johnston but Generals Smith and
Longstreet as well. Almost all that's now left of Magruder's
memory is a roadside marker and motel named for him outside
Williamsburg, Virginia.

It was about this time that Confederate President
Jefferson Davis signed into law the first military draft in
American history; it would be almost a year before U.S.
President Abraham Lincoln would approve such a law for the
North. By then it was as much out of favor as the draft laws of
the next century's Vietnam War. After the federal law was
approved, a mob of 50,000 rioted in New York City, objecting
to the draft.[10] The crowd caused more than a million dollars
in damages before Federal troops ended the fighting days later.

                                    * * *

Edward M. Burruss was from Mississippi, newly recruited to the
Confederate service:

> Richmond is one living, moving mass of soldiers & to
> day the streets show nothing but a continuous stream
> on their way to Yorktown—infantry, cavalry & artil-
> lery.[11]

On April 20, 1862, Confederate troops marched through Richmond, headed for Yorktown to stop McClellan. As they marched, bands played favorite songs of the South at war: "Dixie" (Way down yonder in the land of cotton, old times there are ne'er forgotten / Look away, look away. Look away, Dixie Land), which apparently was written by two freed slaves living in Mount Vernon, Ohio, and "The Bonnie Blue Flag" (Hurrah! Hurrah! for Southern rights, Hurrah! / Hurrah! for the Bonnie Blue Flag that bears a single star), which was an old Irish drinking song rearranged with new words by a New Orleans comedian.

As the Confederate troops paraded past the Spotswood Hotel, one officer looked up and saw a young couple—a man and a woman—watching from a window, waving and cheering. The officer called to the man, "Come along, Sonny; the young lady will spare you," and added "Here's a musket for you." The young man shouted back, "Fine, and have you a leg for me also?" He placed the stump of a leg on the window sill, showing he'd already done his part for the South. The troops who had been loudly cheered stopped and themselves began cheering. They stood at attention, and on their commander's orders, stood at Present Arms to the young veteran.[12] He was among the first of many to come, many to die, many to suffer life-changing wounds.

Young Sallie Brock was thrilled by it all, especially by Brigadier General Robert Toombs. He had been one of the founders of the Confederacy and now served under Joe Johnston. Toombs wore a black slouch hat, Sallie remembered, and a bright red scarf. He led each of his brigade's regiments past the crowds at the Spotswood, just to make certain everyone knew he was on his was to the battle front.[13]

Edward Dicey was a correspondent for England's *Spectator*. General McClellan had allowed him and a small group of other influential citizens (including Nathaniel Haw-

thorne) to go to Virginia to watch Union preparations for the
Peninsula campaign. Just as McClellan had hoped, Dicey and
the others were impressed by the hundreds of supply wagons,
the thousands of men, all clogging the Potomac wharves. When
Dicey tried to return to Virginia, he had to wait on the
southern side of the chain bridge while more men, more
material, crossed. Dicey was suitably impressed, but it all made
him wonder:

> For hours we found it impossible to cross, as a divi-
> sion of 16,000 men were marching over. . . . With
> colors flying and bands playing, regiment after regi-
> ment defiled past us. The men were singing, shouting,
> cheering. . . . [T]hey chanted "John Brown's Hymn,"
> . .and the heavy tramp of a thousand feet beat time to
> that strange weird melody. As the New England
> regiments passed our train, they shouted to tell the
> people at home that we had seen them in Dixie's
> Land and on the way to Richmond. Ah, me! How
> many, I wonder, of those who flitted before us in the
> twilight, came home themselves to tell their own
> story?[14]

Between Williamsburg and Fortress Monroe, stood the Revolutionary War battlefield of Yorktown. Its nineteenth-century
defenses, however, were hopelessly weak; Johnston said so.
Defenses so weak, he added, "No one but McClellan could
have hesitated to attack."[15] And hesitate is what McClellan
continued to do, allowing Johnston's Rebels to fall back.[16]

The end of March saw Elisha Hunt Rhodes (a sergeant
who would rise to colonel) in the 2nd Rhode Island Volunteer
Regiment sitting at the tip of the peninsula, waiting to move
out. He was just twenty years old when he wrote in his diary:

Newport News, Virginia, March 29/62—We are now at
Newport News where the Union Army can be found.
The next place is Yorktown where the Rebels will be
found.

March 31/62—Our tents have come, and we are in
comfort again. Plenty of beef, port, ham, bacon, etc.
Yesterday I had a beefsteak and sweet potatoes. Very
good living for a soldier. . . . I am well and contented
as usual. Camp life agrees with me.

Rhodes's unit moved out during the first week of April,
stopping at Warwick Court House:

Camp Winfield Scott, Va., April 15/62—We are still at
Warwick Court House. The affair that we had with
the Rebels when we first arrived on the night of April
5th was the first time that we have fired upon the
enemy since Bull Run. . . . We are living in the fields
without tents, and every man cooks his own rations.

Camp near Young's Farm, April 30/62—Monday the
Rebel gun boat *Teazer* shelled our Batteries near
Young's Farm, and as it was supposed that they would
land troops, our Regiment was sent down. . . . This
morning we moved to a piece of woods and have a
fine camp. Our Batteries are shelling the Rebels
across the river, and it sounds like a 4th of July
celebration. We can hear the Rebels beat their drums
in their camps, but ours are quiet as we do not want
to show our position.[17]

How could Rhodes hear "the Rebels beat their drums" while
"ours are quiet?" Well, why should the Rebels let the Federals
know just where they were, if the Union army hoped the
Confederates didn't know where *they* were? Unless, of course,

they wanted McClellan to hear them. Unless it was just Prince John Magruder again with his fakery.

On May 3rd, under darkness, the Confederate army slipped away from their positions, retreating northwesterly toward Richmond. It was an army led by some former U.S. army officers, some graduates of the Virginia Military Institute, and some who wore shoulder bars because they were politicians. A couple were lawyers. None knew much about organizing a retreat. Especially not at a time when, for many of the men, their enlistments were up and their officers were campaigning among the troops for reelection.

It was past midnight when Johnston's troops fired their final rounds from the Yorktown batteries. The Confederate army left behind almost as much field artillery and material as it had captured a year earlier at Manassas. They also left Magruder's fake cannon, which the Union soldiers later seemed to enjoy as a joke but which McClellan fumed over.

Stuart and his cavalry were to follow the army, harassing the slow moving Federals. His orders were to reconnoiter, but Stuart did more than that. He and his 1,200 troops rode circles around the Yankees, literally. He headed north, then wheeled east, then south; in three days he rode around the Union army, followed closely—obviously not close enough—by frustrated Federals, including his father-in-law, Brigadier General Philip St. George Cooke.[18]

But what was even more of an harassment to McClellan than the dashing Stuart was the state of the roads. They were a mess. It had rained for days, Virginia rain, a drenching spring rain. The Northern troops shivered and cussed Jeff Davis, slipped in the muck and cussed George McClellan. And the horses and wagons, unable to cuss, bogged down in pastern-high, axle-deep mud. (There is an often-told story about a mule that sank so deep in the mud only its ears were visible.) About the only thing keeping the men going in the cold rain was the daily ration of a quarter-pint of whiskey, handed out at the end of each day's march.

On May 4, the Union army opened fire on the positions formerly held by the Confederates. It was ineffective, to a great extent, because nobody was there, nobody was home, so to speak.

Johnston's army retreated up the Peninsula, and on May 10, the Confederate navy burned everything it couldn't take with it out of Norfolk and Portsmouth, including the ironclad CSS *Virginia*, formerly the USS *Merrimack*. River pilots had advised that the *Virginia* drew too much water, that she could not navigate the channel up the James River to Richmond. The ironclad had engaged in only one battle (that with the USS *Monitor* in Hampton Roads) and was blown up less than three months after being relaunched. She was burned near the mouth of the Elizabeth River, just off Portsmouth.

Slowly, the Confederates fell back. Even more slowly, the Union troops pushed on. On May 15, Confederates along Drewry's Bluff, a bend in the James River below Richmond, repulsed an attack by the Federal fleet, including the *Virginia*'s foe, the *Monitor*. Cannon fire from the Confederates' Fort Darling, along with sharpshooting along the riverbanks, were too much for the Union ships, and they retreated downriver.

General McClellan had promised Commander John Rogers, on board the Federal ship *Galena*, that he would give the fleet "prompt support wherever and whenever required."[19] One Confederate officer later reported "had Commander Rogers been supported by a few brigades, Richmond would have been evacuated." But General McClellan, despite his earlier promise of aid, telegraphed the U.S. War Department, "Am not yet ready to cooperate with [the navy]."[20]

* * *

Four days before McClellan landed at Fortress Monroe, the U.S. Congress passed a law making legal what General Benjamin Butler and others had been doing for months. It forbade the return of fugitive slaves. Butler had termed these runaways "contraband," reasoning that anything Southerners "owned" could be taken away from them. As the Federals advanced up the Peninsula toward Richmond, numbers of slaves escaped from their owners and sought refuge with Union forces.

In the fall of '61, when General Magruder read in a newspaper that the North was about to turn the city of Hampton into a runaway slave settlement, he burned the town to the ground. It was one of the oldest settlements in the nation, dating back to 1610.[21]

Often, as they escaped, the runaways passed on Rebel troop information. One such "contraband" report led McClellan to believe the Rebels had 75,000 men and were expecting 75,000 more.

McClellan might have pushed on through, but apparently he never even considered it. After all, he was outnumbered, he believed. Instead, he focused on a siege. He wrote his wife on May 22, that, if the Rebels stood and fought, they

> must do so in the very outskirts of Richmond, which must in that event suffer terribly, & perhaps be destroyed.

He didn't want that to happen, he added, praying that in the aftermath of a siege—victorious, of course—he would not have to witness what would happen to Richmond—pillage and fire.

On May 24, lead elements of McClellan's forces, part of Brigadier General William F. "Baldy" Smith's division pushed the Rebels out of Mechanicsville, just five miles from the Confederate capital. Union forces could see the spires of

Richmond and hear church bells ringing. The Federals set their watches by the clocks' chimes and bells.

Elisha Hunt Rhodes was

> *Near New Bridge, Chickahominy River, May 24/62*—We left our camp last night for a place called "Ellisons Mills." Just as we reached a bridge over a creek bang goes a gun, and a shot struck within ten feet of me. . . .
> From a hill nearby we can see the spires of the churches in Richmond. Col. Lowe makes an ascension in his balloon [the *Intrepid*] every day. It has rained nearly all day, and we are wet and uncomfortable. . . . [W]e were near a place called Mechanicsville, and I went into the town. The houses were riddled with fire from both sides during the night.
>
> *Near Mechanicsville, Va., June 4th/1862*—We are still in this position. . . . Great battles are being fought, but we are not being called upon. Our time will come.[22]

In *Tales of a Wayside Inn, The Student's Tale*, Henry Wadsworth Longfellow wrote: "All things come round to him who will but wait."[23]

Elisha Rhodes didn't have to wait long. The Seven Days' Battles had come to Richmond.

The War in the West

II

Shiloh, Bloody Shiloh

While Richmond's citizens waited for McClellan, their neighbors westward looked to an areas around an old log cabin meeting house. After Fort Donelson, Albert Sidney Johnston concentrated his troops at the rail center of Corinth, Mississippi, reinforcing his Army of Tennessee, named for the state. On March 4th, General Halleck relieved Grant of command, sending him the following communique:

> You will place Major-General C. F. Smith in command of [the] expedition, and remain yourself at Fort Henry. Why do you not obey my orders to report strength and positions of your command?[1]

Grant himself looked on it as a sort of imprisonment:

> I was left virtually in arrest on board a steamer without even a guard, for about a week, when I was released and ordered to resume my command.[2]

48

Halleck was just forty-seven, only eight years Grant's senior, but he looked and seemed far older. Then, too, Halleck was everything Grant wasn't: a success. He had graduated from both Union College and West Point, and he was a successful scholar and lecturer on warfare. A lawyer; a businessman; a man of authority, despite his deceivingly puffy eyes.[3] But he had problems as a leader. He apparently thought the way to spur on a subordinate was to nag at him. And he was a man who saw Grant—now that Grant had won at Fort Donelson—as a rival. After that victory, Halleck had requested that General George McClellan promote Buell, Grant, and Pope to major generals. Buell and Pope, of course, had had nothing to do with the Donelson victory. And while Halleck realized Grant deserved promotion, he just didn't want to single out a man he saw as his rival.

Lincoln did; he sent only Grant's promotion on for Senate approval, ignoring Buell and Pope. Later, when Halleck hinted that Grant was often drunk, neglecting his duties, Lincoln told a group of congressmen that if stories of Grant's drinking were true, he would like to know Grant's brand of whiskey so he could supply it to his other officers.[4]

Grant survived an investigation and was returned to his troops on March 13. He commanded the Union's Army of *the* Tennessee, named, as was the North's custom, after the river. He took aim on Johnston and moved his army to Pittsburg Landing, a spot William Tecumseh Sherman thought a fine place for a battle. Grant agreed and planned to meet the Rebels there, twenty-five miles from Corinth.

Grant's army was made up of new, untried troops, most hardly able to load their rifles. They waited in the woods of Pittsburg Landing for Don Carlos Buell's Army of the Ohio to join them with another 25,000 men. Grant believed that when Lew Wallace brought up his 5,000 troops from a camp down river at Crump's Landing, the Federals would be ready for Johnston.

Johnston knew this, and knew that to win against Grant he had to surprise the Union forces before Buell and Wallace arrived. So, early on April 3, the Rebels moved toward Pittsburg Landing. But there were delays, misplaced orders, bad roads, and mass confusion. Troops assigned to the rear wound up in front. Units strayed, got lost, strayed again. They reached their designated points well after dawn on April 4.

And the rain. There was so much rain that what roads there were, were impassable. Johnston postponed the attack for twenty-four hours, until April 6.

That same rain almost killed Grant. He was riding back and forth in the dark, impatiently checking his troops, when his horse slipped in the mud and fell. Grant's leg was pinned underneath. But the rain that *caused* the horse to fall, *saved* Grant. The ground was soggy and soft, and the general was helped to his feet. His leg wasn't broken but was so badly swollen that his boot had to be cut off. The injury was so painful that he spent the first day of the battle hobbling around on crutches. "My ankle was so much swollen from the fall," he said, "and the bruise so painful, that I could get no rest."[5]

Grant had consulted with William Tecumseh Sherman, and General Sherman had assured him there would be no attack any time soon:

> I do not apprehend anything like an attack on our position.[6]

Perhaps some "picket firing," he added, but nothing more. When one of his front-line officers claimed there were thousands of Rebels out there in the woods, an angry Sherman told him:

Take your damned regiment back to Ohio. Beauregard is not such a fool as to leave his base of operations and attack us in ours.[7]

Pierre Gustave Toutant Beauregard, the South's hero of
Manassas, was second in command of the Southern forces in
the west and drew up the plan for battle. He had studied
artillery at West Point under Robert Anderson. That was the
same Major Anderson who later commanded Union troops at
Fort Sumter. And the same Beauregard who ordered Rebel
artillery to fire on Fort Sumter and forced Anderson to
surrender.

Friday's confusion made even Beauregard believe the
battle was lost. There wasn't much chance the Union would be
surprised. Feisty Braxton Bragg agreed. As did Leonidis Polk,
perhaps a better Episcopal bishop than general. Only former
U.S. Vice President John C. Breckinridge (the man who had
lost the election to Lincoln in 1860) wanted to continue the
attack.[8]

Like the troops from the North, the Rebels were raw
and scared. After a day of marching in hard rain, they wanted
to be certain their weapons would fire, so they tested them, and
all through the night you could hear the "pop-pop-pop" of rifle
fire. They flushed a deer from cover and chased after it,
laughing and cheering.

But surprise or not, Union reinforcements or not, on
Saturday night, Johnston told his officers he was determined to
go ahead:

Gentlemen, we shall attack. . . . We will water our
horses in the Tennessee River![9]

Members of the 2nd Texas weren't too happy with the thought
of attacking. They'd been issued new uniforms made of undyed

white wool, and they asked, "Do the generals expect us to be killed and want us to wear our burial shrouds?"[10]

Forty thousand Confederates in gray and butternut brown (and at least some Texans in off-white) formed up in four parallel lines: William Hardee, Braxton Bragg, Leonidas Polk, and John C. Breckinridge. Bragg was on the right, pushing his troops toward the Tennessee River to block any retreat.

The Confederate lines were three miles wide and over a mile deep. The strategy—typical of the time—was more like medieval warfare or that of the Napoleonic Age than the nineteenth century. Men marched side by side, stopped perhaps less than one hundred yards away from the enemy, and fired away. The tactic had worked when the weapons were smooth-bore and shotgun-like. But Civil War weapons were rifled, more accurate, and much more deadly. Using an eighteenth century tactic assured slaughter during nineteenth century battles.

Over the next two days the Rebels faced 63,000 Federals in blue: W. H. L. Wallace with what may have been the Union's finest corps; Steven Hurlbut, noted for his anti-Semitism; John McClernand, whom many saw as the hope for the future, a boy wonder, and Benjamin Prentiss, a man who took orders very seriously. They were spread around Shiloh Church, their backs to the river.

It was 5:14 in the morning, a beautiful Sunday, clear and cool after the storm.

Grant's injured leg had kept him awake most of the night. He was having breakfast in Savannah and heard sounds coming from Sherman's camp at Shiloh Methodist-Episcopal meetinghouse. But they weren't the peelings of a church bell. Instead, they were the first shots of battle, with the 6th Mississippi leading the way.

Beauregard should have been right, but despite everything, the Federal troops *were* surprised. Many literally were caught with their pants down, still in bed. Others gathered around cook fires, leisurely preparing a breakfast they'd never enjoy.[11]

Even Sherman was caught sleeping. William Tecumseh Sherman was just back in service after being relieved of command for being afraid and nervous, too certain the enemy was always there when he wasn't. He may even have been insane. But, when the enemy really *was* there, really *was* attacking, Sherman didn't believe the men under him. And they were afraid to press the truth.[12]

Almost too late, they rousted Sherman from bed. Seeing what was going on around him, he shouted, "My god! We are being attacked!"[13] The next moment, an orderly standing beside Sherman was killed.

The surprised and frightened Union soldiers hid under the bluffs of the Tennessee River. By mid-morning, 5,000 Union bluecoats huddled there. Meanwhile, the always hungry Confederates stopped to eat the beans and cornbread their Union opponents had cooked for their own interrupted breakfast. It gave Prentiss time to organize a defense.

After the initial surprise, it was a cat and dog fight. Neither the generals nor the private soldiers knew their jobs. What happened, happened through pure determination to fight, not to retreat.

But Johnston's plan was working. They were pushing the Federals back all over, except for Prentiss's hard core of resistance near a sunken road. He had regrouped his men there and Grant ordered him to hold on at all costs.

Twelve times Braxton Bragg threw his men in against the Union line. Twelve times Ben Prentiss beat them back, 18,000 Confederates against 4,500 Federals. The fighting was hot and heavy, but the Confederate charge was piecemeal: one unit at a time, not a concerted action. Every time the Confederates charged they were hit by a barrage of Union fire; like bees the bullets buzzed and whizzed around them, leading one soldier to call it a "Hornets' Nest." The name stuck.

Some Union soldiers resorted to an old camp tale to explain the Confederates' bravery. Beauregard, they believed, had issued the Rebels a concoction of whiskey and gunpowder, priming them, as it were, for battle.[14]

Brigade after brigade of Rebels rushed against the Union center, but each time they were hit by deadly crossfire and each time they were forced back. No longer were they fighting men, but boys not long from schools and farm and factories. Now fighting, now shedding tears, now dying.

In the saying of the times, thousands of raw recruits "saw the elephant," they saw combat for the first time, and for most, it was a horrifying experience. Friends they'd known for years suddenly died right beside them. And they realized they, too, might fall.

Ten-year-old John Clem of the 22nd Michigan was right in the middle, a drummer boy, beating out orders until an artillery shell destroyed his drum. But "Johnny Shiloh," as they came to call him, wasn't hurt and went on to fight again.[15]

It was mid-afternoon now, mid-afternoon of a day out of hell, surrounded by beauty. Off toward the right of this hell, peach trees bloomed in an orchard near the Hamburg Road, blossoms fluttering in the spring breeze.

Johnston heard of a brigade refusing to fight, and he changed roles, a change that hurt the Southern cause. He changed from being a *commander* to a *fighter*, personally leading the assault, a mistake in any battle. He charged into the peach orchard across an open valley, on a bay horse called "Fire-eater," riding between two ridges swept by fire, exposing himself to enemy fire. "Fire-eater" was shot four times before the big horse stumbled and fell. Quickly, Union riflemen targeted on Johnston, and a minié ball ripped through his clothing. Another tore the sole of a boot. A third ball hit him behind the knee, a minor wound, he believed, and the general continued the fight, ordering his division surgeon to attend the other wounded first, the *Federal* wounded.

When blood began spurting from around Johnston's knee, he realized it wasn't a minor wound. It was, instead, a severed leg artery. Johnston always carried a tourniquet with him, but no one thought to use it to save his life.

His aide asked, "General, are you wounded?" And Johnston answered, "Yes, and I fear seriously."[16] They were his final words. He lay back, apparently in very little pain, and died.[17] For Albert Sidney Johnston—sixty-one years old, Kentucky-born, veteran of war after war after war—the battle was over.

He was not alone. Near the peach orchard, dozens from both sides died even while they drank in desperation from a mud hole. So many, bleeding so profusely, they stained the water red. So many, the mud hole became known as "Bloody Pond."

It was late afternoon when infantry General Daniel Ruggles acted on his own, without orders, to gather an artillery force. He aimed sixty Confederate cannon on the Federals, pouring down fire onto the Hornets' Nest.[18]

Rebels flanked Prentiss on both sides and the Union officer finally surrendered the 2,200 men left under him, less than half of those who'd begun the day beside Prentiss. He'd been fighting for nearly twelve hours.

Confederate officers and men stopped and strained to see the men who had held the Hornet's Nest. They crowded around their captives and looked on in awe as Prentiss was led away. Their curiosity was as costly as their early morning hunger had been, because it gave the Union time to regroup.

Slowly, the day's fighting ground down. With Johnston's death, Beauregard took command of the Confederate forces, and he believed Grant's men were too tired to fight. He really *hoped* they would give up and slip across the river during the night, because Beauregard knew his own men were exhausted. He decided to wait until the next day to press his advantage. That night he slept in the same bed General Sherman had been rousted from that morning.

But Grant wasn't about to give up and told his men: "Retreat? No I propose to attack at daylight and whip them."[19]

It was a miserable night for everybody. First a drizzle, then a torrent—rain, falling on the 95,000 living and the 2,000 dead. The wounded huddled together for warmth, crying out through the night; their cries frightened and disturbed their comrades who couldn't help. Lightning startled them. Thunder and riverboat cannon pounded down on the Rebel troops.

Early on April 7, General Buell's reinforcements arrived. Grant greeted the reinforcements by ordering the Union army military band to play a rousing song: "Dixie!"

Scouts had reported the Union reinforcements to Nathan Bedford Forrest, and Forrest wanted to have no more to do with the battle. He couldn't find Beauregard to warn him, and his fellow officers ignored Forrest's plea. Finally, he gave up, predicting, "We'll be whipped like Hell."[20]

Beauregard had just 25,000 effective men left, and they were discouraged by Sunday's deadly stalemate and the night's rain. They were also badly shaken by the sight of so many of their fellows lying dead in the morning sun.

One Confederate soldier wrote:

> You could never form an idea of the horrors of actual war unless you saw the battlefields while the conflict is progressing. Death in every awful form, if really be death, is a pleasant sight in comparison to the fearful and mortally wounded. Some crying, oh, my wife, my children, others, my Mother, my sisters, my brother,

etc. [A]ny and all of these you will hear while some
pray to God to have mercy and others die cursing the
"Yankee sons of b-----s."[21]

As Buell's fresh troops attacked, the tired and worn Confederates could only retreat. Fiercely, stubbornly, they gave back the
land they'd paid for only yesterday with so many lives.

Beauregard was just as discouraged as his men. What
was nearly a victory on Sunday morning became defeat on
Monday afternoon.

Both sides claimed they won the Battle of Shiloh. But
who did? Long before he became chief justice of the U.S.
Supreme Court, Oliver Wendell Holmes was a junior officer in
the eastern theater. When he heard about the Battle of Shiloh,
or as the Union called it, the Battle of Pittsburg Landing,
Holmes believed it was "rather an equivocal victory after
all."[22]

If occupying the field means victory, then Grant's Union
forces were the winners: they held the ground. If human losses
are considered, then it was a draw; and both sides lost.

They unceremoniously buried their dead in separate
Union and Confederate trenches. Hospitals on both sides were
jammed, and urgent calls went out for doctors and nurses. In
two days, the Union suffered more than 13,000 casualties,
including 1,754 deaths. The Confederacy tallied more than
9,700, including 1,728 deaths.

Who, then, was the real winner of the Battle of Shiloh?
Shiloh, bloody Shiloh.

5

Phenomenally Mismanaged

The well-documented stories of inflation in the Civil War South were facts of everyday life in Richmond. "Oh, the extortioners!" Richmond's J. B. Jones complained in May 1862. "Meats of all kinds are selling at 50 cts. per pound," a price he would welcome three years later.[1] It was the same with other commodities: "Butter, 75 cts.; coffee, $1.50; tea, $10; boots, $30 per pair; shoes, $18; ladies' shoes, $15; shirts, $6 each." The Confederate Congress had issued an order fixing maximum prices on certain articles, but apparently it never was enforced: "Houses that rented for $400 last year, are $1000 now. Boarding from $30 to $40 per month." And complaining, Jones added, "does more harm than good."

There is no such thing as a short war when you not only oppose the fighting but find yourself trapped behind enemy lines. Like Jones and his family, Frank West and his wife, Mary Andrews West, disapproved of secession; unlike Jones they

58

objected to the war itself. Yet, they chose not to leave the South and lived in Richmond under siege for four years. They fought to survive while the city fought off invasion. Frank "kept out [of the army] by acting as a compositor or editor" on the Richmond *Whig*.[2] He, as had many others both North and South, had vowed not to take part in the fighting. Frank and Mary were Southerners who had chosen to support the Union but also had chosen to remain in the land of the Confederacy. They became as much prisoners of the Union siege as did Confederate loyalists.

It could not have been an easy choice and certainly it was not an easy existence. However, they were somewhat prepared: "When the war was first commenced, I had a little sum of money in bank [*sic*] and some State Stock." Mary West converted most of her funds into perhaps the most valuable articles any survivor of any war could own; she bought food and clothing. As she later explained to her sister, Clara, "Save shoes and one pair of gloves, we have not bought one article of clothing" since the war began.

* * *

Women North and South, including those of Richmond, were very much a part of the war. Many sewed, raised money, recruited troops. Some shared camp life with loved ones. Thirty-two hundred women, including author Louisa May Alcott, nursed the Union sick and dying. The number was only slightly lower for the Confederate injured. Some women fought, disguised as men. Rose O'Neal Greenhow was a spy who informed Confederate General Beauregard about Union troops marching to Manassas. Elizabeth "Crazy Bet" Van Lew was a spy for the Union, living in Richmond, helping inmates escape from Libby Prison.

When one woman was asked if she wanted her sons to join the army, she replied:

> Wanted 'em to go? If they hadn't 'a' gone, they shouldn't 'a' stayed where I was. Them Yankees mustn't come a-nigh Richmond![3]

* * *

Things were looking so desperate along the Virginia Peninsula in late April of 1863 that the Confederate government prepared to abandon Richmond. On May 13, President Davis sent his wife and children to safety in Raleigh, North Carolina. But for most people in the city, there was no avenue to safety; they had to stick it out.

Richmond was to be defeated at all costs, the Union seemed to declare, and that cost would be high on both sides of the battle line. With the Confederate army digging in around the city, war clerk John Jones believed, "we are now so strong that no one fears the results when the great battle takes place."[4] He added, "McClellan has delayed too long, and he is doomed to defeat." Troops march into the city, and the army "has them out in such a manner and at such times as it eludes the observation of the spies."[5]

They marched east, where on May 31 approximately 84,000 men fought the Battle of Seven Pines (the Battle of Fair Oaks, the Yankees called it), their numbers divided about equally, North and South. Frequently, it's difficult to say which side wins a battle, and the Battle of Seven Pines was one of

that kind. It was "phenomenally mismanaged" on the Confederate side, one Southern officer admitted.[6]

A Richmond resident, Constance Cary Harrison (whose
very name carries memories of F.F.V.—First Families of
Virginia—saw the Battle of Seven Pines in a different light:

> In face of recent reverses, we in Richmond had begun
> to feel like the prisoner of the Inquisition in Poe's
> story, cast into a dungeon of slowly contracting walls.
> With the sound of guns, therefore, in the direction of
> Seven Pines, every heart leaped as if deliverance were
> at hand. And yet there was no joy in the wild pulsa-
> tion, since those to whom we looked for succor were
> our own flesh and blood, barring the way to a foe of
> superior numbers, abundantly provided, as we were
> not, with all the equipments of modern warfare, and
> backed by a mighty nation as determined as ourselves
> to win. Hardly a family in the town whose father, son,
> or brother was not part and parcel of the defending
> army.[7]

Two days after the battle, Colonel David A. Weisiger of the
12th Virginia Volunteer Infantry wrote his wife:

> Oh! My dearest I have had a very hard time, but the
> sufferings in the way of hardship is nothing to what I
> have suffered in mind at seeing some of my best men
> and brave boys shot down before my face.[8]

For Weisiger, it was a short but fearful experience:

> We were in action about half an hour and lost ten
> men killed, twenty-seven wounded, and seventy-five
> missing. You just ought to see me, muddy and dirty
> up to my knees, without a change of clothing as my
> horse after being shot ran off.

That was June 25, the first day of what later was called the Seven Days' Battles—Seven Pines, Mechanicsville, Gaines' Mill, Savage's Station, Malvern Hill. Won or lost, and there are arguments on each side (the North's claim to victory was based on the Federals suffering fewer casualties), the Seven Days' Battles gave Richmond breathing space and time, an eight-week peace. General Joseph E. Johnston was wounded at Seven Pines, yet in his place the Confederacy received its greatest hero: General Robert E. Lee, took command.

Lincoln had offered Lee the command of all Union troops; Lee had declined, saying he would stand by his state of Virginia. He resigned his U.S. commission, saying he hoped never to have to draw his sword again. Virginia Governor Letcher, however, had other ideas and invited Lee to Richmond. Robert E. Lee left his ailing wife at their home in Arlington, one of the last times he would be able to call the mansion home. He traveled to Richmond by train, wearing civilian clothes and a silk hat.

Lee was fifty-four years old, five-feet-eleven-inches, and he weighed just under 170 pounds. His black hair was grizzled with gray; only later did it turn the now-familiar white. And only later did he grow a beard. When he met with Governor Letcher he was smooth shaven except for a short mustache, which, unlike his hair, was still predominately black. Letcher offered Lee a position as commander-in-chief of all Virginia military forces, army and navy. Lee accepted but later became Jefferson Davis's military advisor, a post he gave up after the Battle of Seven Pines.

Son of Revolutionary War hero Light-Horse Harry Lee, he was himself the leader of Federal troops at Harpers Ferry when abolitionist John Brown was captured. When he took over from Johnston at Seven Pines, Lee was exactly what the South's forces needed. "What a change!" J. B. Jones exclaimed and predicted a "career of glory for our country."[9] And Jones added, "no one now dreams of the loss of the capital."

Lee's new troops weren't so sure. They nicknamed him "Granny Lee," because he moved slowly, deliberately, and because, as in most other armies, most other times, he was considerably older than the soldiers serving under him. They also called him "King of Spades," when he made them dig in around Richmond. It was, however, those same fortifications Lee made them build that saved their lives. And saved Richmond.

* * *

"Richmond" gave Robert E. Lee a lot of trouble. Not the city, though it was trouble enough for the new Confederate commander and would be for the four years the North held the city under siege. In this case, "Richmond" was a horse, a bay stallion presented to him by admirers. And "Richmond" just didn't like other horses, strange horses. When General Lee rode "Richmond" by himself, things went fine, but when there were other horses around, "Richmond" squealed and bucked.

The gray horse Lee generally rode, the one most familiar to us, was "Jeff Davis," later to be called "Greenbrier," later to be called "Traveller." Same horse, different names. "Traveller" and "Richmond" never did get along. Richmond, the city, however, loved "Traveller" enough later to name an alley after him.

* * *

Lee knew McClellan was hoping to bring in even more troops, and the new Rebel commander knew he had to act before those troops arrived. He believed the Federal wing north of the Chickahominy River was the spot to test the Union army.

Lee sent Jeb Stuart and his cavalry to reconnoiter, and on June 12, he began his now-famous "Ride Around McClellan," a three-day, hundred-mile encirclement of the Army of the Potomac. Aside from proving Stuart could get the job done, it proved Lee had been correct; the Union northern flank was unprotected.

Immediately, Lee ordered Stonewall Jackson to bring his 18,500 men in from the Shenandoah Valley and take the Federal's supply base at White House Landing on the Pamunkey River. Generals D. H. Hill and James Longstreet would assist, bringing the total Confederate force to 55,000. Prince John Magruder would be left with 30,000 men, holding the direct line to Richmond, south of the Chickahominy.

McClellan had twice the number of Magruder's troops but arguably half the courage. On June 25, McClellan pushed his army toward New Bridge, touching off the Battle of Oak Grove. By itself, Oak Grove was small; however, it marked the opening of the Seven Days' Battles.

All the next morning, General Lee watched and waited for Jackson to advance, but Stonewall had gotten a late start that day. When he did move out, he found the Union cavalry blocking his way. When he did reach his objective, it was so late he quit for the day.

Lee's plan for June 27 was to have Jackson continue his push on to White House Landing. Unfortunately for the Rebel strategy, the Federals had not remained where Lee thought they were. The Union's supply base had been moved, thanks, in part, to Stuart's Ride, which alerted them to Rebel intentions.

When Lee spoke with Jackson that afternoon, he asked Stonewall if his men could stand the heavy fighting currently underway at Boatswain's Creek. Jackson, whom Lee had just mildly rebuked for being late, said, "They can stand almost anything; they can stand that!"[10]

Finally, the Confederate army was coordinated, the first time the Rebel army had been able to muster so many men together at one time. It was the Battle of Gaines' Mill, and saw Brigadier General John Bell Hood's Texas regiment send the Union army packing across the river. It cost the South 8,800 men and the North another 6,800, the bloodiest fighting in the Seven Days' Battles. It scared McClellan into ordering his men to abandon their forward positions and to withdraw to a fortified camp twenty-six miles from Richmond.

The Little Napoleon headed for Harrison's Landing, and Lee tried to stop him. As the Union army headed back down the Peninsula, they ran into a bottleneck at Glendale Junction and had trouble getting to the single small road leading across the James River near Malvern Hill.

General Lee sent two columns, A. P. Hill and Long-street, on a wide sweep southeast. But since it would take them a while—probably until June 30—to get there, it was up to John Magruder to pin down the Federals on the Williamsburg Road. McClellan's troops easily fought off Magruder's smaller army, and by mid-morning the next day, all of the Union army's men and wagons had crossed White Oak Swamp.

When Stonewall Jackson got his men across the swamp (McClellan's troops had had the foresight to destroy the only available bridge over the swamp), he was so tired he suggested, "Let us at once [go] to bed, and see if tomorrow we cannot do something."[11] Meanwhile, Major General Benjamin Huger had run into a problem, a confusion of trees Union troops had cut down to hamper the Rebels. Instead of going over or even through the tangled mess, Huger insisted his lead brigade build a new road around it. The delay meant Lee had 9,000 fewer troops in his force as they headed toward Malvern Hill.

Malvern Hill is a large plateau, a mile and a-half long, about three-quarters of a mile wide, perhaps 100 feet high, all yellow at the time with ripe wheat, all protected by swamps and ravines and creeks around it. General Daniel Harvey Hill didn't like the setup. He told General Lee, "If General McClellan is there in force, we had better let him alone." Longstreet was at that meeting and was confident, too confident: "Don't get scared, now that we have him whipped."[12] To his later regret, Lee agreed with Longstreet.

Adding to the confusion were the names of roads in the area; several were known to military mapmakers as "Quaker Road," even though they had other, local, names. (Sometimes, the name of a road simply depended on which way you faced. As an example, locals would face Richmond and call it "Richmond Road." But heading east, they'd call it "Williamsburg Road," or wherever else they intended to go.) Going on the advice of *his* mapmaker, John Magruder marched his three divisions obliquely away from the coming battle.

Longstreet rode off after Magruder to correct the problem. It was a touchy situation. Magruder still felt slighted, because he'd been replaced after fooling McClellan into a stand-off. Longstreet chose not to order Magruder to change direction, but to convince Prince John of the mistake. It was three hours later when Magruder was finally persuaded and got his troops straightened out.

When they got everybody near where they were supposed to be, and got the battle started, it nearly was a disaster. Union General Fitz-John Porter had 250 pieces of artillery aimed at the Rebels, all pounding away. Twelve-pound shot rained down on the Confederates; General Longstreet couldn't even get his own artillery set up to fire.

General Lee apparently believed Brigadier General Lewis Armistead had successfully flanked the Union troops; he hadn't, but that didn't stop Lee, who told his men to "press

forward your whole line and follow up Armistead's success."[13]
The Rebels charged. The Federals beat them back. "It was not
war,"[14] according to Lieutenant General Daniel Harvey Hill an
officer known as sharp-tongued but distinguished and one often
described as "dyspeptic," which apparently in the nineteenth
century meant he was subject to ulcers[15]). As Hill later remembered, "it was murder." Earlier, he had discovered troops
of General Robert Toombs (a political, rather than military,
appointee) wandering around aimlessly and had to take
command. That night Hill found Toombs and shouted, "For
shame! Rally your troops! Where were you when I was riding
up and down your line, rallying your troops?"   Malvern Hill
saw 5,400 Southerners slaughtered.

Totaled up, the Seven Days' Battles cost Lee 21,000—
nearly one-fourth of his force. They cost McClellan 16,000.
Nevertheless, the Battles forced McClellan away from Richmond and back down the Peninsula. "Little Mac's" plan to
capture the Confederate capital ended.

Robert E. Lee moved the action toward Washington.
But Richmond still remained under siege.

* * *

The summer of 1862 was one of great decisions for Abraham
Lincoln and the North. One such decision dealt with slavery.
There may be as many reasons for the war as there are
historians to write about them. But one of the chief causes, of
course, was Southern slavery, or as a Southerner might prefer,
the North's desire to overthrow that "peculiar institution."

In one of the great decisions of that summer, one that
would greatly affect Richmond, Lincoln told his cabinet on July
22, 1862, that he would free the slaves. Just one member of that

cabinet dissented, Montgomery Blair, and then only to suggest freedom come *after* the election that fall. Any earlier, Blair believed, and the Republican Party would lose control of Congress.[16] Politics, as usual, prevailed.

When a group of clergymen approached Lincoln on September 13, calling for immediate freedom for slaves, Lincoln told them, "Slavery is the root of the rebellion [but under the present circumstances] I cannot even enforce the Constitution in the rebel states," much less enforce their emancipation.[17]

Emancipation would come, President Lincoln decided, only after the North won a decisive battle. The Seven Days' Battles weren't; the Second Battle of Manassas on August 29, 1862, certainly wasn't, either; that was another Southern victory.

Finally, reason enough—victory enough—four days after Lincoln's meeting with the demanding clergy. It came along Antietam Creek near a small Maryland town called Sharpsburg. It came with 6,000 dead or dying, another 17,000 wounded. It saw almost one-third of all the Confederate forces that marched into Maryland that late summer having to be carried out. They fought in a cornfield, and afterward the crop looked as if it had been "struck by a storm of bloody hail," one witness said. They fought by a whitewashed Dunker Church, in the shelter of a sunken road, along a line soon called Bloody Lane. A few hundred Georgia troops, firing from high ground, prevented Union Major General Ambrose Burnside's four divisions from crossing the graceful arched bridge over Antietam Creek for three hours. Five hundred Rebels holding back 13,000 Federals.

The rebels fought despite the infamous "Lost Orders." Two men, one of them Pvt. B. W. Mitchell of the 27th Infantry, were resting in the field where, just recently, Robert E. Lee had had his headquarters. Mitchell found three cigars, wrapped in paper. Just as they were about to light up to celebrate their find, they noticed, scrawled on the wrapping paper, the words "Headquarters, Army of Northern Virginia." It was a copy of

Lee's Special Order No. 191, the Confederate invasion plan, certainly an all-time military jackpot.

Quickly, the note was rushed up the chain of command to General McClellan, who cried out to an aide, "Here is a paper with which if I cannot whip Bobbie Lee, I will be willing to go home."[18]

Despite having Lee's battle plan in his hands, once more McClellan hesitated, afraid of Confederate reserves that were not there. After Burnside's regiments finally crossed Rohrbach Bridge—the bridge that quickly took Burnside's name—Union troops began pushing the Confederates back toward Sharpsburg, threatening to cut off their retreat over the Potomac.

It was an opportunity for McClellan and a crisis for Lee. Again, McClellan hesitated and refused to order Fitz-John Porter's 5th Corps into action. They were, Porter said, "the last reserve of the last army of the Republic."[19] So, McClellan refused to give the order that could have given him an overwhelming victory and possibly brought an early end to the war. His hesitation allowed Rebel General A. P. Hill to arrive with reinforcements from Harper's Ferry.

That night, survivors of the Battle of Antietam heard cries of the dead and wounded.

"No tongue can tell, no mind conceive, no pen portray the horrible sights I witnessed this morning," a soldier from Pennsylvania wrote home. The Battle of Antietam saw more casualties—four times the number—than were suffered by American troops during the invasion of Normandy on World War II's D-Day, 1944.[20] And yet, the two sides fought to a virtual draw. Federal troops lost twice the number as did the Confederates, but the South could not afford giving up one for two. By reason of percentages, then, it was something of a Northern victory, and the Confederate troops from the top down knew it.

The day after the battle, Lee stood defiantly behind his lines, almost asking that the attack be resumed. But Union General McClellan declined. Finally, Lee turned his army back toward Virginia; he knew who had won. His army knew as well. When the Confederate band began playing "Maryland, My Maryland." It was the same song the band had played as it marched *into* Maryland, hoping to rally to the Confederacy a wavering people who had remained in the Union. But this time the Southern troops hissed and booed, and the band changed tunes, playing "Carry Me Back to Old Virginny."

The victory, however, was enough for Lincoln to make up his mind. He would issue his Emancipation Proclamation on the first of the new year.

6

Somebody's Darling

As the Army of Northern Virginia crossed the border back toward Richmond, they wore what many called "multiforms," ragged uniforms—some gray, some blue, some brown. Very few wore anything vaguely resembling a complete uniform. They wore a little of this, a little of that, merely clothing they had found or, if they were lucky, had been sent to them by a loved one. Some items they took from the dead or dying lying on battlefields.[1]

* * *

The year wore on and the Union army outside Richmond was stalled for lack of leadership. Now there was a new fear, that "there will be no fighting around Richmond until McClellan *digs* his way out of it."[2] For the moment, Confederate troops camped around the city could relax and dream of the future, and residents of Richmond could bury the dead who arrived by ones and twos, by tens and twenties, almost every day. They were "our best and brightest young men," Sallie Putnam wrote. She and other Southern ladies would minister to the sick and dying, singing as they did:

> Into a ward of the white-washed hills
> Where the dead and dying lay;
> Wounded by bayonets, shells and balls,
> Somebody's darling was borne one day.
> Somebody's darling so young and so brave,
> Wearing yet on his sweet, pale face,
> Soon to be laid in the dust of the grave,
> The lingering light of his boyhood grace.[3]

"There was scarcely a family that had not had some one of its number in the field," Putnam wrote, and "mothers nervously watched for any who might bring them news of their boys."[4] All too often those mothers and fathers and sisters and brothers heard the news most feared. "Every family received the bodies of the wounded or dead," she added, "and every house was a house of mourning."[5] Sallie was only sixteen at the time war began; childhood quickly vanished in Richmond under siege.

"Young wives clasped their children to their bosoms," the grown Sallie Putnam remembered years later. In agony, they "imagined themselves widows and their little ones orphans." In times of peace, death is usually greeted one by one. In times of war, singular death becomes plural.

As the dead arrived in Richmond, the bodies were stuffed into pine boxes for shipment home. Soon demand outran supply, and frequently bodies were left piled on depot platforms so long that complaints were made to authorities about the stench.

Constance Cary Harrison witnessed the arrival of casualties:

> From one scene of death and suffering to another we passed during those days. . . .
> Day by day we were called to our windows by the wailing dirge of a military band preceding a soldier's funeral. One could not number those sad pageants: the coffin crowned with cap and sword and gloves, the riderless horse following with empty boots fixed in the stirrups of an army saddle; such soldiers as could be spared from the front marching after with armies reversed and crepe-enfolded banners; the passers-by standing with bare, bent heads. . . . [T]he green hillsides of lovely Hollywood [Cemetery] were frequently upturned to find resting-places for the heroic dead. So much taxed for time and for attendants were those who officiated that it was not unusual to perform the last rites for the departed at night.[6]

Richmond's old Hollywood Cemetery had to be expanded; it was past the point of overflowing. Hollywood Cemetery (so named because of its many holly bushes) became the final resting place for 18,000 Confederate soldiers. No longer was there time to prepare each headstone; unused housing shingles were scratched with the names of the deceased, and line upon line of "Somebody's Darlings" inhabited the cemeteries of the South.

John Tyler, the tenth president of the United States, Richmond's representative to the Confederate Congress (as well as an outspoken delegate to the Secession Convention), died on January 18, 1862, at the age of seventy-one. His death came just a few months shy of the twentieth anniversary of his inaugural in Washington.

He had fought hard to preserve the Union, but when it
became obvious the South would break away, he fought hard to
make permanent the Confederate government. He was buried
at Hollywood Cemetery.

As was James Monroe, the fifth president of the United
States of America. As would be Jefferson Davis, the only
president of the Confederate States of America. As would be
Fitzhugh Lee and Jeb Stuart and George Pickett. As would be
18,000 other Confederate soldiers, most of whom died while
"recuperating" at Richmond military hospitals.

In April of '64, another—far younger—individual was
buried in Hollywood Cemetery: Joseph Even Davis. "Little Joe"
was barely five years old—"the good child of the house, so
gentle and affectionate," Mary Chesnut wrote—when he fell
from the high north piazza of the Confederate White House,
landing on the brick pavement below. Mrs. Chesnut rushed to
the White House and spoke with a Davis family friend who told
her, "[L]ittle Jeff" [Jefferson Davis, Jr.] was kneeling down by
his brother. And he called out to her in great distress, ". . .I
have said all the prayers I know how, but God will not wake
Joe."[7] "Little Jeff" wasn't the only one grieving:

> As I sat in the drawing room, I could hear the tramp
> of Mr. Davis's step as he walked up and down the
> room above—not another sound. The whole house
> was silent as death.

Richmond children jammed into Hollywood Cemetery to honor
one of their own. "Immense crowd at the funeral," Mary
Chesnut wrote:

> Sympathetic but shoving and pushing rudely, thou-
> sands of children. Each child had a green bough or

a bunch of flowers to throw on little Joe's grave, which was already a mass of white flowers, crosses, &c&c.[8]

The president of the United States could understand the grief felt by the president of the Confederacy. Just a year earlier, in 1862, twelve-year-old Willie Lincoln died of typhoid.

As Davis had "walked up and down the room above" where his son lay dead, Lincoln had stayed by his son's body all night before the burial.

* * *

There are other Civil War-era cemeteries in Richmond: Shockoe, where 577 Union and 220 Confederate soldiers were taken after dying at the Alms House Hospital across the street. Oakwood Cemetery, a frequent site for duels between hot-blooded Southern men, and where 17,000 Confederate soldiers would be buried, their blood gone cold. And the Hebrew Cemetery, where, on June 26, 1862, Confederate War Department clerk John B. Jones joined a crowd looking northeast, toward Mechanicsville. It was his first sight of battle.

He saw regimental bands, the fifes and drums of A. P. Hill's Light Division, music playing while Hill's men made ready for an expected Federal assault. About three o'clock, Jones heard the battle begin—cannon firing, rifles popping. They sounded like "driving hail," Sallie Putnam wrote.[9]

Jones remained standing on the high ground of the Hebrew Cemetery through the early evening. Cannon fire continued, lighting the Richmond sky until about nine o'clock. When the sounds of battle died down, Jones wandered back toward his Clay Street home, hoping to learn which side had won.[10]

The fighting he witnessed at long distance was part of the Seven Days' Battles, and the South had been victorious. Jones rejoiced at seeing his first battle. That and for the fact that Richmond was once more safe.

It helps in rejoicing, of course, when the first battle you witness is one your side wins.

The War in the West

III

Stones River

Not long after the sounds of battle faded at Shiloh, they were heard again south of New Orleans. In mid-April, Admiral-to-be David Glasgow Farragut and Commander David Dixon Porter attacked Rebel forts at Jackson and St. Philip, seventy-five miles south of New Orleans. To get to New Orleans, to end the Confederate trade pouring into and out of the South's largest city, the North must first get past the two stout brick and mortar forts down river.

For six days—sometimes pounded by as many as 3,000 shells a day—the Rebels held on. So, early on the morning of the 24th, Farragut decided to run past the forts. The Confederates opened fire, between eighty and ninety guns against Farragut's fleet with nearly twice as many. Three rebel gunboats tried to ram the Federal fleet; they managed to sink one, the USS *Varuna*, a ten-gun sloop. Meanwhile, the Confederates pushed fire-rafts into the middle of the battle—flaming pitch and pine. Cannon and mortar fire lit up the sky in what was later called "the greatest fireworks display in American

history."[1] he Union fleet got through, but not without damage.
Four ships were destroyed; they all were heavily pounded. In
manpower, 147 casualties were recorded in less than ninety
minutes. Still, it worked, and the Union fleet headed upriver for
Farragut's main target: New Orleans.

In Richmond, Mary Chesnut confided to her diary:

April 26, 1862.
Doleful dumps—alarm bells ringing. Telegrams say
the mortar fleet has passed the forts at New Orleans
. . . . Down into the very depth of despair are we.

April 27, 1862.
New Orleans gone—and with it the Confederacy. Are
we not cut in two?
The Confederacy done to death by the politicians.
What wonder we are lost. Those wretched creatures
the Congress and the legislature could never rise to
the greatness of the occasion. They seem to think they
were in a neighborhood squabble. . . . The soldiers
have done their duty.

April 29, 1862.
Grand smash. News from New Orleans fatal to us.
Met [Francis] Weston [a wealthy rice planter]—he
wanted to know where he could find a place of safety
for two hundred negroes. I looked in his face to see
if he were in earnest—then to see if he were sane
. . . . Apparently all the white men of the family had
felt bound to stay at home to take care of them.
There are people who still believe negroes to be
property.
War seems a game of chess—but we have an unequal
number of pawns to begin with. We had knights,
kings, queens, bishops, and castles enough. But our
skillful generals—whenever they cannot arrange the

board to suit them exactly, they burn everything up
and march away. We want them to *save* the *country*.
They seem to think their whole duty is to destroy
ships and *save* the *army*. . . .
The citizens of New Orleans say they were deserted
by the army.[2]

The Tennessee-born Farragut was sixty years old at the time, an
aging but still active flag officer who already had forty-nine
years of naval service behind him.[3] Each year on his birthday,
he proved he was still healthy and active by turning handsprings
as his men watched.[4] His philosophy: "Conquer, or be conquered."

Conquering New Orleans wasn't difficult for Farragut.
The Confederate garrison consisted of just 3,000 short-term
militia.[5] They marched out of the city without firing a shot, but
they carried away everything they could, setting fire to most of
the military supplies they left behind. The people of New
Orleans took care of the remainder, burning two ironclads
under construction and as many as 35,000 bales of cotton. They
dumped hundreds of barrels of sugar and molasses into city
streets.[6]

To control New Orleans, the Union army sent in
General Benjamin Butler, and he quickly earned two nick-
names. The ladies of New Orleans quite often and quite
literally showered abuse on the Union soldiers. Even David
Farragut wasn't immune; one woman standing on a French
Quarter balcony, dumped the contents of her chamber pot on
Farragut's head, one of many such indignities accorded Union
troops. On May 15, General Butler issued an order that ladies
who insulted Northern troops "shall be regarded and held liable
to be treated as a woman of the town plying her avocation."[7]
Quickly, the general became known as "Beast Butler."

About the same time, he took on another sobriquet: "Spoons." That nickname he gained because of his alleged prowess at collecting Southern silverware without the nicety of reimbursing the owners.

* * *

So, the Union owned New Orleans, but there still was Vicksburg higher up the Mississippi River, with rail lines linking the eastern and western sections of the Confederacy. It was important, and leaders of both sides knew it. According to Abe Lincoln, "We can take all the [other] ports of the Confederacy, and they can still defy us from Vicksburg."[8] Jefferson Davis agreed: "Vicksburg is the nail that holds the South's two halves together."

To protect the city, the Confederate army formed a 56,000-man defensive ring around Vicksburg with John C. Pemberton in charge of the garrison. Pemberton was a Pennsylvania-born Quaker and the citizens didn't like him very much because of that. They wanted a Southern-born leader in charge. He was not very well liked and not very sure of himself. After all, he had conflicting orders from his commander-in-chief, President Jefferson Davis, and his commander in the field, General Joseph E. Johnston.

The Union army had its own problems, thanks to Henry Halleck, Grant's superior. For some reason—possibly out of jealousy—once more Halleck relieved Grant of command. All Grant could do was wait, and he began drinking again, threatening to go home. General Sherman had to talk Grant into staying with the army.

Finally, Lincoln overruled Halleck and restored Grant to command, saying, "I can't spare this man. He fights."[9]

Once back on duty, Grant was anxious to attack the fortified city, but capturing Vicksburg wouldn't be easy. For two and a-half months he tried. In October he attacked from Holly Spring, hoping to work down the Mississippi Central Railroad. It didn't work. He dug a canal (it was Lincoln's idea; he'd once made a trip down the Mississippi and considered himself something of an expert on the river) to link a curl in the river and cut Vicksburg off from the Mississippi. That didn't work either. He tried cutting through the swamp, and it was another failure.[10]

Of course, the Confederates weren't sitting still while Grant worked out other plans. Major General Earl Van Dorn led his cavalry on a ride around the Federal lines, capturing Grant's stores at Holly Springs. This left Grant hanging in the breeze with no supplies. He took it as a lesson: he could get along very well, thank you, simply by foraging—living off the land.

Next, Sherman sailed up the Yazoo River northeast of Vicksburg to attack Rebel defenses overlooking Chickasaw Bayou. That's when he ran into trouble. A narrow causeway was the only high ground in the swamp, and when Sherman tried to cross it, one-third of his 32,000 men didn't make it to the other side. The Confederates lost only 200 men in the skirmish, but Sherman counted nearly 1,800 casualties. The bruised, battered, and waterlogged bluecoats pulled back, and Sherman was forced to call off the bayou attack.[11]

* * *

With the battle for Vicksburg stalled, the focus in the western theatre turned to Tennessee.

William S. Rosecrans commanded the Union Army of the Cumberland. He was a man much like George McClellan, preferring large, well-supplied armies. Also like McClellan, he didn't like to rush into a fight. He was known to be bulldog tough, but also slow and methodical. His men called him "Old Rosy." When "Old Rosy" delayed, postponed, and lingered, Lincoln told him either to march on the Rebels or give up the army, almost the same order Lincoln had given McClellan earlier in the year on the Virginia Peninsula.

Rosecrans had taken up headquarters in Nashville, with a 45,000-man force ready to meet Confederate General Braxton Bragg.

Bragg had 8,000 fewer infantrymen than Rosecrans, but he made up for it with a twenty-six-year-old cavalry officer named Joseph Wheeler. While the Union army was mired in December mud, Wheeler rode completely around the enemy rear, wreaking havoc and capturing much of Rosecrans's ammunition to turn on the Union troops.[12]

Then came one of those memorable moments in the war, two days before the end of the year 1862. Rosecrans's and Bragg's armies were camped only a few hundred yards apart, at Stones River, near Tennessee, Murfreesboro. That night a battle broke out—a battle of the bands. Union musicians played "Yankee Doodle" and "Hail Columbia." The Confederates answered with "Dixie" and "The Bonnie Blue Flag."

One band—and it's not certain which—began playing the sentimental "Home Sweet Home" and the other joined in. Then men from both sides started singing. They sang about home, of pleasures and palaces. That night they sang together. The next day, they tried to kill each other.[13]

New Year's Eve was bitterly cold. The Rebels under Breckinridge, Polk, and Hardee were stretched from the Nashville Turnpike to Triune Road, north of Murfreesboro. The Union forces Philip Sheridan, Colonel William Hazen, and

Major General Thomas Crittenden totaled 43,000 men, all ready for a fight.

Both Rosecrans and Bragg planned to attack the other army's left side.

At daybreak, Confederate troops charged the Federal camp. Just as at Shiloh, the Confederates caught the enemy at breakfast, 13,000 rebels swooping down, driving the bluecoats toward the junction of the Nashville and Chattanooga Railroad and the Nashville Pike.[14] To one Union private, it looked like the whole Confederate army coming down on him.[15] Another said it was "like a flock of woodpeckers in a hail storm."[16]

Edward Wood was a private with the Chicago Board of Trade Battery of the Union army when he wrote home about the Battle of Stones River:

> Dear Brother Will,
> You will think when you have read this that I have become an inveterate grumbler, but all our former experience, when compared with what we have undergone since leaving Nashville, seems but a pleasure excursion. I had no idea what powers of endurance man possessed until I saw them tested as I think I now have, to the uttermost. . . .
> The rebs formed in the woods in front of us, and three times during the day charged on us, we pouring in all the time a continuous shower of shell and canister. At one time they got within 200 feet of us when the pioneers who were supporting us sprang to their feet and poured in a volley of musketry which was too much for them. They broke and ran.[17]

"Old Rosy" was at his best, riding among his troops, urging them on. He was splattered with blood when an aide was beheaded by a cannonball, but it didn't stop him.[18]

Steadily, the Confederates pushed the Union army toward the river, and the Federals' far right crumpled. Breckinridge moved his Rebel force across Stones River, hoping to fold the Union line back onto itself. It was a do-or-die attack at the Round Forest. Fighting was so fierce, the Union center became known as "Hell's Half Acre."[19]

Phil Sheridan was about the only thing keeping the Rebels from making it a complete rout. All three of his brigade commanders were killed in the New Year's Eve fight. More than one-third of his men were casualties, and yet they slowed the Confederate tide, beating off the Rebels with bayonets when their ammunition ran out.[20]

Finally, the fighting tapered off, and as 1862 came to an end, the night was filled with the sound of wounded men crying. One night they sang together. The next, they cried out in death.

There wasn't much fighting on New Year's Day, 1863. Both sides shivered and reinforced their positions.

On January 2, the Rebels began the day by easily pushing Union troops off a hill overlooking the battlefield. They followed the enemy and that was a mistake. One witness said the Confederates "opened the doors of hell, and the devil himself was there to greet them."[21] Union cannon pounded the Rebel troops, and the South lost 1,700 men in just forty-five minutes.

General Bragg decided it was too many to continue, and he pulled back. Rosecrans, however, decided to hold on where he was. Thirty-one percent of his army was killed or wounded, and the Union Army of the Cumberland was crippled by what it claimed was a victory—the battle it called Stones River.

Bragg's casualties were fewer—about 10,000—but he ordered his men to clear the field. The South also claimed a victory, calling it the Battle of Murfreesboro.[22]

A young Murfreesboro woman witnesses the battle and the later Confederate retreat. She later wrote:

Who of us that were there does not remember it? It
was the grandest, saddest sight we ever saw. . . .
No other sound broke the stillness. . .only the ceaseless foot-steps of the retreating heroes, that followed
each other in rapid succession, disturbed the breath-
less silence. . . .
Not a word was spoken.
[I] saw amid the dreary, falling rain, the dim out lines
of a gallant army that was passing away! and leaving
their homes to the mercy of a bloodthirsty enemy and
dropped bitter, burning tears.[23]

Whoever won the battle, the fighting reinforced the Union's
hold on Kentucky and gave Lincoln some welcome news at a
time when Federal troops north of Richmond were losing the
Battle of Fredericksburg.

7

A Thief and Harlot Riot

As 1862 wound down in the east, Robert E. Lee was camped at Fredericksburg, about halfway between Richmond and Washington, D.C., waiting for the Union army to attack. Only it wouldn't be George McClellan doing the attacking (as if he ever had). On November 7, Abe Lincoln fired McClellan. The Little Napoleon had been too late too many times, the final time coming after Antietam when—as usual—he hesitated before chasing Lee's Army of Northern Virginia. Lincoln wasn't at all happy with McClellan.

Lincoln named Major General Ambrose Burnside to command the Army of the Potomac, and even Burnside was surprised. He didn't think he was unqualified to command, and he was right.

Lee, however, welcomed Burnside and told James Longstreet he was sorry to see McClellan go:

[W]e always understood each other so well. I fear they
may continue to make changes till they find someone
whom I don't understand.[1]

Burnside rushed his troops south, an unwieldy army of 110,000
men. As he hurried after Lee, he ordered his engineers to bring
up pontoons to build a bridge over the Rappahannock River.
But his orders were unclear and his commander, "Old Brains"
Henry Halleck couldn't figure out where Burnside planned to
make the crossing.

For a week, Burnside (the man from whom we take the
name for men's occasionally fashionable sideburns) waited. Lee
didn't; the "King of Spades" dug in—75,000 men in hills along
the southern bank of the Rappahannock River. He would have
been happy to wait there all winter; not so Ambrose Burnside.
He knew official Washington wanted quick action, so as soon
as the engineers built the bridge, he would cross over and
attack.

The Union general believed his Confederate opponent
would expect him to cross the river somewhere either above or
below the city of Fredericksburg; therefore, he would do what
Lee did not expect, cross over right in the middle of town. The
only part of the operation that surprised General Lee was the
fact that Burnside would charge right into the heart of the
waiting Rebel troops.

James Longstreet's artillery corps was spread out over
four miles of high ground with a sweeping field of fire over the
river and a wide stretch of open fields. Anyone crossing the
river had to come under the Confederate guns. "A chicken
could not live on that field when we open on it," he was told.[2]

Finally, in the middle of the night on December 11,
Burnside's engineers pushed their pontoons into the middle of
the icy river. At first light, Rebel sharpshooters went to work,
picking off the engineers until the Federals sent three regiments

over by boat to clear out the town in house-to-house fighting. Not much damage to the either army, but it delayed Union forces until Stonewall Jackson's corps could connect with Longstreet and extend the Confederate lines. Burnside's already dangerous position became deadly.

The Battle of Fredericksburg, December 13, 1862, saw Burnside assault Lee's forces head-on, time and time again, and time and time again the Rebels pushed them back. The blue-clad Federals charged into a storm of cannon and rifle fire.

Union General William B. Franklin took on Jackson's right flank, while other Federal troops battled Longstreet on the left. The idea was for Franklin to turn Jackson in like a hinge, but again Burnside issued confusing orders and again it was fatal.

Gordon Meade's Pennsylvania division found a small gap in Jackson's line and pushed through, but Franklin failed to send in reserves to support the push and, when Jackson double-timed his own reserves to the front, they drove Meade back. All across the field, Confederate forces were winning. Robert E. Lee stood at his command post, watching his men successfully defend their lines. He said to Longstreet:

> It is well that war is so terrible, or we should grow too fond of it.[3]

Fifteen Union brigades challenged the Rebels at a stone wall below Marye's Heights. Georgia and South Carolina riflemen waited, 2,500 of them. Their ranks were three and four deep. The first rank fired and handed their spent weapons to the rear; from there they were quickly reloaded and sent back to the men ahead. Almost continuous fire on the onrushing Federals. In Richmond, they heard the sounds of battle.

As night came, the cold crept in, and more than 8,000 Union men lay dead and dying in front of that stone wall. Not one man had safely reached it.

Sgt. Richard Rowland Kirkland of the 2nd South Carolina Volunteers was just nineteen at Fredericksburg. He stood behind that wall, saw men die and heard their cries for help. Time after time he risked enemy fire by climbing over the stone wall, taking water and kind words to the Union wounded. Both sides saluted Kirkland as "The Angel of Marye's Heights."

Not all Confederate soldiers were so charitable. In the middle of the night, hundreds went among the Federal dead, stripping them of any clothing the Rebels could use.

Poet and author and sometime war correspondent Walt Whitman was also at Fredericksburg. As a nurse, he tended the wounded in a large brick mansion the Union used as a hospital. (The mansion, "Chatham," was built by William Fitzhugh, three generations back in Robert E. Lee's ancestry; General Lee even named one of his sons after the home's builder.) In *Specimen Days*, Whitman wrote:

> Outdoors, at the foot of a tree, within ten yards of the front of the house, I noticed a heap of amputated feet, legs, arms, hands, etc., a full load for a one-horse cart.

Other sites, not so good as that brick mansion, were also used as hospitals:

> These are merely tents, and sometimes very poor ones, the wounded lying on the ground, lucky if their blankets are spread on layers of pine or hemlock twigs, or small leaves. No cots, not even a mattress. It is pretty cold. The ground is frozen hard and there is occasional snow. I do not see that I can do much good to these wounded and dying; but I cannot leave

them. Once in a while some youngster holds on to me convulsively, and I do what I can for him; at any rate stop with him and sit with him for hours, if he wishes it.

The Union suffered 12,653 casualties at the Battle of Fredericksburg. The South lost 5,322.

* * *

January 1, 1863, was a Thursday. Snow was on the ground in Richmond and the siege continued. Privation continued. "The disaffection is intense and widespread among the politicians of 1860," John Jones believed, "and the consternation and despair are expanding among the people."[4] He and his family went to St. Paul's church for New Year's services. "Dr. Charles Minnegerode preached a sermon against the croakers," those who complained about the war, the government, the prices, and the short supply of food. "Thus we begin the new year," Jones added; "Heaven only knows how we shall end it!" That end was two years down the line, but obviously, even in 1863, all was not going well.

* * *

In Washington, that New Year's Day, 1863, Abraham Lincoln fulfilled his pledge to sign the Emancipation Proclamation. More than 3 million men, women, and children "are and henceforth shall be free," it read.

The proclamation termed emancipation an "act of justice," but called on slaves to "abstain from all violence."

"Fellow citizens," Lincoln wrote, "we cannot escape history. . . . In giving freedom to the slave, we assure freedom to the free."[5]

It left nearly half a million slaves still under bondage in Maryland, Delaware, and Missouri; it left another 275,000 in bondage in Union-occupied Tennessee, Louisiana, and Virginia. In Union-held New Orleans, at least one black continued to own slaves. (Julia Grant, General Grant's wife, still owned four slaves, including one—also named Julia—who went along as Mrs. Grant's personal servant whenever she visited her husband's army headquarters; the other three, she rented out.)

Some Federal soldiers were jubilant over the freeing of the slaves. Others were plainly horrified by it. For most, it was just another part of the war.[6] But well-liked or not, effective or not, the Proclamation turned Union forces into an army of liberation and stopped forever any thoughts of England coming in on the Rebels' side.

As for Richmond, the Emancipation Proclamation left up to Federal troops the job of enforcing freedom in the city.

But first, they had to get there.

* * *

On January 25, 1863, Abe Lincoln decided Ambrose Burnside was right; he was not up to commanding the army. So, once again Lincoln changed commanders, replacing Burnside with Joe Hooker, Fightin' Joe Hooker, if we are to believe the name he was given at the Battle of Williamsburg (actually, it was a mistake; a reporter wired his editor the story of the battle, heading it "Fighting—Joe Hooker." The editor dropped the

hyphen and it became Joe's nickname by default). Whatever his
nickname, Joe Hooker was a tenacious fighter, but he drank
too much. He also wanted a dictator to run the country. Three
days after he put Hooker in charge of the Union army, Lincoln
sent him a letter:

> I believe you to be a brave and skillful soldier, which,
> of course, I like. I also believe you do not mix politics
> with your profession, in which you are right. You have
> confidence in yourself, which is valuable, if not an
> indispensable quality. You are ambitious, which,
> within reasonable bounds, does good rather than
> harm. . . .
> I have heard. . .of your saying recently that both the
> army and the Government needed a dictator. Of
> course it was not for this, but in spite of it, that I have
> given you the command. Only those dictators who
> gain successes can set up dictators. What I now ask of
> you is military success, and I will risk the dictator-
> ship.[7]

Hooker claimed he appreciated the letter, saying it was the kind
a loving father would send his errant son. He would abide by
it and make Father Abraham proud.

Lincoln was right about one thing; Hooker had confidence. He said, "My plan is perfect," and warned: "May God
have mercy on General Lee, for I will have none."[8] Hooker's
self-confidence may have been based on numbers. He had
130,000 troops, including nearly 12,000 cavalry. His artillery
boasted of at least 400 guns.[9] Robert E. Lee had about 65,000
men and 220 guns; he had sent James Longstreet with part of
his army foraging for supplies.

Joe Hooker was said to play a mean game of poker, but
Bobbie Lee was an even better gambler as far as war was concerned. He left Jubal Early with 10,000 men and, with just

55,000 troops, called Hooker's bet near a mansion called Chancellorsville on May 1.

The mansion was a two-storied, dormered building at the intersection of the Orange Turnpike and Ely's Ford Road. It was in what is now known as Virginia's "Horse and Whiskey Country," rolling hills with some cleared farm areas, some areas of heavy woods—scrub oak, pine, all tangled with underbrush. Hooker used the mansion for his headquarters.

Thomas J. "Stonewall" Jackson and his men met Hooker's forces a few miles east of Chancellorsville at a spot where the undergrowth gave way to open country. It was an area more suitable to the Federals' superior number to that of the Rebels, but Hooker ordered his men back to a defensive position around the mansion; he hadn't put up much of a fight, much less given God a chance to have mercy on General Lee.

Hooker's corps commanders protested the retreat but obeyed. His second in command, Major General Darius Couch of the 2nd Corps, later wrote that, Hooker claimed "the advantages gained by the successive marches of his lieutenants were to culminate in fighting a defensive battle in that nest of thickets (around Chancellorsville). . . . I retired from his (Hooker's) presence with the belief that my commanding general was a whipped man."[10]

Couch also was a very confused general. First ordered into battle, then ordered back, then he was given a third order from Fightin' Joe: "Hold on until 5 o'clock." Couch was not only confused, he was exasperated by it all. He sent back a reply: "Tell Hooker he is too late, the enemy are already on my right and rear. I am in full retreat."

Joe Hooker was at least up to the battle of words. He answered, "It is all right, Couch, I have got Lee just where I want him; he must fight me on my own ground."

That night Lee and Stonewall Jackson sat on empty hardtack boxes pulled up near a campfire, discussing plans for the next day's fight. As they talked, Jeb Stuart rode up with information about Hooker's army. Fightin' Joe's right flank was "up in the air," that is, not properly anchored against attack.

Proponents of both Lee and Jackson say their man originated the plan of attack. Whoever did, it was a brilliant decision. Jackson would take his 28,000-man corps on a flanking movement and leave Lee with only 14,000 men against Hooker's army of more than 100,000. Lee's men, however, would be well screened by the heavy forest. Using a local guide, the son of Colonel Charles C. Wellford, who owned the Catherine Furnace near the battle site (the furnace had been built earlier in the century, abandoned, then reopened to manufacture weapons for the Confederacy), Jackson took his men on a twelve-mile march over back roads. Hooker apparently didn't hear Jackson's men heading around his flank, because he had sent them on a raid to scare Richmond. The scare didn't work, and Hooker knew nothing of Jackson's movement.

Facing Jackson were two disparate Union officers. Daniel Sickles headed up the 3rd Corps. He was a Tammany Hall, New York Democrat, a political appointee who had a reputation for philandering. When his wife decided to do a bit of philandering on her own in 1859, Sickles killed her lover on the streets of Washington. He was tried for murder but acquitted, the first known successful plea in America of temporary insanity.

The commander of the Union's 11th Corps was Oliver O. Howard, a West Point graduate with a distinguished combat record; he had lost an arm in the Seven Days' Battles. No philanderer he, but rather a monogamous church-going teetotaler known as The Christian Soldier.

About 4:00 A.M. Jackson's troops filed past General Lee. Jackson sat slumped on his horse, "Little Sorrel." Lee sat tall on "Traveller." Jackson and Lee spoke briefly, the last time Lee would see Jackson alive.

By mid-afternoon, Jackson sent Lee a message saying he had met the enemy at Chancellor's Tavern. It was O. O. Howard and his 11th Corps, and he hit them while they were at ease, preparing an early dinner.

The Rebels' uniforms were even more tattered than usual because of the briars and brush they'd marched through, and they charged, yelling and screaming, into the Yankees. "Like a cloud of dust driven before a spring shower," Howard later wrote, "the startled rabbits, squirrels, quail and other game [came] flying wildly hither and thither in evident terror."[11] Jackson pushed Howard back for several miles before The Christian Soldier could improvise a new line of defense.

Lee's two remaining divisions had attacked Hooker's front, and for several hours into the night fighting flared and died, flared and died again.

Major General Robert Emmett Rodes's division had been one of the first to attack Howard, and now his men had to pull back to reorganize. It was about 9 P.M. when his men began moving back into position.

Despite the hour, Stonewall Jackson rode out to make a personal reconnaissance of the situation. It is his usual practice not to rely solely on the reports of others. General A. P. Hill was with him, as were several other members of his staff. East on the Orange Plank Road, along other, smaller trails, Jackson rode "Little Sorrel." They were beyond the Confederate picket lines when they turned back. A group of nervous North Carolinians heard the approaching horsemen and fired first one shot, then a volley. General Hill shouted, "Cease firing!" but "Little Sorrel" bolted and ran into the woods. More firing, other horses reared in fright. More screams that the Rebels were firing on their own men. The Carolinians didn't believe it: "It's a lie; pour it into them, boys!"[12]

Two of Jackson's staff were killed. When A. P. Hill found Stonewall he saw Jackson had been hit in several places.

His left arm hung limp. "Very painful," Jackson told Hill, "my arm is broken."

Jackson's men found a litter and carried him along the road. Union artillery fire blasted the road; one litter bearer was killed and another ran off.

Stonewall didn't want it known he had been injured; just say it was some Confederate officer, he told his staff. But it didn't take long for the word to reach his men. As Jackson was being carried back into his lines, he was approached by Major General W. Dorsey Pender. "Ah, General," Pender said, "I am sorry to see you have been wounded. The lines here are so much broken that I fear we will have to fall back." He couldn't move, but that didn't prevent Jackson from issuing an order: "You must hold your ground, General Pender! You must hold your ground, sir!" It was Pender's North Carolinians who had shot Jackson.

When they finally found an ambulance for Stonewall, it was already occupied by two other officers. One of the two gave up his ride and Jackson was taken to the home of a nearby minister where he was offered whiskey to ease his pain. Jackson's surgeon, Dr. Hunter Holmes McGuire, found him there and administered a shot of morphine. Dr. McGuire observed that Jackson already had lost a lot of blood. As Jackson was put back in the ambulance, Dr. McGuire went with him, holding a finger on the general's artery. Slowly, the wagon moved over the four miles of bumpy road to a field hospital just erected near the Wilderness Tavern. There, in a tent, he was examined more closely. His left arm was shattered and several bones on his right hand had been fractured. The bullet was removed from just under the skin.

Then Dr. McGuire administered chloroform and amputated Jackson's left arm about two inches below the shoulder.

For the next two days, May 3 and 4, Jackson remained at the field hospital.

When Robert E. Lee heard about Jackson's wounds, he wrote Stonewall:

> Could I have directed events, I should have chosen for the good of the country to be disabled in your stead. I congratulate you upon the victory, which is due to your skill and energy.

Receiving the note, Jackson said, "General Lee is very kind, but he should give the praise to God."[13]

Late Monday Jackson was taken to Guinea's Station, staying at a friend's home, the plantation owned by Thomas Chandler. He was placed in a small, three-room office building next to the main house. All seemed to be going well with his convalescence until Jackson contracted pleural pneumonia. He died at 3:15 P.M., May 10, his last feverish words: "No, no, let us pass over the river and rest under the shade of the trees."

The next day, the general's body was taken to Richmond. Flags were lowered to half-staff, businesses and government offices were closed, and crowds lined the streets as the Great Stonewall was carried to the Virginia Governor's Mansion at the corner of Governor and Capitol Streets.

Only a few prominent people were allowed in, among them Constance Cary Harrison:

> Two sentries paced to and fro in the moonlight streaming through the. . .windows. . . . A lamp burned dimly at one end of the hall, but we saw distinctly the white outline of the quiet face in its dreamless slumber. [14]

They laid him in the Mansion's reception room, with the star-crossed "Stainless Flag" of the Confederacy as his pall. In life he had been a bewildering man, a man loved and hated, one holding a strong belief in his God and in himself. A man who, almost as much at Robert E. Lee, was the military strength of the Confederacy.

The next day, with guns booming, they bore Jackson through Richmond on a plumed funeral carriage. His horse, "Little Sorrel," pranced behind him. Two regiments of Pickett's men formed the escort. Then came wounded men from the Stonewall Brigade, heading the mourners. And President Davis in his carriage. And Secretary of State Judah Benjamin. And Secretary of War James Seddon. The rest of the cabinet, on foot. Department clerks, state and city officials, thousands of citizens and soldiers.[15]

Jackson's funeral was the last—perhaps the greatest—of the military funerals in Richmond under siege. Down Governor Street to Main, through the western gates of Capitol Square. They laid him in state in the Hall of Representatives. Garlands of spring flowers and white lilies. Twenty-thousand or more filed by for a last look at the Great Stonewall. Until finally, he was taken to a train and carried to Lexington for interment.

A few days before Jackson's death, as he lay in that plantation office building, a note from General Lee was read to Stonewall: "You have lost your left arm, but I have lost my right."

* * *

As for the Battle of Chancellorsville, Jeb Stuart took over as Jackson's temporary successor. He prepared to launch an all-out attack on Hooker's forces at Hazel Grove. But Hooker ordered Hazel Grove abandoned. The most intense fighting was near a homestead called Fairview, brigade after brigade of

Rebels challenging the Federals' position. The Union guns began to run out of ammunition, but Hooker refused to resupply them.

Stuart reunited his troops with Lee at Fairview and surged toward the Chancellorsville clearing, and Hooker withdrew northward to a shrunken defensive line.

It was a major victory for Robert E. Lee, and his exhausted troops cheered as he rode into the clearing around the burning mansion at Chancellorsville. It was, however, an expensive victory. Confederate forces suffered 13,000 casualties—22 percent of Lee's army. Hooker lost 17,000—15 percent of his force.

But the South lost Thomas Jonathan "Stonewall" Jackson, and he could never be replaced, if not for his military brilliance, then for the confidence he inspired in his men.

Chancellorsville was such a victory that it gave Lee confidence, too much confidence. He would move north, into Pennsylvania, and it would prove to be an exceptional error.

* * *

On January 1, 1861, the Richmond *Daily Dispatch* sold for one cent per copy, and classified advertising offered lump coal at six dollars per load. By November, 1864, daily newspapers were twenty cents each, and coal was ninety dollars per load.[16]

When J. B. Jones took a job as Confederate war department clerk, issuing passports first in Montgomery and later in Richmond, he was paid $1,200 a year, probably an average salary for 1861. In 1864, he and one son, who by then also was a war department clerk, earned $4,000 each, "yet we cannot subsist and clothe the family; for, alas, the paper money is $30 for one in specie!"[17] Salaries were constantly wrangled

over in Congress and reported in newspapers. After much
debate, associate justices of the Confederate Supreme Court
were paid $5,500 per year.[18] No matter their salaries, no
matter how often those salaries were increased, Richmond
residents could not keep pace with inflation; it became increasingly difficult to buy sufficient food with the dwindling value of
the Confederate dollar.

In March of 1863, the Confederate Congress created
commissions to control prices. The idea didn't work. The
situation became much worse before it became even a little
better.

* * *

Changes were everywhere. Before the war began, the *Dispatch*
of January 3, 1861, carried notices of "Reliable Drugs" for sale,
recommendations that, if "you go rifle shooting, use your rifle
in a scientific manner," and a reminder that "Death loves a
shining mark; Gentlemen with brandied noses will take warning." By February 6, 1863, the tone of the newspaper changed,
and the *Enquirer* offered notices of "Substitutes Wanted." The
shooting was being done in war, not in hunting.

As capital of a rebellion, Richmond was no stranger to
war and its accompanying distress. On March 12, 1863, the
editor of the *Sentinel* wrote of "The Future of Our Confederacy." There are "gloomy and despondent people," he declared, "who apprehend disputes, quarrels, secession, and
disunion among the Confederate States themselves." But they
will prove wrong, he added, and predicted the ultimate result
"will be the independence of the South." At that point, however, the Confederacy was halfway through its short existence,
halfway between Fort Sumter and Appomattox. He saw no

probable termination of the circumstances, causes, and necessities which had banded the Confederate States together, [and we] perceive no reason to fear the dissolution of our Confederacy.[19]

Perhaps no dissolution yet, but there were other problems. Lee's army along the Rappahannock River was reduced to half rations. Inside Richmond's seven hills, the situation was worse.

* * *

As the size of the Confederate army increased, so did its demand for food. Some farmers and speculators withheld crops, hoping to drive up the prices beyond their already heady altitudes. To add to the problems, weather in the spring of 1863 was less than helpful. Nearly a foot of snow fell March 19-21, and when it melted, roads already damaged by heavy military use became impassable.

There was and is much confusion over what took place next. There's even confusion over when it happened. In writing of the events nearly twenty-five years later, the editors of the Richmond *Dispatch* said it occurred on April 1 and blamed outside agitators (a phrase that came into vogue again in the 1960s), possibly Union sympathizers.[20] We don't really know about "outside agitators" (Richmond City Council's own reports of the incident make no mention of them), but we do know there were several inaccuracies in that report. The event actually occurred on April 2, 1863, and what it was, was a riot. The city simply had run out of bread.

The people of Richmond, as the twentieth century saying goes, were mad as Hell and weren't going to take it any more. They took the situation into their own hands. On the night of

April 1, a group of women met. They agreed to demand food,
and if their demand wasn't met, they would take supplies by
force. Carry axes and hatchets, their leaders said.

On the next day, women and children met, John Jones
said, "as if by concert" at a Baptist church near the Tredegar
Iron Works where many of their husbands and fathers
worked.[21] They marched to the governor's mansion to com-
plain. Governor John Letcher did little to assuage their anger,
so they rioted, in street after street the women rioted. There
were "but few men among them, and these were mostly foreign
residents, with exemptions [from fighting] in their pockets,"
Jones wrote. Sallie Putnam called it a "disgraceful riot, to
which, in order to conceal the real designs of a lawless mob
engaged in it, was given the name 'bread riot.'"[22]

Mrs. Sara A. Pryor was another Richmond resident who,
like Sallie Putnam and John Jones, kept a diary. She was more
sympathetic to the rioters than was Sallie. Mrs. Pryor told of
meeting a young woman of eighteen, emaciated by hunger:

> As she raised her hand to remove her sunbonnet, her
> loose calico sleeve slipped up and revealed a mere
> skeleton of an arm. She perceived my expression as I
> looked at it and hastily pulled down her sleeve with a
> short laugh. 'This is all that's left of me!' she said. 'It
> seems real funny, don't it?'[23]

Where are you going?

> We are going to the bakeries and each of us will take
> a loaf of bread. That is little enough for the govern-
> ment to give us after it has taken our men.[24]

Jones also met someone that day, perhaps the same young
woman as Mrs. Pryor, "a young woman, seemingly emaciated,
but yet with a smile." She was, she told Jones, "going to find

something to eat." "I could not, for the life of me," he wrote, "refrain from expressing the hope that [she] might be successful." He even pointed the way for the crowd, sending it "in the right direction to find plenty in the hands of the extortioners."[25] Jones later testified in court about the rioters, who they were and what they had done.

What they did was break into shops and warehouses, shouting, "Bread! Bread! Our children are starving while the rich roll in wealth."[26] First pleas, then shouts, then rioting and violence. The rioters (like rioters before and since) took anything available—food, clothing, jewelry, nearly everything they could lay their hands on. Sallie Putnam blamed the few men among the rioters for this thievery, saying they carried away "immense loads of cotton cloth, woolen goods, and other articles." The women's "cry for bread," she claimed, soon gave way to men stealing clothing, shoes, dry goods, and jewelry.[27]

Accounts differ as to what happened next, whether Virginia Governor Letcher or Confederate President Davis stepped in to calm the crowd that had grown to more than 5,000. Most likely, it was Letcher. One account, printed years later, has him meeting the crowd on Main Street, between 13th and 15th, and speaking to the rioters for about five minutes.[28] A cart was overturned, or maybe it was a rice barrel (eyewitness reports vary); the governor climbed up and warned the crowd that if they didn't leave within five minutes, the troops would open fire. Dramatically, he took out his watch to mark the time. Equally dramatically, the guard loaded its weapons. Other accounts have Jefferson Davis acting out this scene; some say Davis met the mob around 13th and Cary Streets, delivered a quiet, nonthreatening speech, and the crowd dispersed. Richmond Mayor Joseph Mayo may also have tried to calm down the rioters.

John Monclure Daniel of the Richmond *Examiner* called the mob "a handful of prostitutes, professional thieves, Irish and Yankee hags, gallows-birds from all lands but our own."[29]

Sallie Putnam saw the rioters armed "with pistols, knives, hammers, hatchets, axes, and every other weapon which could be made useful in their defense or might subserve their designs in breaking into stores for the purpose of thieving."[30]

By 11:00 A.M. the Bread Riot was over; it had lasted about two hours. It wasn't President Davis or Governor Letcher or even Mayor Mayo who calmed down the crowd. It was the armed Confederate regular troops who did the job.

A total of forty-four women and twenty-nine men were arrested. Most of the charges were later dropped; many of the accused were found innocent, and in some cases they skipped bail. Only twelve women are known to have been convicted of any charge and most of those charges were misdemeanors. Men, however, were sentenced to serve time in the state penitentiary on felony charges.[31] For some, this was almost a trip home; they lived in an area of Richmond known as "Penitentiary Bottom." The fate of some of those arrested isn't known because a fire later destroyed many court records.

Richmond, of course, wasn't alone in its starvation. The people of Atlanta rioted March 16, demanding bread; Salisbury, North Carolina, saw a flour riot on March 18; March 25 saw a bread riot in Mobile, Alabama; and on April 1, another bread riot took place in Petersburg, just minutes away from Richmond by rail. Perhaps Richmonders took lessons from those earlier riots. Perhaps, some of the participants of the Petersburg event rode with the news to Richmond to riot again.

The various riots caused some historians, then and now, to claim a Union conspiracy. After all, the discontent seemed to travel in a line northward from Atlanta to Salisbury to Petersburg to Richmond. Noted Civil War historian Bruce Catton, however, not only discounts the conspiracy theory, he feels the Richmond Bread Riot "meant nothing in particular."[32] If by "nothing in particular," it's meant that Richmond's Bread Riot wasn't unusual, then there is no argument.

But still the hunger and discontent continued. A year after the Richmond Bread Riot, Randolph County, Alabama, farmers complained to President Jefferson Davis, telling of the growing number of indigent families and "deaths from starvation."

> Women riots have taken place in Several parts of the County in which Govt wheat and corn has been seized to prevent starvation of themselves and families. Where it will end unless relief is afforded we cannot tell.[33]

Richmond newspapers carried reports of most of the earlier events, but when it came time for their own, their story changed, or rather, the whole story wasn't run. In fact, the riot so shocked the Confederate government that it tried unsuccessfully to suppress the news. J. B. Jones even recorded in his diary that "No account of yesterday's riots appeared in the paper today."[34] That isn't entirely incorrect; the day after the Bread Riot, the *Dispatch* carried a lead editorial that bannered "Sufferings in the North."[35] But the *Examiner* reported the Richmond Bread Riot on April 3 and again on April 4, the latter, strangely, copying accounts from Danville and Lynchburg newspapers. The out-of-town papers, so the *Examiner* declared, were "flaming accounts of a thief-and-harlot riot."[36] The editor also told of reports carried in northern newspapers, "the work of exaggeration" best left to the Yankees. On April 23, the *Examiner* reprinted a New York *Herald* account of the riot that said the "leading men of the city [Richmond] attempted to circulate the report that the women were 'Irish and Yankee hags.'" The New York *Herald*'s comment was a quote from the Richmond *Examiner* itself.

In her memoirs, Sallie Putnam claimed that "no demonstration of the kind was afterwards made during the war."[37] That also is not entirely accurate. There were other demonstrations in Richmond, although they never reached the magnitude of the Bread Riot. Crowds gathered on several occasions, complaining of high prices, complaining of conditions in general. Even on the day after the riot, April 3, other mobs—apparently not connected with the Bread Riot—roamed the city but were quickly dispersed.

By then, the military was taking no chances. Cannon were brought into Richmond from various other Virginia cities, including Lynchburg, cannons that "will run easily on the streets."[38] "They will be easily, very easily drawn, being light," according to a letter from Captain Peter G. Goghlan, keeper of the state armory.

Rumors were everywhere, widespread claims of another bread riot planned for Friday, April 10, and troops under the command of Major Gerald Elzey were called in to reinforce the city police and Confederate units guarding the city.[39] Soon, however, the people of Richmond settled down, and as Jones added to his diary on the evening of the riot, "All is quiet now . . .and I understand the government is issuing rice to the people."[40]

8

The Greatest Extortioners

To Richmonders under siege, surviving became more than just rioting for bread; it became something of a full-time job, with the frequent food shortages, continually rising prices, and the steady preference—sometimes by the government, sometimes by the people themselves, sometimes by both—for supplies to go first to the army and later to civilians. Nearly everyone and everything felt the effects of the war. "Our churches were stripped of their cushions," Mrs. Putnam remembered, the cushions torn apart and used as beds in hospitals. Private homes also gave up pillows for hospital use, and "carpets and curtains were cut up for blankets for soldiers." Often troops on their way to the front lines were given help and food.

As she wrote:

Many times the dinner was taken from the table and distributed to soldiers in their march through our

streets, when perhaps there was nothing in the larder
with which to prepare another for the self-sacrificing
family which had so generously disposed of the
principal meal of the day.[1]

Not all soldiers were lucky enough to be offered food as they
marched on to the war outside the city. And some didn't wait
to be offered; they took what they wanted. The *Dispatch* of
June 16, 1864, wrote:

Four turkeys and seventeen hens were stolen from
Mr. Charles Longest [who] was aroused by the squa-
lling of the chickens just as the thieves were leaving
the premises.[2]

And, the same issue reported, "between two and three thousand dollars worth of bacon" was stolen from a smoke house in
Manchester, south of the city.

Of passing note here were the PIGs of Richmond under
siege, not the porcine variety, but the police. In the 1960s and
1970s, the word "pig" was a derogatory term for police. At the
same time, the phrase "blind pig" was used for something
illegal, usually an after-hours place to buy alcoholic beverages.
The two terms—pig and blind pig—may have had their
origination in Civil War Richmond. The Richmond police were
called the Public Guard and wore a "P.G." insignia on their
hats. Now, a blind pig is one without an eye, as in P (no I) G.
PIG And a police officer who does not see an illegal drinking
establishment, also is a "blind pig."[3]

* * *

By the end of 1863, not only food prices were high; clothing was equally expensive and hard to find. "A genteel suit of clothes cannot be had now for less than $700," Jones wrote, "and a pair of boots, $200 if good."[4] Sallie Putnam said the women of Richmond "were actively interested in discovering the coloring properties of roots, barks, and berries [and] we beheld the Southern gentlemen clad in homespun suits, and our ladies wearing domestic dresses that challenged manufacture."

If Jones's boots for men were $200, Putnam's "balmoral boots for ladies brought two hundred to two hundred and fifty dollars," and she added, "We hardly dare trust ourselves to give the price of ladies hats."[5] Empty larders and closets became commonplace.

In her postwar letter to her sister Clara, Mary Andrews West blamed the farmers who have been "the greatest extortioners." It was the speculators, she added, "speculators of all kinds [who] kept up the prices of everything." There were numerous reports of high food prices. J. B. Jones told of "an opossum dressed for cooking, with a card in its mouth marked, 'price, $20.'"[6] "How," Mary West asked, "were the salaried portion of the community to live. . . ?"[7]

And yet, there were those who managed to live well. They even partied, though the parties were somewhat changed; they entertained, although that too was different. Not all of those who lived well could have been extortioners or speculators. Some—again, like the Wests—prepared for the worst and were ready when their expectations were met. Mary West told Clara that when relatives outside Richmond heard of their condition, very quickly "we would be bountifully supplied." Food and other items, then, were there, only finding and paying for them were the prevalent problems.

Writer after writer, witness after witness, told of the hunger, of deprivation, of starvation, and of the simple wants of the city's residents. Writing thirty years after the war—thirty

years in which, to be sure, good times and bad became inter-
mixed in his mind—a long-time resident of Richmond told of
the many changes in the still important social life in the
Confederate capital city. For many months, Edward M. Alfriend
wrote, Richmond was "an extremely gay, bright, and happy
city."[8] But as the war, death, dying, privation, and inflation all
progressed, "its miseries tightened their bloody grasp upon the
city, happiness was nearly destroyed, and the hearts of the
people were made to bleed."[9]

Civil War Richmond's "style of living was quite as simple
as our dress," Sallie Putnam agreed, but attempts were made to
continue social life, albeit with major changes from prewar fashion. Often, one family would dine with friends, using a system
referred to as "banting." "The inducement to accept the kind
invitation" to dine, Putnam said, frequently was "I'll give you a
nice coffee" to which the banting reply was "Will you give me
something sweet?" "There was," she wrote, "something romantic, something novel in this mode of life, and the remembrance,
though associated with much that is painful, is on the whole
rather pleasant."[10] Was Sallie Putnam's remembrance just that,
a glorification of something that occurred during an under-
standably important period of her life? As the siege continued,
"something novel" would become her standard of living.

The South in general, and perhaps Virginia in particular,
had long been noted for its hospitality. In a Richmond under
siege, banting wasn't the only change. The biggest came in the
form of "starvation parties," begun, it is believed by Hetty Cary,
a Baltimore cousin of a well-to-do Richmond family. She
started things rolling by paying thirty dollars for music, but
served neither food nor drink.[11] Edward Alfriend tells us "The
young ladies of the city, accompanied by their male escorts,
would assemble at a fashionable residence that before the war
had been the abode of wealth, and have music and plenty of
dancing, but not a morsel of food or a drop of drink was seen."

It became a "popular and universal" form of entertainment; "the ladies were simply dressed, many of them without jewelry, because the women of the South had long ago given their jewelry to the Confederate cause."[12] Neither food nor wine was served, Alfriend said, "because the host could not get it, or could not afford it."

Starvation parties apparently were frequent and well attended, often by government and military leaders. That sometimes included General Robert E. Lee, taking time off from the nearby war to visit his arthritic wife at their home on Franklin Street, between 7th and 8th Streets. On such occasions, Alfriend wrote years later, "he was not only the cynosure of all eyes, but the young ladies all crowded around him, and he kissed every one of them." As Alfriend put it, "This was esteemed his privilege, and he seemed to enjoy the exercise of it." Yankee General Sherman may later deem war akin to Hell, but Southern gentleman General Lee, for the moment at least, found some entertainment attached to it.

But as time and the siege progressed, dining became increasingly difficult. Boarding houses closed, hotels stopped serving the *table d'hote*, and more and more families "lived and slept in a single room, cooking at the grate meals which, when winter came, consisted often only of potatoes."[13]

Years after the events, Sallie Putnam recalled that "Richmond. . .had never known such a scarcity of food, never known such absolute want of the necessities of life."[14] Sending a servant to the market often resulted in his return with an empty basket "or something so miserable in appearance that the stomach revolted, probably at the sight."

John Jones, whose family included his wife, two daughters, two sons often at home from the war, a hired servant, a cat, and a parrot, concluded that there "really is no scarcity of anything but meat."[15] He believed high prices prevented the purchase of food. "I have not seen a rat or mouse for months," he added, "and lean cats are wandering past every day in quest of new homes."[16] The Jones family cat apparently didn't leave home but was fed by a daughter who frequently gave up her share of meat.

However, as the war continued and privation progressed, large packs of dogs roamed the city. Some, it may be supposed, were like the cats Jones saw, looking for new owners. Others, according to later reports, had turned feral.

Jones, and no doubt many others to judge by newspaper advertisements, supplemented food purchases with gardens. He planted early but grew tomatoes ("maturing very slowly, but there will be an abundance, saving me $10 per week for ten weeks"), lima beans ("very full, and some of them will be fit to pull in few days"), potatoes (although they were "green as grass"), cabbages (the seeds at one time cost him ten dollars an ounce), parsnips, and red peppers. "No doubt," Farmer Jones recorded, "the little garden, 25 by 50, will be worth $150 to me."[17] Richmond's changeable weather didn't help matters; on April 2, one year after the Bread Riot, Jones wrote in his diary: "I set out sixty-eight cabbage-plants yesterday. They are now under the snow!"[18] So many times he would add: "Thank Providence, we still have health."

Two things he could not grow: flour and coffee. Mrs. Jones solved the beverage problem:

> My wife has obviated one of the difficulties of the blockade, by a substitute for coffee, which I like very well. It is simply *corn meal, toasted like coffee,* and served in the same manner. It costs five or six pounds—coffee, $2.50.[19]

Flour wasn't so easy to "obviate," and that same basic ingredient of the 1863 Bread Riot continued its upward price spiral: $40 per barrel on August 4, 1863; $50 on August 6; $70 by

October 22; $400 per barrel on May 22, 1864; and $1,500 per barrel on March 20, 1865.[20] If Sallie Putnam's comment was true that the April 2, 1863, Bread Riot was the only one the city suffered, one must wonder why.

In fact, prices on everything soared. "Confederate money was almost valueless," Alfriend recalled; "Its purchasing power had so depreciated that it used to be said it took a basketful to go to market." Thus, he easily could add, "I know of some who lived for days on soup and bread."[21] Jones, in fact, wrote in May of 1864 that "unless government feeds the people here, some of us may starve."[22] And day by day, the population increased. Some came unwillingly.

* * *

Robert Goodyear was a sergeant with Company B, 27th Connecticut Volunteer Infantry. He was captured near Fredericksburg and marched to Richmond:

> It does seem that victory is not destined to crown the efforts of the Potomac army. And I can attribute it to no other reason than to the corruption and wickedness existing in it.
> Still we hope on—trusting and praying that God in His own good time will give us the victory and crown our efforts with an honorable and permanent peace.[23]

* * *

The weather in late April 1863 was anything but spring-like. Hailstones as big as hen's eggs (in the twentieth century, we'd describe them as being "golf ball size") devastated Richmond's war gardens.

* * *

Not long after Robert Goodyear wrote about trusting God, a small village about 100 miles north of Richmond saw the largest cavalry battle of the war. In fact, the Battle of Brandy Station on June 9, 1863, was the largest cavalry battle ever fought in the Western Hemisphere—20,000 Union and Confederate horsemen. Robert E. Lee's son Rooney was wounded; General Wade Hampton's brother Frank was killed. In the end, Rebel General Jeb Stuart was the winner. More or less.

It was, however, a turning point for the Union cavalry. Up till then, the Federal cavalry was decidedly (and confessedly) inferior to the Confederate cavalry. The Battle of Brandy Station gave them self-confidence that, according to one of Stuart's aides, "enabled them to contest so fiercely the subsequent battlefields of June, July, and October."[24]

It began when Stuart wanted to show off his new command, five cavalry brigades of 9,536 officers and men. It was more than he had ever commanded and he wanted, not only General Lee, but the ladies of northern Virginia to see them. And him.

Stuart moved his headquarters from Orange to Culpeper, and in a long field near Brandy Station, ordered his men to set the stage for a pageant. The field was close to the Orange and Alexandria Railroad; Stuart wanted the train stopped. Spectators would use the train for seats. There would be a ball on June 4, the night before the pageant; another would be held the next day. Each of Stuart's staff officers was ordered to purchase a new uniform for the extravaganza. It would be quite the social event.

One problem: at the last minute, Lee could not attend because of duties elsewhere. Well, there would be enough young ladies to dote on the dashing Stuart to make up for General Lee's absence.

At 10 A.M., bugles sounded, and Stuart's troopers moved out in columns of squadrons, passing Jeb's review, then doubling back. Blank charges were fired to simulate the repelling of attackers. Rebel horsemen galloped by, rebel yells were screamed, young ladies swayed and swooned. Oh, it was a grand day to be in Stuart's cavalry. That is, the young ladies swooned if they were accompanied by some awkward swain. If their parents were in tow, they were able to ward off attacks of "the vapors."

It all went so well that Stuart ordered a repeat performance for June 8. General Lee would be able to attend after all. The second performance went equally well, despite grumbling by the enlisted men, who had not been invited to attend either of the grand balls.

Following the review, the spectators left and the men packed their equipment, ready to move out early the next day. Jeb Stuart spent the night sleeping in an open wagon, surrounded by the sweet smell of uncut clover. All was right with his world.

Early on June 9, Stuart awakened to the sounds of rifle fire, the all too familiar pop-pop-pop. Then an answering echo. This was not some pageant; the Federals were on the south side of the Rappahannock River. General Stuart, however, wasn't worried.

An aide, Brigadier General William "Grumble" Jones, tried to warn Stuart but the warning was ignored. "Tell General

Jones to attend to the Yankees in his front," Stuart said, "and I'll watch the flanks."

"So he thinks they ain't coming, does he," Jones answered. "Well, let him alone; he'll damn soon see for himself."[25]

The Federals already were at Brandy, about 10,000 of them. They had crossed the Rappahannock River to find out what General Lee was up to, and they had caught Jeb Stuart napping. Or, to be more precise, caught him still glorying in his two-day pageant. It took all day, and a lot of charging back and forth, for Stuart to win. It was not a dazzling victory, and that embarrassed him.

But the ever-flamboyant Stuart ordered his men to establish his headquarters at the top of Fleetwood Hill (the actual site of the Battle of Brandy Station) in order to be able to say he had held his ground against the Yankee horsemen. Even that didn't work out exactly as planned; the top of the hill was "covered so thickly with the dead horses and men, and the blue bottle flies were swarming so thick over the blood stains on the ground that there was not room enough to pitch the tents among them," General W. W. Blackford later remembered.[26] Stuart had to consent to camp elsewhere.

Usually, Richmond newspapers praised Stuart. Not this time; they attacked him:

> The more the circumstances of the late affair at Brandy Station are considered, the less pleasant do they appear. . . . If the war was a tournament, invented and supported for the pleasure of a few vain and weak-headed officers [this disaster] might be dismissed with compassion. . . . The Confederate cavalry was carelessly strewn over the country, with the Rappahannock only between it and the enemy who has already proved his enterprise to our cost.[27]

* * *

Normally, however, Richmond newspapers carried little, if any, news of the war in the surrounding trenches, whether to keep it from the enemy, to keep it from their local readers, or because they couldn't obtain the news isn't certain. Sometimes, however, such news crept into their reporting:

> June 21, 1863—
> Not much of interest in the last few days. The firing yesterday morning from 4 to 10 O'Clock was the heaviest we had. . . .

> June 25, 1863—
> Some of our boys have been doing some pretty gallant little deeds within the past two weeks. Some parties charged outside our works killed and captured a few Yankees.[28]

The tide of war flowed away from Richmond, and it flowed in a deadly manner. General Lee and his troops crossed the Potomac at Harpers Ferry. It was near where, a few short years earlier, he had led Union troops in capturing John Brown. This time he planned a general invasion of Pennsylvania.

Despite objections from President Davis, who wanted to keep the troops around the Confederate capital, Lee again took the war to the North, to fight the Yankees in their own backyard, and to take the death and destruction out of Virginia. Not incidentally, it was also a shopping trip of sorts; many of his men lacked shoes, and the general had heard of large stores of footwear in Pennsylvania. His march took him to Gettysburg to check reports of a large supply of footwear just waiting for his men to take.

Lee's troops crossed the Potomac into Maryland on June 16, 1863. At the same time, a group of ladies—"mostly young and guileless"—were traveling into Virginia for a picnic. To keep their uniforms dry, many of the Confederate troops removed their uniforms—trousers and shoes—and wrapped them into balls, carrying them over their heads along with their cartridge boxes. What underwear they wore was tattered and full of holes. The two groups met in mid-stream, heading in opposite directions. The gentle ladies blushed and hid their faces in their shawls, averting their looks to avoid embarrassment. It truly must have been quite a sight for the "young and guileless" ladies of Maryland. After all, "50,000 men without their trousers on can't be passed in review every day of the week."[29]

It may have been the only light-hearted moment of the Pennsylvania campaign.

For the battle itself, the two armies met as with so many other occasions, at a time and place neither side had chosen: Gettysburg.

9

Butchers, Quacks, and Claude Minié

"I believe the Doctors kill more than they cour [*sic*]," an Alabama soldier wrote.[1] He may not have been far off. Certainly, Civil War doctors didn't have very good reputations. Some were called "butchers," while others were referred to as "jackasses." That same Alabama soldier believed "doctors haint Got half Sence.[2]

One officer complained that in every regiment "there were not less than a dozen doctors from whom our men had as much fear as from their Northern enemies." During a two-month period of 1862, of the 580 amputations done in Richmond hospitals, 245 ended in death.[3]

Nearly every available building, public and not so public, was turned into a hospital. The City Alms House, located between 2nd and 4th Streets opposite Shockoe Cemetery and completed just before the war, was rented to the Confederate

government and became known as General Hospital No. 1, or
Alms House Hospital. A private tobacco warehouse on Grace
Street between 17th and 18th Streets became General Hospital
No. 2. The Union Hotel was General Hospital No. 10.

In all, there were more than twenty-five hospitals in the
city during the siege, including the new, if hastily built, Chimborazo Hospital on Church Hill. Chimborazo was named after a
mountain in South America and was one of the largest hospitals
in the world—then or at any other point in history.[4] It was
opened in October of 1861 and covered over forty acres. It had
a capacity of more than 3,000, divided into five divisions, each
with its own laundry, kitchen, and bathhouse. It even had its
own herd of cattle—200 at one time—to provide fresh milk.
Over its history, it treated more than 76,000 Confederate sick
and wounded.[5]

Phoebe Yates Pember was a matron at Chimborazo
Hospital, and in her postwar account of living in Richmond
under siege told of her part in running the facility:

> Soon after the breaking out of the Southern war, the
> need of hospitals, properly organized and arranged,
> began to be felt, and buildings adapted for the pur-
> pose were secured by the government. . . .
> [S]oon rumors began to circulate that there was some-
> thing wrong in hospital administration, and Congress,
> desirous of remedying omissions, passed a law by
> which matrons were appointed. They had no official
> recognition, ranking even below stewards from a mili-
> tary point of view. Their pay was almost nominal from
> the depreciated nature of the currency.[6]

To save money, Richmond's many small hospitals later were
reorganized into a few large ones, some better than others. The
Camp Jackson Hospital and the de Sales Hospital on Brooke
Avenue operated by the Sisters of Charity and Mercy were not

only large, both were praised. Clean and cool in the summer, well supplied with clear, cold water the year-round, and their patients were well cared for.

The William H. Grant Tobacco Factory was turned into General Hospital No. 12 and held up to 100 patients at a time. One story has it that the patients at No. 12 were sometimes *too* well cared for. In their eagerness to help, Richmond women often rushed to the factory-turned-hospital. When one of the city's young ladies and asked an ailing soldier, "Can't I do something for you, Sir?" she was taken aback by his reply: "No, thank you, ma'am." Obviously disappointed, she pressed on: "Can't I wash your face for you?" The soldier gave up and said, "Well, if you insist, ma'am, but 14 other ladies have washed it already today."[7]

Grant Hospital, or Wayside as it later was called, gained a reputation, in part because of notices it placed in Richmond newspapers:

> Sick and disabled soldiers on furlough or honorably discharged with the service, who are temporarily detained in Richmond, Va., will be comfortably provided with food, quarters and attention at the Wayside Hospital, corner of Franklin and 19th.[8]

Whether a hospital building was new or a converted warehouse, the care given the sick and wounded was chancy at best, ranging from inadequate to useless, and in some cases, harmful. War had developed technically; now more efficient ways existed to kill and maim; however, there were precious few ways to save lives. The medical community didn't know the meaning of the word *antisepsis*, much less how to practice it. Wounds were dressed with nonsterilized material—often used and re-used—for sterilization in general had not entered most doctors' minds. A surgeon's instruments might not be so much as rinsed or wiped off between operations and neither would be the physician's hands. Tales are legion of doctors' blood-covered coat lapels, in some cases the blood being worn as a badge of honor by the surgeon. Wounds were expected to suppurate, and doctors spoke of "laudable pus" as a good sign of healing.[9]

Low-velocity, high-caliber rifles tore flesh and broke bones, taking many lives. Often it wasn't the bullet itself that killed. Rather, it was the minute piece of septic cloth it carried along with it—the soldier's own dirty uniform—that killed with the bacteria that rode along with it.

If antiseptic surgery was unknown, antibiotics were undreamed of. For every Union or Confederate soldier who died of battlefield wounds, two died of diseases. And it must be remembered that the Battle of Antietam alone took 6,000 lives. The number to die of disease was staggering.

Chloroform and ether were used whenever possible. However, thousands of amputations were performed without pain killer, especially in the South where many medical supplies were specifically prohibited by the Union's blockade. During the Shenandoah Valley campaign Stonewall Jackson's troops captured 15,000 cases of chloroform. It helped Southern surgeons but it still wasn't nearly enough.

Sometimes a soldier might be given a shot or two of whiskey before a blood-soaked surgeon would lop off a leg or arm (they raced the clock in order to complete the operation before shock set in). For others, it was just the opposite. In the North, thousands became addicted to pain-killing drugs administered as they recuperated from amputations.

Dying on the battlefield was bad enough, and most recognized that as coming with war. But dying in camp or in hospital galled them. John Pierson was a Federal officer who voiced his complaints in a letter to his wife:

We have lost several men of the 10th by Sickness and must go [on] unless better care can be had for the Sick. I do not mind seeing a man shot down in Battle but it is exceedingly painful to see them suffer for want of proper care in the Hospitals.[10]

Of course, a war of disease wasn't new. There's good evidence that, from the time the first white man visited North America until the time of the Jamestown, Virginia settlement, as much as 90 percent of the aboriginal population of North and South America succumbed to European-brought diseases.[11] It is what might be called "the kindergarten syndrome." A child, surrounded only by family and friends, may live her short existence virtually disease free. But just wait until she starts kindergarten. Coming into contact with strangers means everything from runny noses and chicken pox to—remember the 1940s and 1950s?—polio and head lice, all spread among new friends.

During the American Revolution, as troops from various colonies gathered, one of the first and longest lasting battles George Washington fought was disease among his regiments.

The situation hadn't changed much by the time the Civil War began. Where new groups of people gathered, new—and often more virulent—diseases followed. New arrivals to Richmond—soldiers, visitors, the wounded, prisoners, or refugees alike—brought with them several such new strains of disease. They carried what are now described as childhood diseases: measles, mumps, and tonsillitis. They also carried non-childhood but equally formidable diseases: typhoid, dysentery, and pneumonia.

And as with George Washington's troops, Civil War-era soldiers carried smallpox wherever they went.

In November of 1862, Richmonders faced a major outbreak of smallpox. The City (Alms House) Hospital was filled with smallpox patients; in another hospital, there were

seventy-five cases of the disease. Two additional hospitals had
to be built to handle pox patients, and the Richmond City
Council asked that smallpox patients be removed outside the
city to limit further contamination.[12]

While smallpox raged inside the Richmond city limits,
outside the city still another disease took its toll of Union
troops—venereal disease. There were as many cases of venereal
disease as of measles, mumps, and tonsillitis combined.[13]

Confederate soldiers (and civilians, for that matter)
didn't have to leave the city to contract a not-so-sociable social
disease. They only had to walk across 10th Street from the
YMCA hospital to enjoy the alleged charms and definite
diseases carried by the ladies of the evening. There, across from
the Young Men's Christian Association, was located one of
Civil War Richmond's largest houses of prostitution. The ladies
were often referred to as "Cyprians" by local newspapers, and
were seen soliciting from the windows—soldiers, visitors, or
hospital workers, any male passing nearby. It was a problem
certainly not confined to Richmond or the Confederacy as a
whole, certainly not confined to the Civil War, but it was just
one more problem faced by Richmond under siege.

* * *

Claude Minié had a lot to do with wounds during the Civil
War. He was a French army captain who, in 1848, perfected a
bullet small enough to be easily rammed down a muzzle-loaded
rifle, but one whose wooden plug base expanded when fired. It
was, of course, the minié ball, though it wasn't really round
enough to officially be a ball. Round or not, it was superior to
the old poured-shot bullet that might rattle around in the rifle
after it was fired. But these new bullets were expensive. Leave

it to an American, James H. Burton of the Harper's Ferry Armory, to come up with a cheaper product. His had a deep cavity in the base of the bullet. It filled with gas that expanded when fired.

Back in 1858, Virginia had a large stock of flintlock muskets stored in the Richmond Armory. All it took was a percussion lock substituted for the flintlock, grooving the barrel, adding a sight, and the state militia had modernized rifles, just waiting for the new improved minié balls. The cost wasn't bad, either: $1.50 per rifle.

Cheap bullets made for even cheaper lives.

* * *

By mid-1864, the smallpox epidemic was over in the city. From a military hospital just outside Richmond, hospital steward Luther L. Swank wrote to his sister Katie that, while "others are dying. . .and being killed almost daily [he] enjoyed better health during the whole season" than ever he had done before.[14] Perhaps he knew something about smallpox that others, obviously less fortunate than he, did not.

Swank certainly was a survivor. He even gained weight and attributed it to the abundance of food available in the city's markets. Prices were high, he agreed, but food was available to those who knew how to get it. He appended a list to his mother "so that she can draw a contrast between ours and yours." Beef sold at $3.50 per pound, tomatoes at $2.00 per half peck, butter beans at $4.00 per quart, and butter sold at $5.50 per pound. He wrote his family later and again listed market prices. The second time those prices were higher: butter at $11.00 per pound, and by late October, a head of cabbage sold for $2.00.

At the time, Confederate war clerk J. B. Jones earned $4,000 per year, roughly seventy-seven Confederate dollars per week.

"Let this schedule of prices," Luther wrote, "make you contented to exist out of Old Va. until this cruel war is 'over' and then [we] will return to our allegiance to the old 'mother of Statesmen' and great generals and brave soldiers. . . ."[15] He closed with the comment: "I'll stop now and eat dinner. Bill of fare, Beef—loaf of bread & sweet." Obviously, Swank not only knew how to avoid the smallpox, he knew how to obtain more rations than most other Richmonders under siege.

Generally, the hospitalized wounded, like others living in Richmond, often found food hard to come by:

> The rations became so small. . .that every every ounce of flour was valuable, and there were days when it was necessary to refuse with aching heart and brimming eyes the request of decent, manly-looking fellows for a piece of dry corn-bread. If given it would have robbed the rightful owner of part of his scanty rations.[16]

* * *

The siege continued. In the beginning, there was fear that it might last six or even twelve months. In reality, the siege lasted almost the entire length of the war. A saying at the time was that the Union soldier who had so easily marched into Mexico a few years earlier could not so easily march into Richmond. The Southern-born generals who had led them into Mexico were keeping them out of the Confederate capital. Luther

Swank, John Jones, and Sallie Putnam would be besieged in Richmond not for six or twelve months but for four years.

The War in the West

IV

Vicksburg

Vicksburg—the "Gibraltar of the West"—remained, like Richmond, the object of the Union army's interest. Confederate General Pemberton's troops were safely inside the Rebel lines, but being safe also meant they were trapped and couldn't get out. And Grant came up with a new plan to get in: he would march south below Vicksburg, then turn northeast, swing back west, and attack the city from its land side. He remembered when he'd been forced to live off the land, and this time he traveled light, foraging as he moved.[1] In three weeks, he marched 180 miles, fighting and winning five battles along the way, and keeping reinforcements out of Vicksburg.[2]

It went well for Grant. Living off the land worked. Some of his men had never eaten so well, and local residents didn't like it. When a Southern plantation owner rode up on a mule and complained to Grant that Union troops had stolen everything from him, Grant told him, "Well, those men didn't belong to my division. Because if they *were* my men, they wouldn't have left you that mule."[3]

On May 19, Grant's entire army charged Pemberton's defenses. They reached the open areas in front of Vicksburg, but Confederate cannon fire drove them back. It was another stalemate.

Each side tried to "out camp" the other, to wait until the other gave up. The Union army couldn't get in, and the South couldn't reinforce the city. Which left only one solution. Like Richmond to the east, Vicksburg became a city under siege.

Confederate and Federal cannon traded fire. Union troops dug in, bored like gophers, one soldier said, "with a spade in one hand and a gun in the other." Many residents abandoned their homes and did a bit of boring themselves, dug caves in the soft soil of the Mississippi bluffs, even laying carpets over the dirt floors, moving furniture from their parlor to their new subterranean home, filling nooks and crannies and niches carved in the cave walls with books and flowers.[4]

Soon, the people of Vicksburg were desperately short of food; officials imposed rationing: two biscuits, two slices of bacon, a few peas, and a spoonful of rice per day."[5] They turned to eating dogs and cats and even rats. One Vicksburg newspaper, the *Daily Citizen*, wrote of "the luxury of mule-meat and fricasseed kitten."[6]

* * *

Truces, usually unofficial, often not even acknowledged, took place at Vicksburg as well as at many other places when the two sides were close together. Such momentary halting of the war allowed soldiers on both sides to bury their dead. Sometimes men of both armies found themselves bathing in the same creek at the same time, and bathing was something neither side got enough of, given conditions and time. Such informal truces would see men from Indiana trade with men from Alabama—clothing and pocket knives. Men from Virginia might trade with troops from New York—tobacco for playing cards, an often sought-after article among Southerners. "[K]nives spoons pipes money and most everything," was traded during these unofficial truces."[7]

Writing about one such occasion outside Vicksburg, a Wisconsin trooper claimed that "if the settlement of this war was left to the Enlisted men of both sides, we would soon go home."[8] A Pennsylvania soldier claimed these unofficial truces worried the officers, because "they are afraid we will get to think and wont [sic] fight." The only thing keeping the war going, he believed, was the greed of the officers who "wait till they make enough money and then Resign."[9]

* * *

Union cannon endlessly bombarded Vicksburg, and the tension of the siege was so heavy there was talk of setting up an asylum for those driven crazy by the attack. One resident noted:

> All day and all night the shells from the mortars are falling around us, and all day from the guns around the fortifications. . . . It is a most discouraging sort of warfare.[10]

The *Daily Citizen* continued to publish, but it had to be printed on wallpaper, the only paper left. Yet still, it claimed:

Johnston is coming. Our lines will soon be opened,
the enemy driven away, the siege raised.[11]

All this waiting bored Grant, and when he was bored, he drank.
Sherman again had to step in to help, saying later, "Grant stood
by me when I was crazy, and I stood by him when he was
drunk."[12]

Drinking water was the problem for the Confederates in
Vicksburg. It was running out. Thirst became as much an
enemy as Grant's army.

Week after week the siege dragged on. Day after day the
Union army bombarded the city. Hour after hour the Confederates weakened without reinforcements. Pemberton knew it was
almost over and told his men that unless the siege was raised
soon, unless he received supplies, they'd have to surrender. And
the Vicksburg newspaper asked, "Where is General Johnston?"

Well, he was in Jackson, Mississippi, holding an army of
only 25,000 men. He believed Vicksburg was already lost and
didn't want to waste men in battle trying to save it. Finally,
Jefferson Davis pressured him, and Johnston gently probed
Sherman's troops. It was a feeble probe against a strong enemy.
And it was too late.

On the afternoon of July 3, Brigadier General John
Bowen rode out of Vicksburg under a flag of truce and told
Grant that Pemberton wanted to discuss surrender terms.
Bowen rode out of Vicksburg at about the same time, half a
continent away, General Pickett made his disastrous charge at
Gettysburg. And like Pickett's charge, it signaled an end: the
forty-seven-day siege of Vicksburg was over.

Pemberton hoped meeting with Grant on the Fourth of
July would bring better terms. He received better terms, all
right, but it had nothing to do with the nation's birthday. Grant
couldn't demand unconditional surrender as he had at Fort
Donelson, because to do so would leave him with 31,000

Confederate prisoners to guard and feed, so he offered the Rebels parole, hoping they'd go home, to fight no more.

The American flag again flew over Vicksburg's court-house, giving the Union, one soldier said, "the most glorious Fourth I ever spent."[13] The people of Vicksburg didn't see it that way, and the next time they celebrated the Fourth of July was in 1944, eighty-one years later—another time, another war.

Five days after Vicksburg fell, Union troops captured Fort Hudson, Louisiana, isolating Texas, Arkansas, and western Louisiana from the rest of the Confederacy, and leaving Lincoln to say, "The Father of Waters again goes unvexed to the sea."[14]

10

The Saddest Day of My Life

First reports in Richmond saw Lee and the Army of Northern Virginia as the winners at Gettysburg, and Southern pride overflowed. The *Examiner* not only called this "victory" a good omen but believed it to be a sign of what should have been done earlier. "From the beginning," the editor wrote, "the true policy of the South has been invasion." It was written four days *after* the Confederate defeat at Gettysburg but two days *before* the true outcome was known:

> The present movement of General Lee. . .will be of infinite value as disclosing. . .the easy susceptibility of the North to invasion. . . . We can. . .carry our armies far into the enemy's country, exacting peace by blows leveled at his vitals.[1]

Robert E. Lee wanted to ease the suffering war had caused in Virginia. Not incidentally, he hoped to find fresh supplies for the Confederacy—food, horses, perhaps even Union guns.

As General Lee headed north across the Potomac, Jeb Stuart, with his commander's permission, decided to ride around Union General Hooker, just as he once had ridden around General McClellan. But this time the Union army was spread out further, and the ride took Stuart farther afield. It took him ten days to complete the circuit, ten days in which Lee had no idea where Stuart was and, consequently, no idea what he faced at Gettysburg—"I am in ignorance as to what we have in front of us." Lee desperately missed Stonewall Jackson; he just as desperately needed information from Stuart who finally arrived on the evening of the second day of the Battle of Gettysburg.

Robert E. Lee would later call it "one of the saddest [days] of my life." It can easily be argued that Lee was poorly served at Gettysburg by his lieutenants—Ewell was irresolute, Stuart missing, Longstreet gave poor advice. General Lee himself would only say, "It is I that have lost this fight"

One of the early casualties was Edward Hallock Ketcham. He and his brother, Second Lieutenant John Townsend Ketcham, though Quakers, served with Company M, 4th New York Cavalry. "I cannot believe he is dead," John wrote his mother on July 6, 1863:

> Don't let it kill thee, mother! Thee and I are all that is left of us. . . . Edward was the first man killed in the regiment.
>
> They were lying on the ground, behind a small mill, in front of our batteries, making apart of the outer line of battle. It is always necessary in such time for someone to keep a lookout to watch the movements of the enemy. As the men all lay on their faces, Edward was

sitting up to look; a sharpshooter's bullet probably struck him in the temple, and went through his head. He put up his hand and said: 'Oh!' and fell on his elbow, quite dead. . . .

I went out at night, to look for [him], but could not find him. The next morning our line advanced, and I went out to the tree; and there, on his back, his hands peacefully on his breast, lay all that was left of the brother I had lived so closely with all my life.[2]

It began when two Rebel brigades stumbled upon a small group of dismounted Union cavalry, a thin line commanded by Brigadier General John Buford. His dismounted cavalry stood between the Confederates and those desperately needed shoes stored in a Gettysburg warehouse.

Rebel commander Henry Heth and his superior, A. P. Hill, believed the Union line was nothing more than a group of local militia, so they swarmed across Wiloughby Run, anxious for the footwear. Swarmed right into Buford's troops now armed with breech-loading Spencer repeating rifles. Union troops were able to get off eight to ten shots for every three the Rebels—if they were fast—could load and fire. Buford stopped the Confederates even before they realized they were in a major battle.

Major General George Meade had only recently taken over from Joe Wheeler (Fightin' Joe had resigned after losing at Chancellorsville) as commander of the Union troops. He sent General John Reynolds marching in from the south. With Buford, Reynolds climbed to the top of the cupola at the Gettysburg Seminary to survey the surrounding area. There, at McPherson's Woods, they saw what they believed to be a good place to make a stand. Back on the ground, Reynolds rode toward the wood, shouting, "Forward, for God's sake! Forward," hoping to get there before the advancing Rebel troops.

Almost immediately, a Southern sniper shot and killed Reynolds, a minié ball behind the ear.

Abner Doubleday (he of baseball-inventing claim) took over Reynolds's command. As the mass of Confederates under Brigadier General James Archer climbed the slop in the face of Union fire, the Rebels were joined by another brigade under Jefferson Davis's nephew, Joseph. At the crest of the ridge they were hit by what many believed to be the finest unit in Meade's army: The Iron Brigade ("First Brigade, First Division, First Corps of the First Army of the Republic"). They still wore the peculiar black hats first issued when they were mustered in. And then the Rebels knew they faced more than just Buford. The Confederates were beaten back.

Before he could get away, Archer was captured, the first of Lee's generals ever to be taken prisoner, and ironically, he was handed over to an old friend, Union Major General Doubleday. Doubleday reached out his hand in greeting. "Archer," he said, "I'm glad to see you!" But the Confederate wouldn't take the offered hand: "Well, I'm not glad to see you by a damn sight."[3]

Over the next three days—July 1 through 3—place names and events would be written into America's memory: Cemetery Ridge, The Devil's Den, Little Round Top. And Pickett's Charge.

* * *

The first day of Gettysburg was, by far, not the worst. But that night, New York *Times* correspondent Samuel Wilkeson sat beside the body of his dead son; Lieutenant Bayard Wilkeson had been killed that day, and Samuel wrote his dispatch while his son's blood was still moist:

Who can write the history of a battle whose eyes are immovably fastened upon a central figure of transcendingly absorbing interest—the dead body of an oldest born, crushed by a shell in a position where a battery should never have been sent, and abandoned to death in a building where surgeons dared not stay. . . ?

For such details as I have the heart for. The battle commenced at daylight, on the side of the horseshoe position, exactly opposite that which [Confederate Major General Richard] Ewell had sworn to crush through. Musketry preceded the rising of the sun. A thick wood veiled this fight, but out of the heavy darkness arose the smoke and surging and swelling of the fire. . . .

Eleven o'clock—twelve o'clock—one o'clock. In the shadow cast by [a] tiny farmhouse, sixteen by twenty, where General Meade had made his headquarters, lay wearied staff officers and tired reporters. . . .In the midst of [a bird's] warbling a shell screamed over the house, instantly followed by another and another, and in a moment the air was full of the most complete artillery prelude to an infantry battle that was ever exhibited. Every size and form of shell known to British and to American gunnery shrieked, moaned, whirled, whistled, and wrathfully fluttered over our ground. . . .Through the midst of the storm of screaming and exploding shells an ambulance, driven by its frenzied conductor at full speed, presented to all of us the marvelous spectacle of a horse going rapidly on three legs. A hinder one had been shot off at the hock. . . .During the fire the houses at twenty and thirty feet distant were receiving their death, and soldiers in Federal blue were torn to pieces in the road and died with peculiar yells that blend the extorted cry of pain with horror and despair. Not an orderly, not an ambulance, not a straggler was to be

seen upon the plain swept by this tempest of orches-
tral death thirty minutes after it commenced.[4]

And the second day came. Again, two great armies faced each other. Artillery and infantry, this day amid the rocks of the Devil's Den and Little Round Top.

Longstreet wanted Lee to take a defensive position, to stand between the Union army and Washington, D.C., to make the Federals attack him. Lee rejected the idea; once more—as it had so successfully at the Battle of Chancellorsville—the Army of Northern Virginia would attack.

On one end of Meade's fishhook-shaped line was Culp's Hill. The bend in the hook included Cemetery Hill; the shank ran down Cemetery Ridge and ended in two rocky knobs—Big and Little Round Top. When General Richard Ewell told Lee he would not be able to take his target, Culp's Hill, Lee decided to go after the southern end of the fishhook, the Round Tops. It was Longstreet's assignment, but the man Lee called "my old War-horse" pouted and delayed, not pushing off until four o'clock.

John Bell Hood's division led the way among the huge boulders that came to be known as the Devil's Den. Union grapeshot struck Hood, permanently injuring the Kentuckian's left arm. His men seized the wooded Big Round Top, then charged north for the open slopes of Little Round Top.

For a while, only Union General Gouveneur Warren, Meade's chief of engineers, and a signal corps soldier stood atop the knob. Quickly, Warren persuaded the 5th Corps commander to send a brigade to the crest of the hill. On the far left was Colonel Joshua L. Chamberlain of the 20th Maine. Just a year before he was teaching rhetoric and modern languages at Bowdoin College; when the school refused to release him to join the army, Chamberlain took a leave of absence. To study in Europe, he said. But his studies were on the battlefields of America, and his first big lesson came at Gettysburg.

For two hours the 20th Maine withstood repeated assaults. Smoke. Noise. Terror. One-third of Chamberlain's men were injured and many of those still able to fight were out of ammunition; they had carried only sixty rounds per man. Chamberlain's order: Fix bayonets! Charge downhill, into the surprised and exhausted Confederates. Stab. Punch. Jab. Charge again. Colonel William Oates said, "When the signal was given, we ran like a herd of wild cattle, right through the line of dismounted [Rebel] cavalry."[5]

No way now for the Confederates to retreat in an orderly manner, simply run or give up. Scores of Alabamians surrendered to Chamberlain's men.

Through the Peach Orchard, the Wheat Field, over by the Devil's Den, first by inches, then feet and yards, the Rebels rallied and slowly drove back the Union. But not at Little Round Top. Chamberlain and his 20th Maine held on.

All day, the Rebel assault had gone on piecemeal. For once, the actions of the Army of Northern Virginia were uncoordinated, disjointed, while Meade's forces acted with coolness and clarity.

Each side, that second day of Gettysburg, lost 9,000 men. The two-day total was up to nearly 35,000. And still the battle was not decided. Day Three was yet to come.

* * *

John L. Burns was the Gettysburg town constable. He was seventy-two years old but didn't like the idea of Rebels traipsing around his town. Burns gathered up his ancient musket, dressed himself in a blue swallowtail coat with large brass buttons and a yellow vest. He wore a bell-crowned, broad-brimmed hat. And he went to war. Or, rather, he went back to war; he'd served his country earlier in the War of 1812 and the Mexican War. He'd even volunteered for the Civil War but was rejected because of his age. "I know how to fight," he said, "I have fit [sic] before."

Now, he marched up to Major E. P. Halstead's 7th Wisconsin troops and demanded to know, "Which way are the Rebels? Where are our troops?"

Burns refused a suggestion that any fighting he might do be done in the woods where there was more cover; he joined a line of skirmishers in the open field. When they quit the field, Burns joined another unit; they quit, so he joined another, finally winding up fighting side by side with the Iron Brigade.

Burns was wounded three times that day and was captured by the Confederates. The Rebels let him go after the battle and Burns walked back to his Gettysburg home where he recovered from his wounds

Much later, author Bret Harte wrote about John L. Burns, and the old man became a national hero. He died in 1872, at the age of eighty-one. Later still, the state of Pennsylvania raised a statue to him. It was 1903, the fortieth anniversary of the Battle of Gettysburg.

* * *

The night of July 2. Both armies were hurt. Neither could really say it had won the day or was even ahead of the game. Two days of fighting saw each side holding a strong position. Meanwhile, the casualty list grew.

General Meade met with his officers; he wanted their opinions on what Federal troops should do the following

day—go or stay. Major General Oliver O. Howard recommended a wait-and-see attitude; if Lee didn't attack, then the Federal
troops should. Major General Winfield Scott Hancock agreed
to an attack, but only if their own lines of communications were
cut. General Meade decided he would stay and fight it out, but
would wait for the enemy to attack first. He expected it to
come in the center of the Union front.

Over in the Rebel camp, James Longstreet once more
recommended a conservative, defensive stance. Not Robert E.
Lee. He would attack, and just as Meade had predicted, head-
on into the Union center. In his report, Lee wrote:

> The general plan was unchanged. Longstreet, rein-
> forced by Pickett's three brigades, which arrived near
> the battlefield on the afternoon of the 2nd, was
> ordered to attack the next morning, and General
> Ewell was ordered to attack the enemy's right at the
> same time. The latter during the night reinforced
> General Johnson with two brigades from Rodes' and
> one from Early's divisions.[6]

In other words, it would be a concerted, three-pronged attack.
Years later, Longstreet claimed those were not the orders Lee
had given him on the night of July 2. He said General Lee had
not told him of the plan until the morning of July 3. It is worth
noting, however, that Longstreet never challenged Lee's version
of the orders until years after Lee had died. When he told *his*
version of what happened, Longstreet claimed he said to Lee:

> General, I have been a soldier all my life. I have been
> with soldiers engaged in fights by couples, by squads,
> companies, regiments and armies, and should know,
> as well as anyone, what soldiers can do.

Longstreet said he looked out at the field his men would have
to cross and told Lee:

> It is my opinion that no 15,000 men ever arrayed for
> battle can take that position.[7]

July 3 was a Friday. General Ewell renewed his attack on
Culp's Hill. After five hours of slugging it out, the Rebels were
forced back.

That left it up to a planned artillery barrage and a mile-
long charge by General George Pickett on Cemetery Ridge.

By one o'clock, the fighting had died out, and the
battlefield was quiet. Waiting. Waiting.

Pickett sat, writing a poem to his wife, Mary. Lewis
Armistead—"Lo," his friends called him, short for Lothario,
something the shy Virginian surely wasn't, a fact his friends
knew very well—stood tall, with steel-gray hair despite his
young age. He asked that a package be sent to Mira—Almira
Hancock—the wife of his closet friend, Winfield Scott Hancock.
Hancock now stood on the opposite side of the battlefield,
wearing a Union-blue uniform with major general's insignia.
Armistead had been booted out of West Point during his
second year following a dining hall fracas in which he hit Jubal
Early over the head with a plate.

Walking over to where George Pickett sat, Lo Armistead
took his West Point ring off his pinky finger (the customary
finger on which to wear them at the time). Pressing the ring
into Pickett's hand he told his fellow Virginian to give it to
Pickett's wife as a remembrance.

General Longstreet was to signal the artillery attack with
two quick cannon shots. Brigadier General E. Porter Alexander
was in charge of the Confederate artillery. He was just twenty-
six and not too comfortable around the higher-ranking Longstreet. He claimed Longstreet told him:

> If the artillery fire does not have the effect to drive
> off the enemy or greatly demoralize him, so as to
> make our efforts pretty certain, I would prefer that
> you should not advise General Pickett to make the
> charge. I shall rely a great deal on your good judg-
> ment to determine the matter, and shall expect you to
> let General Pickett know when the moment offers.[8]

Alexander, however, wanted the decision to be made by
someone else, preferably General Lee. By messenger, he ques-
tioned Longstreet but was given what he felt was an equivocal
reply. It was up to Alexander to start the barrage that would
start Pickett's charge.

As planned, Longstreet fired two signal cannon to begin
the barrage. For twenty-five minutes, 130 Confederate cannon
blasted away. Then, Alexander sent Pickett a message to
George Pickett:

> If you are coming at all you must come at once, or I
> cannot give you proper support.[9]

Nothing happened. Minutes passed. Alexander sent another
message to Pickett:

> For God's sake, come quick. . . . [C]ome quick, or my
> ammunition won't let me support you properly.[10]

Pickett took the note to Longstreet and asked if he should
advance. But Longstreet refused to give the order and, without
saying a word, turned his face away. Pickett saluted, said, "I am
going to move forward, sir," and he galloped off to his division
and into history.

"As valiant as Pickett's charge" that day became a
martial metaphor. He was thirty-eight at the time. He'd been
last in his class at West Point in 1846, the same class as George

McClellan and Stonewall Jackson. He'd fought in Mexico but resigned his Federal commission to become a Confederate brigadier general. He wore his hair long, in highly perfumed ringlets. Once, when some admiring women asked General Lee for a lock of his hair, Lee suggested they ask Pickett instead; he had more of it.

"Up, men, and to your posts," Pickett shouted, "Don't forget you are from Old Virginia!"[11] Pickett himself did not charge; he and his aides watched from a nearby farmhouse. It wasn't a pretty sight.

It was three o'clock that Friday when the Confederates stepped off in perfectly dressed rank after rank, still pretending it was the Age of Napoleon, pretending as well the enemy had been leveled by the artillery barrage. Flags flying, 12,500 Confederate soldiers marched side-by-side; another 2,500 waited in reserve.

A mile-wide spectacle for history to record.

Arthur Fremantle was a lieutenant colonel in the British army, come to observe and, as it turned out, to praise the Confederacy and predict a Southern victory. He stood beside Old Pete Longstreet and cried, "I wouldn't have missed this for anything!" Longstreet sat atop a split-rail fence, turned and laughed at the Englishman. "The devil you wouldn't!" he said, "I would like to have missed it very much; we've attacked and been repulsed."[12]

Someone remarked that it was a beautiful day for a battle. All too soon, a Native American saying proved true: it was a good day to die.

They charged in the open, no place to hide, just the knee-high grass and a few stone walls.

The line of Rebels had covered about 300 yards when the Union cannon opened fire. The Confederate line wavered but marched on. In the rear, Longstreet still sat on that split—

rail fence, crouching forward, watching his men march bravely into the thickly flying cannon balls.

Union troops knelt at the top of the ridge, firing volley after volley into the oncoming Rebel ranks. The Federal artillery switched from ball to canister, and shards of steel whistled into the men massed and trudging across the open field. Smoke and dust. Thirst and dying. More screams, more whistling canister and ball. More death.

Lew Armistead ordered his men to increase to double-time. More gaps in the Confederate line, and by the hundreds young men—young boys, really—fell dead. Others huddled in fear and cried for deliverance. The Rebel line stalled. Armistead skewered his old black felt hat on the tip of his sword, raised it high into the air, and cried out, "Virginians! With me! With me!"

To the stone wall the Virginians charged, and the Federals fell back. It was the High Water Mark of the Confederacy, some would say. But at that high water mark, a blast of hell-hot air and searing steel doubled Armistead over. He was suddenly tired and had to hold onto a Federal cannon just recently captured by his men. Some were there with him, those same men, only now many lay lifeless.

The High Water Mark of the Confederacy receded.

The battered Rebels slowly returned to their lines, some limping, some crawling, some being helped by comrades, all still under Federal fire.

James Longstreet continued to sit, watching and watching. That British observer, Arthur Fremantle, later wrote:

> No person could have been more calm or self-pos-
> sessed than General Longstreet under these trying
> circumstances, aggravated as they now were by the
> movements of the enemy, who began to show a strong
> disposition to advance. I could now thoroughly

> appreciate the term bulldog, which I had heard
> applied to him by the soldiers. Difficulties seem to
> make no other impression on him than to make him
> a little more savage.[13]

In truth, James Longstreet anguished over the defeat. But, then, his anguish could go only so far; he wasn't responsible, he had advised against the charge.

Everywhere, men lay wounded and dying. Of the 14,000 Virginian troops who made that mile-long charge, only half returned. Two-thirds of Pickett's division, almost all Virginians—gone, all gone. When told to prepare for a counterattack, Pickett said he could not, "I have no division now."[14]

The Battle of Gettysburg saw 28,000 Confederate casualties, 23,000 for the Union. More than 51,000 casualties over the three-day period. Thirty-thousand of them dead. The single most costly battle in American warfare.

The survivors stumbled in a daze, stumbled back to their camps, stumbled back as General Robert E. Lee rode among them on his big horse, Traveller. "It is all my fault," Lee said to them, trying to rally his men against an expected counterattack from Union General Meade. "It is I who have lost this fight," he said, "and you must help me out of it the best way you can. All good men must rally."[15] Around General Lee, as Fremantle wrote, were men who said "We've not lot confidence in the old man: this day's work won't do him any harm. 'Uncle Robert' will get us into Washington yet; you bet he will!'"[16]

However, Lee's attempts to rally his men failed, and it was just as well. There was no rally, just as there was no counterattack. Meade had held command of the Union army for just six days. He believed his victory had been a narrow one. He believed his artillery was low on ammunition. He believed Lee would try another charge. So he waited, not knowing, even, that his own cavalry had stopped the vaunted Jeb Stuart three

miles from the battle scene. He didn't follow up the Union
army's advantage. "We have done well enough," he told a
fellow officer.[17] He would wait for the next day, July 4, to
chase after the Confederate army. But the Fourth of July came
with rain—a hailstorm, and Meade called off the attack.

Back in Richmond, the townspeople were puzzled. Lose
to the North? Why, it was well known that one Southern boy
could whip a dozen "damnyankees." Perhaps it was a shortage
of ammunition. Perhaps the Northern press was lying. Yes, that
was it; the press was lying.

Or perhaps not. It was all too real.

The Army of Northern Virginia lost nearly a third of its
men. The North could and did draw on an ever larger number
of men, but the defeat at Gettysburg was disastrous for Lee;
never again would the South have the strength to mount an
offensive into the North.

* * *

Long after Gettysburg, Lewis Armistead's package reached
Almira Hancock; it was his personal Bible.

* * *

From Elisha Hunt Rhodes's diary:

> *July 5th 1863*—Glorious news! We have won the
> victory (at Gettysburg), thank God, and the Rebel
> Army is fleeing to Virginia. . . . We have thousands of
> prisoners, and they seem to be stupefied with the

news. . . . Every house we see is a hospital, and the road is covered with the arms and equipment thrown away by the Rebels.[18]

July 6th 1863—Today we have slowly continued the pursuit, passing through Fairfield and Liberty and encamping at Emmitsburg. Everything denotes Lee is trying to cross the Potomac. I hope we shall catch him before he reaches Virginia.[19]

They didn't of course, but the Confederate march back to Virginia was no Sunday walk in the park. Florence McCarthy was a chaplain with the 7th Virginia Volunteer Infantry. Six days after the final day at Gettysburg, he was in Williamsport, Maryland, writing home:

Dear Sister:
Williamsport is a one-horse town. . . . At the present Ewell's Corps is at Hagerstown, Picket's [*sic*] is here, and I have no conception where the remainder of the army is. . . .
I have been marched nearly to death. In coming from Gettysburg here, we marched three days and two nights without stopping except long enough to cook food. Most of the time it rained and the roads were perfectly awful. My socks have given out, I can buy none, beg none, steal none, and it is a matter of impossibility to get a piece of clothing washed. I am lousy and dirty and have no hope of changing flannel for weeks to come. . . .
We passed through Berryville, Virginia. The ladies were very kind and polite to the soldiers, but appeared to me to be rich, unrefined and ugly. . . .
Some few of the Pennsylvania people showed some spirits. One old woman beat our men out of her garden with a stick. A girl in Chambersburg took

water and a broom and washed the pavement where our men had laid their haversacks. But as a general thing, they are the most cringing mean-spirited people on earth.

Our men have strict orders to take nothing without paying, but they do just as they please, which is not a twentieth part as bad as they did in Virginia. The chickens, hogs and vegetables are being consumed rapidly. The [crops] in some places will be ruined by camps and by stock, but we have not hurt them enough to talk about.

The Battle of Gettysburg was the most awful of the war.[20]

The failure at Gettysburg finally hit home in Richmond on July 14. That was when the first of many long trains of wounded rolled into the capital city. The war Robert E. Lee had tried to take to the North had come back home to Virginia.

The War in the West

V

Chickamauga and Chattanooga

Richmond grieved over the fall of Vicksburg and mourned the defeat at Gettysburg but didn't pay much attention to General Braxton Bragg and Lookout Mountain.

All through the summer of Vicksburg's siege, Union General Rosecrans looked toward Chattanooga. Like Vicksburg, it was important, both as an east-west rail and a north-south river connection.

Bragg was about fifty miles away in Tullahoma, a strong base he'd used since the Battle of Stones River.

In late June, after Lincoln repeatedly demanded he drive Bragg out of Tennessee, Rosecrans sent his Army of the Cumberland sweeping down from Murfressboro in a broad front—McMinnville, Manchester, and Tullahoma. It was a complex maneuver and it confused Bragg. The Rebels pulled out for safer ground at Chattanooga. But they weren't safe for long.

In September, Rosecrans sent Thomas Crittenden with a small force across the Tennessee River, just where Bragg expected an attack. But Rosecrans wasn't attacking Chattanooga, merely feinting. He had turned his main army south, around the Confederate left flank.

It fooled Bragg into believing the whole Union army was coming at him from the northeast.

Bragg had been in Chattanooga for weeks after being forced out of his camp at Tullahoma, but apparently he wasn't ready to defend the city. So, on September 8, he pulled out without a fight. The Confederate troops headed south, toward Lafayette, twenty-two miles away.

This time it was Rosecrans's turn to be fooled. He saw Bragg on the move and believed the Confederates were in full retreat, so he spread his army over a fourteen-mile front to take advantage of an expected rout. But Bragg wasn't retreating, just re*concentrating*, and Rosecrans's move weakened the Union force.

It was then that the two sides met, at a small, insignificant creek the Cherokee Indians called "the river of death." Chickamauga.

Bragg had more than 71,000 men standing on the creek's eastern bank.

Rosecrans waited on the western bank, with fewer than 60,000 Union troops.

Mid-morning on Saturday, September 19, Confederate cavalry under Nathan Bedford Forrest ran into a Federal infantry unit at Reed's Bridge Road, setting off the bloodiest battle in the western theatre. Hard fighting, and hard times, had come to northwestern Georgia at the River of Death.

The Rebel troops came on with that strange, almost indescribable yell, and, as usual, it shocked Federal ears. Gradually, the Confederates pushed the hard-pressed Union forces back to the Lafayette Road. But Rosecrans's bluecoats refused to break. They stood and fought.

Eleven-year-old John Clem—the boy earlier called
"Johnny Shiloh"—was still with the army. This time he rode
atop a caisson, behind a cannon. He carried a rifle, cut down to
fit his size. The U.S. army had refused to recognize him in any
official capacity, even refused to pay him, but Johnny was a
favorite of the officer corps and they took up a collection each
month to pay Clem out of their own pockets. Johnny was more
than just a boy with a drum this time. When a Confederate
colonel ordered Johnny to surrender, Clem refused and shot
the Rebel officer. "Johnny Shiloh" became the "Drummer Boy
of Chickamauga."

The first day of Chickamauga ended with neither side
having the upper hand, both sides worn out, tired and frazzled.

It was almost midnight when the Union corps commanders met in Widow Glenn's dimly lit cabin between the
Lafayette and Dry Valley Roads. It had been a long, hard day
for everybody. Rosecrans was haggard and drained. He knew
his men couldn't hold out much longer against the larger
Confederate force. The Army of the Cumberland had fought
bravely that Saturday. Rosecrans believed they'd be just as
brave on Sunday and be just as successful. They would hold a
line running from Missionary Ridge to Reed's Bridge Road.

The Confederate troops had also fought bravely, and
their officers held even higher hopes. Lieutenant General
James Longstreet was on his way with 12,000 veterans of the
war in Virginia. He was Robert E. Lee's "Old Warhorse" whose
friends called "Old Pete."

But while Rosecrans met with his officers, Longstreet
was trying to find Bragg. Old Pete was lost, and he stumbled in
among Union pickets and was almost killed before he managed
to ride off.

The next morning, by a quirk of fate—just as at Gettysburg—the Union attacked from the *south*, while the Confederates charged from the *north*. It was September 20. Longstreet

had finally located Bragg and was on the Rebel left wing. Polk was to the right. D. H. Hill was supposed to open the day's fighting, but Bragg's orders didn't get to him until well after daybreak. Even then, Hill took his time, and it was after 9:30—four hours behind schedule—when he began the attack on Thomas.

Once begun, the fighting was fierce and confused, mainly fought in heavy timber. The Rebels slowly inched around Thomas, and he sent a message to Rosecrans, calling for reinforcements. As he rode up to Rosecrans's headquarters, the messenger thought he saw a wide gap between two Federal divisions and told Rosecrans. But there *was* no gap; because of their dark blue uniforms, the messenger just didn't see the troops hidden in the woods. Rosecrans didn't check the report and ordered Brigadier General Thomas Wood to close up on Joseph Reynolds's division. Wood marched around the Federal troops hidden in the trees, creating a gap where none had existed.

And 16,000 Rebel soldiers screamed into that gap, catching the Yankees in a sledgehammer attack. The Union troops pulled back, the worst Federal retreat since the great skedaddle at Manassas, and Rosecrans joined them, running for safety along Dry Valley Road, heading for Chattanooga, eight miles away. Some Union troops didn't run, however. George Thomas kept about half the army—almost all that was left of it—and made a last-ditch stand at Snodgrass Hill, holding off Longstreet until Rosecrans got away. That action earned Thomas fame as the "Rock of Chickamauga."

The Confederates won one of the bloodiest battles of the war, but their losses at Chickamauga were staggering, nearly 18,000 casualties. The Union losses were almost as great, more than 16,000 casualties, including one of Abraham Lincoln's brothers-in-law, Benjamin Helm.

Bragg was appalled at the casualties—over a quarter of his effective force—and didn't chase Rosecrans to finish the battle. James Longstreet and Nathan Bedford Forrest argued with Bragg over his order not to push on to Chattanooga. Both believed Bragg had lost his courage.

U.S. Secretary of War Stanton thought the Union might lose all of Tennessee because of Rosecrans and complained that Rosecrans "ran away from his fighting men and did not stop for 13 miles."

* * *

By mid-October, Grant was in command of the Military Division of the Mississippi, and he replaced the running Rosecrans with stand-fast George Thomas. He told his new commander to hold Chattanooga at all costs. Thomas promised to do just that, claiming, "We will hold the town till we starve."

Which might not be long in coming. The Rebels had cut the Union's supply lines, and Thomas's troops were on half rations of hardtack and meat that came from such emaciated cattle the men called it "beef dried on the hoof."

Outside Chattanooga, Bragg's Southern artillery commanded the heights of Lookout Mountain, while the infantry dug in along Missionary Ridge. When Fightin' Joe Hooker arrived with fresh troops from Virginia, Thomas had close to 72,000 men facing Bragg's 45,000. But, hot-tempered Bedford Forrest was still angry at Bragg's refusal to follow up the Chickamauga victory. He told Bragg, "I have stood your meanness as long as I intend to. You have played the part of a damned scoundrel." He added that if Bragg every again tried "to interfere with me. . . . Or cross my path. . . . It will be at the peril of your life."[1] So, Forrest took his men and rode off to Mississippi.

Jefferson Davis didn't help. He tried to end the trouble among Bragg's men by shifting several generals to other fields of action. Among them, "Old Pete" Longstreet. Davis ordered Longstreet to recapture Knoxville, a move that left Bragg with fewer than 30,000 men.

That was just fine with Grant. He was ready to break out of Chattanooga and was looking for a fight. He found it near Lookout Mountain.

Hooker would attack Bragg's left, while Sherman swept the enemy's right. Grant believed Thomas's men were still tired and demoralized from the Battle of Chickamauga, and he would use them in a secondary role, the Confederate center on Missionary Ridge.

Grant didn't like Thomas. It may have been a matter of Grant looking ahead to a final defeat of the Confederacy while Thomas took each battle one at a time. Even Lincoln apparently didn't like Thomas, a Southerner who preferred to remain with the Union. Once, when Thomas was up for promotion, Lincoln struck his name from the list, saying, "Let the Virginian wait." Even the man's own family disliked him. The South considered him a traitor and confiscated his property; his family disowned him. After the war, he sent money to his sisters when they had financial problems; they turned it down, saying they didn't have a brother.[2]

The Battle of Chattanooga began with Hooker's boys scrambling among the boulders of Lookout Mountain, up hill and over fallen trees, searching for Rebels concealed by the thick, heavy mist. A Union war correspondent called it the "Battle Above the Clouds," and the name stuck.

Clouds or not, the mountain soon became indefensible, and the Rebels fell back off the hill and down the back side of Lookout Mountain. It had been an easy fight for the Union.

They took fewer than 500 casualties, and Bragg was forced to pull his survivors back to Missionary Ridge.

During the night, a Union regiment from Kentucky somehow scratched and clawed its way to the top of Lookout Mountain and raised an American flag. At sunrise on November 25, men on both sides looked up at the Stars and Stripes waving above them.

On the second day of fighting, W. T. Sherman faced Irish-born Patrick Cleburne on the right. Some called it the best division in the Confederate army, and the Union was having trouble fighting in the rocky area near South Chickamauga Creek.

Hooker also hadn't made much headway, and it was clear that Grant's plan wasn't working. That's when he ordered Thomas to make a limited attack on the center of Missionary Ridge. Move to the foot of the ridge and wait, he said. But, against their orders, Thomas's men didn't stop when they got there. Besides, they were sitting ducks for the Rebels firing down from above them and more than just a little mad at being given only a bit part in the day's play. They pushed ahead without orders, or at least no one later claimed to have given the order—a charge that looked as impossible as Pickett's Rebel charge on the Federals at Cemetery Ridge in Gettysburg. Crying "Chickamauga! Chickamauga!" and running up the hill, 23,000 troops rushed forward.

It surprised the Rebels, and it surprised Grant. They were out of formation and out of breath, but the attack cut through the Rebel line. From below, it looked like a race to see which side would make it up the hill first.

The charge up Missionary Ridge was a huge success, but Grant didn't like the idea that someone had made a move without his permission. He wanted to know who had given the order to charge the hill; because he disliked Thomas, he immediately blamed him. Don't look at me, Thomas indicated;

I had nothing to do with it.[3] Nobody owned up to it. Finally, an aide told Grant, "They started without orders and when those fellows get started, all hell can't stop them."[4]

The Federal troops charged so fast, the angle was so steep, that the Confederate artillery couldn't depress their cannon enough to do their own men any good. By ones and twos, Rebel soldiers fell back. Then others followed, throwing down their rifles and packs, and soon they were infected by fear. When they reached the top, Union forces turned the Confederates' own cannon on the retreating Rebel soldiers. And fear turned to panic, the only time the Army of Tennessee did panic. General Bragg tried, but he couldn't rally his men and later wrote:

> [N]o satisfactory excuse can possibly be given for the shameful conduct of our troops. . . . The position was one which ought to have been held by a line of skirmishers.[5]

Bragg knew he was at least partially to blame for both the panic and the defeat. And that's just what it was, a major defeat. The Confederate army suffered 6,000 casualties. One-fifth of Bragg's army was gone. Bragg was also gone; he resigned his command, wiring Jefferson Davis:

> I fear we both erred in the conclusion for me to retain command here after the clamor raised against me.[6]

Chickamauga was a resounding victory for the South. Chattanooga was an even more resounding defeat.

* * *

A week before Chattanooga and Missionary Ridge, President Abraham Lincoln traveled to Gettysburg for the dedication of the national cemetery there. Famed (and long-winded) orator Edward Everett was the keynote speaker. Two hours after Everett began his speech, it was Lincoln's turn. He was to say a few words, and a few is all he spoke. However, his "Gettysburg Address" was not, as myth would have it, written on the back of an envelope as Lincoln rode the train to the battle site; it was prepared well in advance over a period of days. Today, there are at least five, possibly six, authenticated copies of the Address.[7]

By his own words, he either proved himself wrong or provided cause to prolong interest in the speech. It was a Thursday, November 19, 1863, and the world still remembers:

> [We] cannot dedicate—we cannot consecrate—we cannot hallow—this ground. The brave men, living and dead, who struggled here, have consecrated it far above our poor power to add or detract. The world will little note nor long remember what we say here, but it can never forget what they did here. It is for us, the living, rather to be dedicated here to the unfinished work which they who fought here have thus far so nobly advanced.

And for all history lovers, all English teachers, all editors, all those who will not take shortcuts, all who appreciate the power of language—here is that final sentence, seventy-four words long:

> It is for us to be here dedicated to the great task remaining before us—that from these honored dead we take increased devotion to that cause for which they gave the last full measure of devotion; that we here highly resolve that these dead shall not have died

in vain; that this nation, under God, shall have a new
birth of freedom; and that government of the people,
by the people, for the people, shall not perish from
the earth.

This undoubtedly is one of the most moving of all Lincoln's
speeches and ranks among the most powerful of all time. In it,
he makes no mention of North or South, United States of
America or Confederate States of America. He does not
condemn, only blesses.

His emphasis is not on politics or geography, but on
people. Only on people and the government they provide for
themselves.

The men of 1861 did not go to war as Northerners or
Southerners; they went to war as Americans. They volunteered
to defend Southern rights, volunteered to defend the Union.
They marched to war to preserve freedom as they understood
it. In doing so, they left a permanent history of death and dying
for their beliefs, of love and for reverence of cause.

This is the sorrow and the valor and the glory of the
American Civil War.

11

Inflation, Croakers, and Tunnels

By November 1863, the Union army was attacking Charleston, South Carolina, "night and day." From Richmond, Mary Chesnut wrote, "It fairly makes me dizzy [to think of that] everlasting racket they are beating about people's ears down there."[1] Mary, a sometimes confidant to Varina Davis, along with her husband, James, a sometimes aide to President Davis, was a frequent visitor to Richmond, apparently going from one besieged city to the other with inconvenience, perhaps, but little real difficulty.

Meanwhile, complaints and criticism grew and the *Southern Punch* took the complainers to task:

> Some words to Croakers.
> From the moment that the first gun sounded the death knells of the United States at Charleston, to this hour, men have been found who, shaking their wise heads, doubted the final success of this new

government in the greatest Liberty-struggle known to history. . . .

The croakers, always a reconstructionist, happily in a miserable minority, provoked the attention of patriotic Confederate orators, and writers who lashed them with tongue and pen into silence.

To-day, the South presents a solid front to Yankee despotism. In the field, our armies are powerful; at home citizen-soldiers stand ready, everywhere to repel invasion. Soon the Confederacy. . .will gleam with interminable war-like lines.[2]

The "war-like lines" tightened around the Confederate capital. Richmonders heard the cannon firing around Petersburg, but physically the capital city was so far unharmed. Richard J. Sommers tells why it was Petersburg, not Richmond, that took the brunt of Union artillery fire in Virginia. His is a convincing argument. Take Petersburg by force, and you could take Richmond with ease, and the North wanted Richmond kept intact. So the battle lines were drawn south of Richmond, below Petersburg, and the rail center of the latter—if it could be taken by the Yankees—would leave Richmond without an avenue of supply. The Confederate capital would be starved into submission and Richmond would be taken without shelling.[3]

"All interest in the campaign in the vicinity of Richmond having been transferred to the south side of the James [River]," the Richmond *Dispatch* claimed in mid-June of 1864, "it is now generally conceded that the larger portion of Grant's army has been moved to the new field of operation."[4]

The Union army frequently tried, and often succeeded, in cutting off rail communications with Richmond. One day the Yankees would take the lines; the next day the Rebels would take them back. By consensus, the end of Richmond and perforce the end of the Confederacy would come when the rail lines to Richmond could no longer be held by Lee's forces.

Until then, however, life would continue as best it could in
Richmond.

* * *

In the East, the naval blockade was succeeding, and the noose
tightened around Richmond. In the West, the defeated Rebels
were retreating from Chattanooga, and Joe Johnston fell back
toward Atlanta.

Time was running out. The Confederacy had just
eighteen months left to live.

Three years into the war, Federal troops were better
organized, better led, better fed, and better armed than ever
before. Many Union soldiers carried repeating rifles that took
fifteen-shot loads. Rebels said the Yankees could load up on
Sunday and keep shooting all week.

Against this military and industrial might, the Confederate army was increasingly ill-fed, demoralized, and under-
equipped. As one Union soldier put it in a letter home, "I do
think that the most forlorn picture of humanity is a Rebel
Soldier taken prisoner on a very wet day."[5]

The Confederacy was fighting an eighteenth century war
against nineteenth century technology, and it was losing.

When President Jefferson Davis signed into law the
Confederate conscription act in 1862, it applied only to white
males between the ages of eighteen and thirty-five. By early
1864, the Confederate army included both gray-bearded,
middle-aged men and those too young ever to have shaved. The
eligibility had been widened to include those from seventeen
through fifty. And as with the Union army, both older and
younger individuals served. Many Southern states also orga-

nized Junior and Senior Reserves Corps.[6] The Confederate army no longer was exclusively a young men's club.

* * *

For a while, things settled down around Richmond. But not so in the lines around Petersburg. Or, rather, *under* the lines around Petersburg.

Residents of Richmond knew what was going on, or at least had a pretty good idea of it. What they didn't know was when it would happen. What it was, was a Union army tunnel being dug under Confederate lines at Petersburg. It would turn out to be a fiasco, albeit a deadly and exciting one.

The 48th Pennsylvania was made up in part of coal miners, and when peacetime mining engineer-turned-soldier Colonel Henry Pleasants heard some of his men grousing that "we could blow that damn fort out of existence if we could run a mine shaft under it," he put his regiment to work doing just that. They would tunnel under the Rebel redoubt only 150 yards away, set explosives, and when the blast went off, storm the Southern forces. General George Meade didn't think much of the idea but didn't stop Colonel Pleasants. The Pennsylvania miners dug a shaft 511 feet long under the Rebel lines, with several separate tunnels going off in different directions. They rigged a ventilation shaft to create a draft, thereby carrying fresh air to the tunnel. The miners loaded the tunnel with four tons of gunpowder.[7] By mid-July, Southern miners had done a piece of work themselves, digging, tunnelling, probing for the Union project they knew was somewhere around. They heard Yankee picks and shovels but couldn't break through to the enemy's side. Sometimes Union and Rebel tunnels were only feet apart.

Despite his lack of enthusiasm for the tunnel project, General Meade agreed to a diversion, hoping to pull away from the scene several of Lee's units. The big event was scheduled for dawn on Saturday, July 30. Just before the fuse was lit, however, Meade ordered a change in the order of battle; Major General Ambrose Burnside was to send in his white divisions first, apparently because Meade lacked confidence in his inexperienced black troops. General Grant agreed to the change but later testified that Meade believed if the tunnel project went wrong, "it would then be said, and very properly, that we were shoving these people (the black troops) ahead to get killed because we did not care anything about them. But that could not be said if we put white troops in front."[8]

The change in plans demoralized a lot of troops. It didn't help that the officer who was named to lead the assault, James Ledlie, stayed in his tent and got drunk.

So dawn, that July Saturday, almost literally came up like thunder. The gunpowder blew a hole 170 feet long, 60 feet wide, and 30 feet deep. It created The Crater. More than 275 Confederates were buried instantly, an entire Rebel regiment and artillery battalion. And just as quickly, Confederate forces around the Crater ran off.

Instead of charging around the blasted-out hole, Union forces ran *into* the Crater. Ran in and stopped. It was like nothing they had ever seen. They looked around in amazement. Two additional Yankee divisions followed them into The Crater. They, too, stopped and looked around, equally amazed. It didn't help matters that, in planning the affair, no one thought to include ladders with the onrushing troops; once they got in, they had to climb out, hand over dirt daub, all the time ducking Confederate gunfire, holding onto their rifles, fighting back, and generally being scared as hell.

While the Federals stopped to look around, the Rebels stopped running and headed back for the edge of The Crater.

They began shooting the Federals like fish in a barrel. In the end, The Crater remained a no-man's land. And in the end, also, 1,500 Confederates were lost, at least 3,500 Federals were killed or wounded, 1,500 Union troops were taken prisoner, and twenty U.S. flags were captured by the South.

It was, Grant said, "the saddest affair I have ever witnessed in the war."[9]

The Petersburg *Dispatch* called the attempt to undermine Confederate defenses "Grant's imitation earthquake," and said it was no "great shakes after all."[10] And from the Richmond *Whig*:

> Despite the fact that Grant's explosion [*sic*] terrified all the babies and frightened a few of the old ladies of Petersburg, things on the front go on again as usual. We learn from [railroad] passengers last night that a truce lasted yesterday for burying the Yankee dead from 5 o'clock to 8 A.M. After that occasional shelling occurred without material injury to the city.[11]

The Battle of The Crater also marked a change in attitude among Southern troops, at least partially because black troops had been used against them. Phoebe Yates Pember, of Chimborazo Hospital in Richmond, wrote that until The Crater, the Confederate soldiers she treated had not been bitter toward their Northern counterparts. They accepted the fighting, she believed, and she quoted her patients as simply saying, "They fit us, we fit them."

But the white Rebels felt the North's use of black troops was a "mean trick," and that changed the way her hospitalized charges looked:

> Eyes gleamed, and teeth clenched as they showed me the locks of their muskets, to which the blood and

hair still clung, when, after firing, without waiting to re-load, they had clenched the barrels and fought hand to hand.[12]

Down the road a year or so, the Confederacy would try its hand at Phoebe Pember's "mean trick." Down the road a year or so, the Confederacy would recruit its own black troops.

The War in the West

VI

Atlanta

In early March of '64, Lincoln promoted Grant to lieutenant general, the U.S. army's *first* lieutenant general since George Washington. And on May 5, Grant began his Wilderness Campaign in Northern Virginia.

That same day, Sherman lead his army out of Chattanooga and into Georgia. The plan was for Sherman to take Atlanta while Grant took Richmond. Both would get the job done, but neither would have an easy time of it.

Sherman was forty-four, tall, with scraggly red hair and beard. He was energetic. Poet and sometime soldier, sometime war correspondent, Walt Whitman described him as "a bit of stern open air, . .[m]ade up in the image of a man."[1] His close friends called him "Cump." That was short for his middle name, Tecumseh. (He'd actually been named simply Tecumseh Sherman at birth and only later added the William.) The men in the ranks called him "Uncle Billy."

By mid-June, Uncle Billy had pushed Johnston to within thirty miles of Atlanta. And on June 27, he tried to settle things once and for all. But he picked the wrong place and the wrong time—the slopes of Kennesaw Mountain, when Joe Johnston was at his strongest and the thermometer was close to 100 degrees.

Kennesaw Mountain was not a repeat of Chattanooga and Missionary Ridge. This time, Rebel troops didn't panic or run away. Sherman lost 3,000—almost 20 percent of his army. The Confederacy counted only 750 casualties at Kennesaw Mountain, and Johnston returned to his slow retreat.

He still believed the Federal army's 25,000-man superiority would win any all-out battle, so he faded, delayed, and stalled, hoping to persuade the North to give up the fight they plainly were tired of. Johnston believed that if he could hold Sherman off long enough, force Sherman into enough mistakes, then Lincoln would lose the coming election, and the South would be left alone by whoever took over the White House.

Jefferson Davis never did like Johnston and saw only that he was avoiding a fight. On July 17, he fired Johnston and replaced him with John Bell Hood of Texas. Davis believed Hood would fight, not run.

Hood's friends called him "Sam," but he was known to his men as "Old Wooden Head." Hood's left arm hung withered and useless, his sleeve pinned to his coat, thanks to Union grapeshot he received at Gettysburg. In the fall of '63, at Chickamauga, he lost most of his right leg. Outside Atlanta, he was only thirty-three but in no shape to command an army. His men had to strap him to his horse in order for their commander to lead them into battle.

Like Davis, Sherman wanted Hood to come out and fight. Just six days after he took command, Hood gave Sherman what Sherman wanted: he attacked the Union lines in front of Atlanta.

On July 22, Major General James Birdseye McPherson was having breakfast with Sherman when the battle began, but he quickly rode out to lead his men. It was a ride that took him right into the middle of Cleburne's cavalry. The Rebels ordered McPherson to surrender. But he refused, tipped his hat, and rode off. One shot—in the back—and he died almost immediately. Aides recovered McPherson's body and took it to headquarters, laying it in front of his friend and commander, William Tecumseh Sherman. Briefly, they stood by as that crusty "bit of stern open air" openly cried.

John Logan took command of McPherson's troops, and they were angry. They charged the Rebels, crying "McPherson and revenge, Boys! McPherson and revenge." Within minutes, they forced Hood back.

Back to Ezra Church, a small country meeting house two miles west of Atlanta. Hood tried to rally his men there, but the rally failed miserably.

In three battles in just eight days of commanding the Army of Tennessee, Hood lost 15,000 men, two and a-half times as many as Sherman lost. He had no choice then but to do what Joe Johnston before him had done: retreat behind the twelve miles of Atlanta's fortifications and settle in for a long siege.

Meanwhile, Richmond remained under siege as Grant and Lee faced each other over the trenches of Petersburg.

North *and* south, the war was stalled.

* * *

Sherman's solution was to destroy Atlanta by bombardment, and he vowed to turn the city into ruins. Day after day, almost hour after hour, Sherman's cannon hammered away at Atlanta, despite the fact the city was still full of civilians. There were also factories, rail facilities, and other military targets in the city. But Sherman said, "War is war, and not popularity-seeking."[2] Soon, the civilians moved underground, into cellars and caves, what they called "bombproofs," shelters built beneath their homes. It was Vicksburg all over again.

In one day, Sherman's artillery fired 5,000 shells into the city, and the bombardment continued for seventeen long days. Still, the city didn't give up. In fact, the shelling drew the people of Atlanta closer together, giving them a feeling of taking part in the fight, not just witnessing it. Above all, it made them determined to hold on. (Some historians believe this was the case in World War II Germany; Allied bombing drew the people of Germany closer. They also cite the Vietnam War, saying American bombing of the North coalesced rather coerced the population.)

Finally, in late August, the bombardment stopped, and Hood's men checked the Union trenches; they were empty. The people of Atlanta looked around them and celebrated. Everyone hoped Sherman had given up. But they didn't know him very well. He wasn't giving up; he was moving south, hoping to cut the final two rail lines linking Atlanta to the rest of the Confederacy.

If the railroads went, so would the city, and Hood knew he had too few troops left for an adequate defense. He went chasing after Sherman, but didn't make it in time. The last railroad around Atlanta was the Macon and Western Railroad, and when it fell to Union troops, everyone knew it was over.

It was September 1, and Sherman sent his whole force against General William Hardee and the last remaining Southern defenders still inside Atlanta, barely 5,000 men still able to do battle. Patrick Cleburne fought a rear-guard action as he'd done so many times before, and Hardee's troops slipped out of the city to join Hood. By the next day, the Battle for Atlanta was over.

Sherman telegraphed Grant: "Atlanta is ours. . . . And fairly won."[3]

In Richmond, Mary Chesnut wrote of that day in her diary:

> Atlanta gone. Well—that agony is over. Like David when the child was dead, I will get up from my knees, will wash my face and comb my hair. No hope. We will try to have no fear.[4]

She didn't succeed, and later added to her diary:

> I have felt as if all were dead within me forever.
> All was ended now—the hope, the fear, and the sorrow.
> All the aching of heart, the restless unsatisfied longing.
> All of dull, deep pain, and the constant anguish of patience.[5]

Outside Richmond, the entrenched Union troops cheered, and Confederate War Clerk John Jones wrote:

> A dispatch from Petersburg states that there is much cheering in Grant's army for McClellan, the [Democratic] nominee of the Chicago Convention for the Presidency. I think the resolutions of the convention amount to a defiance of President Lincoln, and that their ratification meetings will inaugurate civil war [in the North].[6]

However, Jones didn't believe that was why the Yankees cheered:

I incline to the belief that Hood has met with disaster
at Atlanta. If so, every able-bodied man in that State
will be hunted up for its defense, unless, indeed, the
Union party should be revived there.

The war department clerk was correct:

> September 4th—Showery.
> Atlanta has fallen, and our army has retreated some
> thirty miles. . . .
> The cheering in Grant's camp yesterday was over that
> event. We have not had sufficient generalship and
> enterprise to destroy Sherman's communications.

The loss of Atlanta (among other things) greatly distressed him:

> September 5th
> Clear and warm. . . .
> The loss of Atlanta is a stunning blow.
> I am sick to-day—having been swollen by beans.[7]

The Union lost nearly one-third of its 100,000-man force
outside Atlanta. The Confederate Army of Tennessee once
numbered 53,000 troops, but by the time the city fell, it was
down to 23,000.

Both victory and defeat were costly.

12

Rusty, Dilapidated,
and War Worn

Living is more than obtaining food, having adequate shelter, and avoiding death. Until its own final rail ties to the outside world were cut, and until Union troops marched into Richmond, the city's residents continued to enjoy a more genteel aspect of life—the theatre. Or tried to.

Even fire had not quenched the city's love of theatre. On Christmas night in 1811, the Richmond Theatre burned, and Richmonders built the Monumental Church over the ruins to commemorate the deaths. *East Lynne* played at the Marshall Theatre over the winter of 1858-1859 with an actor described as having "at least the makings of an actor." He was John Wilkes Booth who, somehow, was able to use his acting profession to avoid military service. In January of 1862 when the Marshall Theatre was leveled by fire, the city quickly went to work building another to replace it. The New Richmond

Theatre opened on February 9, 1863. "A lobby entered by several doors from Broad Street," it was reported, and led "to the orchestra and to the parquet. There were two or three galleries [*sic*]. . .the first and dress circle seeming to lead almost under the ceiling. On each side of the stage were tiers of boxes, three on a side."[1]

Not long after the New Richmond Theatre opened, as the audience watched a play unfold, a group of Confederate cavalrymen noisily rode up outside, charged into the theatre and down the aisle, shouting commands and rattling sabres. They located another group of soldiers, rousted them from their seats, and marched them outside. The theatre-going soldiers were part of Jeb Stuart's corps and were absent without leave—AWOL. Stuart was just collecting some of his boys.[2]

In 1864, war or not, several companies played in the various theatres still open in Richmond. Sallie Putnam praised the New Richmond Theatre's "indefatigable manager, Mr. Ogden," but admitted the stock companies playing there during the siege years "ranked in talent somewhat below mediocrity."[3] Entertainment of any quality was welcomed, however, and three weeks prior to Christmas 1863 *The Wrecker's Daughter* and *State Secrets* topped the bill. Many plays, such as the mentioned *State Secrets*, clearly dealt openly with events of the day. Others, *Macbeth* and *The Iron Mask* among them, leave us imagining the reaction of Richmond audiences during time of war.

Then, as now, newspapers frequently carried ads for theatrical performances. The Richmond *Enquirer* carried a notice of *Wife, Or The Tale of Mantua*, running it alongside notices of troop movements ("Gen. Jeff Davis' division occupies our extreme front here"). While one column carried news of the opening of the new term at the Danville Female College ("Tuition in Literary Department for twenty weeks. . . $50"), another carried an ad for "Graceful and Fascinating Dances." A notice of a production of *Joseph and His Court* playing at a local theatre ran along with a reader's objection to conscription of blacks.[4]

The newspapers also reported efforts to trade Southern cotton and tobacco for clothing and food ("King cotton had been bound down in double irons—Lincoln and Blockaders").[5] But all things considered, Richmond readers learned more from their newspapers about actors at their theatres than they did about the war that was at their doorsteps.

Sallie Putnam said Boston had been "facetiously termed the 'Hub of the Universe,'" and certainly "Richmond. . .could style itself the 'Hub of the Confederacy.'"[6] If being a hub meant having opposing armies battle over you, then Richmond certainly filled the bill. Residents of this "hub" continued trying to live life as usual. It wasn't easy by any means.

* * *

The first three years in a human life sees an infant go from squealing baby to rambunctious, running child. Three years in the life of a school boy sees him go from questioning youth to all-knowing academic. Three years in the life of a love affair can see it go from joy to hatred. Three years in the life of a city under siege can see it only go from bad to worse. Atlanta, Charleston, Vicksburg—they all suffered. And so did Richmond.

Still, the summer of 1864 saw residents' spirits soar, and, as Mrs. Putnam put it, "peace and independence seemed dependent only on the endurance of the Southern people."[7] But enduring was growing more difficult. With simply living difficult enough, they weren't too concerned over how things looked.

"Very few of the buildings had been brightened by a fresh application of paint since the commencement of hostilities," Mrs. Putnam wrote, and "where a plank fell off, or a screw got loose, or a gate fell from its hinges, or a bolt gave away, or a lock was broken, it was most likely to remain for a time unrepaired." Carpenters, painters, repairmen, and mechanics were all in the field, "and those left in the city were generally in the employment of the government."[8] Richmond, it seemed, might not last so long as its people. Simply put, the city was, as Sallie Putnam wrote, wearing out, "growing rusty, dilapidated, and beginning to assume a war-worn appearance."

And people, what to do with all the people. The city's population fluctuated greatly over the war years. The official U.S. Census of 1860 lists 39,910 people living in Richmond, 10,739 of whom were slaves. By the time the capital of the Confederacy was moved to Richmond in 1861, it is estimated that the population had increased to nearly 100,000. Toward war's end, as stragglers moved away from the Yankee lines and refugees moved into the city, Richmond's population may have gone as high as 200,000, including troops, the wounded, and the government workers. After the Confederate government and many of its newer citizens evacuated the city, there likely were not more than 8,000 or 9,000 remaining in Richmond. Of this number, many were former slaves, newly freed by the Union army.[9]

During the war, refugees and deserters from both armies were a constant problem in the city. How were they to be fed, since most were without funds? Where were they to be housed? How were they to be controlled when they became hostile, as they sometimes did? Many of the problems were handled by individuals, private charities, and the Richmond city government. The Young Men's Christian Association (YMCA) of Richmond, for example, frequently appealed on behalf of the soldiers' families taking refuge in the city, and the appeal was

Richmond, 1862; looking west, shortly after the start of the war. At left, Confederate troops parade through the streets, a frequent sight as the war progressed. (*Originally published in* Harper's Weekly; *courtesy of the Valentine Museum; Richmond, Virginia.*)

Manchester, Virginia; opposite Richmond on the James River. Taken shortly after the war's end, this picture accurately depicts the style of private homes in Richmond during the siege. (*Eleanor S. Brockenbrough Library, Museum of the Confederacy; Richmond, Virginia.*)

A letter, dated July 24, 1861, from Dr. Hunter Holmes McGuire to his father following the Battle of Manassas. McGuire was chief surgeon to General Thomas "Stonewall" Jackson's command. He later became president of the American Medical Association. At top, McGuire's sketch of the battle. (*Virginia Historical Society; Richmond, Virginia.*)

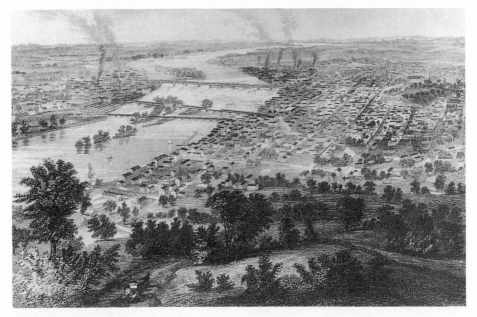

Richmond and vicinity, 1863. At upper right, the Capitol of the Confederate States of America. It presently serves as Virginia's capitol building. (*Valentine Museum; Richmond, Virginia.*)

The White House of the Confederacy at present. It has been restored and decorated with furnishings from the period. The building on the left is the Museum of the Confederacy. (*Author's photograph*)

Scenes of Richmond as depicted in Frank Leslie's *Illustrated News*. Entitled "Sowing and Reaping," the left caption reads, "Southern women hounding their men to rebellion." The right caption says,"Southern women feeling the effects of rebellion and creating bread riots." (*Virginia State Library and Archives; Richmond, Virginia.*)

Tredegar Iron Works, April 1865. The Tredegar Iron Works was one of the largest such manufacturers in the South and continued producing everything from cannons to lighting fixtures throughout the war. (*Library of Congress; Washington, D.C.*)

The Crater located at Petersburg National Battlefield as it is today. On July 30, 1863, after months of digging by a Pennsylvania regiment, Union troops exploded four tons of gunpowder under Confederate lines. The explosion instantly buried more than 275 Rebels. Union troops were also shocked by the blast, allowing the Confederates to regroup. In a counterattack, they killed or wounded 3,500 Federals and captured another 1,500. Neither the Union nor Confederate lines were changed by the battle. (*Author's photograph*)

General Hospital No.1 (Alms House Hospital). Located between 2nd and 4th streets, opposite Shockoe Cemetery, it was just one of more than twenty-five hospitals in Richmond during the siege. Several buildings, public and private, were converted into hospitals as the casualty numbers increased. Not all casualties occurred because of bullets or shelling; at one point, the Alms House Hospital was filled with smallpox victims. (*Valentine Museum; Richmond, Virginia.*)

Poster for the New Richmond Theatre issued shortly before the war's end. Despite the dangers of war and scarce entertainment funds, several Richmond theaters continued to operate throughout the siege. At bottom the poster reads, "The theatre is open every evening." (*Eleanor S. Brockenbrough Library, Museum of the Confederacy; Richmond, Virginia.*)

NEW RICHMOND THEATRE,
(Corner of 7th and Broad Streets.)

This popular resort of amusement, the Manager is happy to announce, notwithstanding the many difficulties against which the Management have had to contend, still continues to offer nightly, BRILLIANT AND ATTRACTIVE PROGRAMMES, diversified by choice selections from the most sterling productions of the Dramatic Repertory; such as

TRAGEDIES, COMEDIES,
PLAYS, DRAMAS, FARCES,
BURLETTAS, OPERAS, &c. &c.

WITH WHICH ARE INTRODUCED

CHARACTERISTIC AND FANCY DANCES, SONGS, BALLADS AND DUETTS,

All presented in a manner unequalled in any other Theatre in the Confederacy.

The Management have directed all their efforts to the composition of a Corps Dramatique, second to none in the Confederacy, and take pleasure in introducing to the public

AN EFFICIENT CORPS DE BALLET.

THE ORCHESTRA

Is composed of the best Musicians in the Confederacy, under the directorship of Professors A. ROSENBURG and M. LOEBMAN, who are conceded to be the best musical caterers in the Confederacy.

☞ THE THEATRE IS OPEN EVERY EVENING. ☜

The Management beg leave to call attention to the elite audiences that nightly crowd the Theatre, as an evidence of the correctness of the performances, and the popularity of the plays selected.

Libby Prison, 1863. In the foreground, stands the prison commandant, Dr. Thomas P. Turner (second from left). Following the war, Turner fled to Mexico and served under Emperor Maximilian. He later returned to the United States and practiced dentistry in New Orleans. (*Valentine Museum; Richmond, Virginia.*)

Richmond at the war's end. Set ablaze and burned by fleeing Confederate soldiers, the former capitol building became a popular spot for Union troops to be photographed. Eventually, those photos were sent home to family and friends as war remembrances. (*Valentine Museum; Richmond, Virginia.*)

Lincoln entering Richmond, April 4, 1865. This wood engraving from a drawing by political cartoonist Thomas Nast shows Lincoln touring Richmond. Lincoln was accompanied by a small troop of Union forces and, while most whites remained indoors, he was surrounded by hundreds of newly freed and appreciative slaves. (*Valentine Museum; Richmond, Virginia.*)

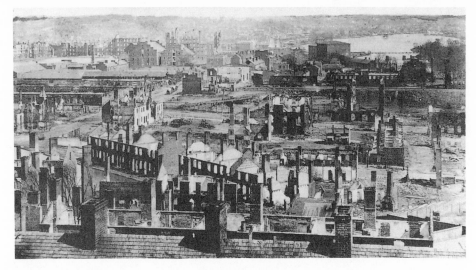

Richmond shortly after war's end. Retreating Confederates turned the city into a "desert," as one newspaper described it, when fires they started in tobacco warehouses spread and eventually set off an explosion at an arsenal. A significant downtown section of the city was wiped out. (*Library of Congress; Washington, D.C.*)

A Hamlet, Indiana, barn. Torn down in 1888, Libby Prison was rebuilt in Chicago and designated the Greater Libby Prison War Museum. Eleven years later, it was torn down again, to be exhibited on a world tour. Crossing Indiana, the eastbound train carrying the prison was wrecked and much of the material wound up as a Hamlet barn. It remained there until the Civil War Centennial in 1963. (*Valentine Museum; Richmond, Virginia.*)

answered time and time again. However, by early July 1864, the supplies gathered by the agency and the remaining funds were so meager that the YMCA felt it could "accomplish but little" in the way of helping the poor.[10] The situation was so desperate that the city council considered taking action against the refugees:

> All persons who are not liable to military duty, and all others whose presence is not, by their being employed in some useful and legitimate occupation, required in the city [are ordered] to leave it and remain away until a change in the state of affairs renders it desirable for them to return.[11]

The resolution was withdrawn only when it was decided it would do more harm (alerting the enemy to just how desperate the situation was) than good (ridding the city of its unwanted human surplus). But the idea would be brought up again later in the siege.

Sallie Brock Putnam was seventeen in 1862 and believed "from the second year of the war, the floating population of the city," as she called the refugees, "quite equalled, if it did not exceed in numbers, the resident inhabitants."[12] There was, she noted, just no place to put this floating population. Even hotels and rooming houses were out of the question. First, they were expensive and few in number, and second, privacy in those that were available was beyond all hope. Landlords had a way of renting a room to one person and then forcing the individual to share it with another. Rooms, Sallie said, were "of india-rubber capacity," stretching and stretching until finally broken.

Regretfully, there is no record of how these new Richmonders lived during the siege, although there are photographs and reports of shack cities on the outskirts of town. Nor is the picture clear of why some homes stayed empty during the war—several diarists note this—apparently unoccupied by either owners, renters, or squatters. In a city overrun with transients, one wonders, with living quarters often going at a premium, why these houses remained empty.

Both the city and Confederate governments attempted to control prices, but apparently neither body attempted to make certain its new residents had places to live.

13

Oh, Lord, How Long, How Long?

Outside the breastworks, the battles raged. Inside the city, thousands of Yankee prisoners were marched in and many times that number of Rebel dead and wounded were carried in. The Northern press wrote of "crushing Lee" and of Union troops eating Christmas dinner in Richmond, but four Christmases would pass before Yankees, other than those held prisoner, would dine in the capital of the Confederacy.

Spring and summer of 1864 saw bitterly fought battles and mounting casualties. In May, Lee and Grant faced each other in the Wilderness, northwest of Richmond.

Henry Morrison was a captain with the 4th Virginia Volunteer Infantry at the Battle of the Wilderness in May of 1864. On the first day of the battle, he wrote his aunt:

> We have been on the march backward and forward in
> the wilderness for two days. . . . I think the fight has
> commenced in earnest now. At this moment, we can
> hear the artillery roaring on our right. Occasionally we
> hear a volley of musketry. The sun is just rising and
> how beautiful![1]

Grant predicted the result of the battle would be "decidedly in
our favor." Lee told President Jefferson Davis that "with the
blessing of God I trust we shall be able to prevent General
Grant from reaching Richmond." Grant was wrong. Lee was
right.

The Battle of the Wilderness began on May 5. Union
troops ran into Rebel soldiers dug in on a ridge along the
Orange Turnpike. For two days the two sides fought in underbrush so heavy men couldn't see who they were fighting;
friendly fire often causing as much damage as the enemy's. It
was the first time General Lee had run up against his new
opponent, U. S. Grant. Lee hoped to trap Grant amidst the
scrub oak and pine the way he had Joe Wheeler a year before.
Grant, however, was no Wheeler, as Lee soon found out.

Lee would hit Grant just as the Union army marched
through the Wilderness, slamming into Grant's flank. In the
heavy undergrowth, the North's 115,000 men (the South
counted about 64,000) wouldn't mean much.

The Rebels knew the terrain—dense, smoke-filled
woods; the Federals had more men—well armed, well trained,
aching for a fight. The firing was so intense it sometimes set the
underbrush on fire.

Both sides held their ground (what they could see of it),
with Grant ready to attack Lee again the next day. Lee also
lunged ahead, even though Old Warhorse Longstreet hadn't yet
arrived from Tennessee. When the fighting broke through into
his field headquarters, Robert E. Lee tried personally to lead

a counterattack from atop "Traveller." Seeing Marse Robert riding his great gray stallion worried the Rebels; he presented too good a target for Yankee marksmen. Members of a Texas unit shouted, "Go back, General Lee, go back!" He finally did, just as one of Longstreet's unit arrived and halted the Union advance.

They fought among the vines, the trees choking the careless; the troops simply couldn't see the enemy until they stumbled upon him. It was noon of the second day when Longstreet finally arrived in force. That wild Rebel yell, and the Confederates drove against the Federal right flank. Suddenly, Longstreet was hit, a bullet in his shoulder—fired by a Rebel soldier. It was minor, however, and he would recover.

With General John B. Gordon of Georgia punching away at the Yankees, the Confederates drove the Federal flank backward. Panic hit the Union troops; an aide even told General Grant that it was all over; Lee was going to beat them in the Wilderness just as Stonewall Jackson had done there a year before. Maybe it was because he was new in the east, maybe it was because of his own ego, but Ulysses S. Grant didn't want to be told how great Robert E. Lee was. He said to the officer who'd brought him the news:

> I am heartily tired of hearing what Lee is doing. Some of you always seem to think he is suddenly going to turn a double somersault, and land on our rear and on both our flanks at the same time. Go back to your command, and try to think what we are going to do ourselves, instead of what Lee is going to do.[2]

The Union suffered more casualties at The Battle of the Wilderness—18,000 for Grant, about 7,500 for Lee—yet it ended in a technical draw. The North was still on the outside of Richmond, looking in. But, despite Lee's seeming victory of numbers, the Battle of the Wilderness changed the way the war would go.

After previous such battles, Union commanders would withdraw behind the nearest river to rest. Not so General Grant. He had told Abe Lincoln "whatever happens, there will be no turning back."[3]

When the Union troops and their supply wagons pulled out, it looked to be a repeat of other actions. But instead of heading back up north, they turned south, toward Spotsylvania Courthouse, a small county seat at the crossroads controlling the shortest route to Richmond.

Jeb Stuart, the pride of Confederate cavalry, waited anxiously. And bandy-legged Phil Sheridan was just as anxious to meet him.

The Federals outnumbered the Rebels two-to-one when they met at a place called Yellow Tavern (named after an old, abandoned, stagecoach inn), just six miles from Richmond. This time, the Union horsemen trampled the Confederates, gunning down many of the Rebels with those rapid-fire repeating carbines. Among the Southern dead, the flamboyant Jeb Stuart.

Stuart's death came a year and a day after the death of Stonewall Jackson.[4] A close friend, Philip Powers, was a captain of the Army of Northern Virginia's quartermaster department. Three days after Stuart's death by a Union cavalryman's bullet, Powers wrote home:

> [T]he news has thrown a gloom upon us all. Since the death of the lamented Jackson, no event, no disaster, has so affected me. Jackson was a great loss to his country and to the cause. Genl. Stuart is a great loss to his country. But to us, who have been intimately associated with him—and to me in particular—his loss is irreparable, for in him, I have lost my best friend in the army.[5]

Stuart and his 1,100 troopers had fought for six hours, holding back the 7,000 Union soldiers headed by Phil Sheridan. The wounded Confederate cavalry officer was taken to the nearby Richmond home of his brother-in-law, Dr. Charles Brewer, and laid in an upstairs room. An aide telegraphed Stuart's wife but she was unable to reach him in time.[6] It was a night of suffering for Stuart; he held to the promise he'd made as a young boy never to touch alcohol, even though it might have eased his suffering.[7] He knew he was dying but remained lucid, at one point offering his horses to his friends and aides, Henry McClellan and Andrew Reid Venable. "[L]et Venable take the gray horse," he told McClellan, "and you take the bay." He asked that a small Confederate flag he carried inside his hat be returned to the Columbia, South Carolina, woman who had made it for him.[8] His spurs he left to Mrs. Lilly Lee, the widow of William Fitzhugh Lee. And his sword, "I leave to my son."

Jefferson Davis learned of Stuart's injury and rushed to the Grace Street home where the young officer lay dying. He asked Stuart how he felt, and was told, "Easy, but willing to die if God and my country think I have fulfilled my destiny and done my duty."[9]

God's reaction isn't known, but that of his country certainly is.

To J. B. Jones, it felt as if "our best generals thus fall around us."[10] Sallie Putnam told how "in bitterness of anguish we turned our stricken hearts to God, and cried out again in the accents of woe, 'Oh, Lord, how long, how long?'"[11]

Throughout the war, Stuart wore a long, flowing black plume in his hat, proclamation of his ties to the Royal Stuarts, pretenders to the throne of Scotland. He was carried to his grave with his hat resting on his casket.

* * *

Back at Spotsylvania Court House, Grant had heard about Federal troops breaking through a Confederate fortification called the Mule Shoe. Whenever the Rebels stopped, they quickly built intricate networks of traverses and breastworks, felled trees with sharpened branches (referred to as abatis), and—yes, General Lee—trenches. The Confederates built such a fortification at Spotsylvania, fieldworks in the shape of a mule's shoe, thus the name.

When twelve New York regiments managed to break through this salient, it gave Grant an idea: if 5,000 men could penetrate this strong, if hastily built fort, what could his entire army do? He found out over the next twenty hours.

It rained that day, hampering the vision of both leaders. Lee saw Grant's supply wagons turning back, or thought he did. And he pulled out twenty-two of his cannon to prepare a counterattack. But the point where those cannon had been was the exact point where Winfield Scott Hancock was preparing to send his 2nd Corps on the morning of May 12.

Hancock's men charged, and Lee realized his mistake. That's when he made another one; he sent the artillery back into the line. They arrived too late to do any good but just in time for the Yankees to capture them. Fifteen-thousand bluecoats swarmed through the salient, pushing through the mist to seize most of the old Stonewall Division. It split Lee's defenses in two.

Again, Robert E. Lee tried to personally lead his men in a comeback. And again, his soldiers shouted him back: "General Lee! To the rear! To the rear!" The Rebel commander finally agreed and the Confederates rallied, pushing the Federals back to the toe of the Mule Shoe. There, the Union army occupied the trenches dug just days before by their Confederate opponents.

Back and forth the battle went, first Rebel, then Yank occupying the breastworks called Bloody Angle. "The flags of both armies waved at the same moment over the same breast-works," a 6th Corps trooper remembered, "while beneath them Federal and Confederate endeavored to drive home the bayonet through the interstices of the logs."[12]

Hand-to-hand fighting, up the parapet and fire down on the enemy; men fired their rifles, then threw them like spears at the enemy before grabbing another rifle handed up from someone behind them.

Fierce, bloody fighting, in the midst of which, Major Eugene Blackford—believe it or not—took time out to write a letter to his sister:

> Tho the shells are bursting all around us and the minié bullets are cheeping just over our heads, we have dug ourselves deep enough into the ground to be tolerably protected and enough for me to write a few lines.[13]

While Blackford wrote home, everyone else in the neighbor-hood grappled at each other in the blood and rain flowing in the trenches, trenches where the dying trampled on the dead, until they themselves fell. When it was over, when the burial detail arrived to perform its gruesome job, it found 150 Rebel soldiers piled two and three deep, so many they simply pushed dirt on top of them.

The Battles of the Wilderness and Spotsylvania opened with a bang; they closed with a whimper. And with a butcher's bill that totaled some 32,000 for the Union and 18,000 for the Confederacy. Proportionately, it was harder on the South, and Lee had to call up six brigades from the Richmond front as reinforcements. Grant, however, learned a lesson: fighting Lee in the East wasn't nearly so easy as fighting Bragg in Tennessee.

From John Jones's diary:

May 21st—
Nothing from Lee, but troops are constantly going to him.
I saw some 10,000 rusty rifles, brought down yesterday from Lee's battlefield. Many bore marks of balls, deeply indenting or perforating the barrels. The ordnance officer says in his report that he has collected many thousand more than were dropped by our killed and wounded. This does not look like a *Federal* victory!

May 22nd—
[T]he war rolls on toward this capital, and yet Lee's headquarters remains in Spottsylvania [*sic*]. A few days more must tell the story. If he cuts Grant's communications, I should not be surprised if that desperate general attempted a bold dash on toward Richmond. I don't think he could take the city—and he would be between two fires.
I saw some of the enemy's wounded this morning, brought down in the cars, dreadfully mutilated. Some had lost a leg and arm—besides sustaining other injuries. But they were cheerful, and uttered not a groan in the removal to the hospital.
Flour is selling as high as $400 per barrel.[14]

By June 3, Ulysses S. Grant was just six miles northwest of Richmond.

The two armies had swung north by northwest of Richmond where they met again at the Battle of Cold Harbor.

There was no harbor at Cold Harbor; there isn't a harbor for miles around, just a strip of land between the Pamunkey and Chickahominy Rivers. The name remembers a tavern where travelers could obtain a place to sleep and something cold to drink, but not a *hot* meal.

However, it was strategically important in the North's plans to take Richmond. At Cold Harbor, as it ever would, Grant's Army of the Potomac outnumbered Lee's Army of Northern Virginia. Almost 50,000 Federal troops launched a massive frontal assault on the Confederates, but the Rebels were well entrenched, and it was a sight of unbelievable slaughter. A member of the 13th New Hampshire Infantry tried to sum up the battle, admitting that language could not describe the fearful picture:

> [R]ushing in the mad plunge of a battle charge, with muskets in hand and gleaming bayonets fixed, thousands of swords flashing, hundreds of battle flags waving, many hundreds of officers shouting loud their words of command and the men screaming and yelling their battle-cries, all mingled with the shrieks of the poor men who are struck in their wild careen—here in ten short minutes ten thousand of them, a thousand men falling in every minute; while along the dense battle lines of more than four miles, huge clouds of gunpowder smoke roll up above the fields and forests.[15]

It wasn't quite that bad, but it was bad enough. Grant believed Lee's forces where tired, always hungry, but so too were his men. "Lee's army is really whipped," he had written Major General Henry Halleck only a few days earlier, adding:

> [T]he prisoners we now take show it, and the action of his [Lee's] army shows it unmistakably. A battle with them outside of entrenchments cannot be had. Our men feel that they have gained the morale over the enemy and attack with confidence.[16]

And he ordered an assault on Lee's well-entrenched lines. It was said to be the bloodiest eight minutes of the war—7,000 Union casualties and 1,500 Confederate were killed or wounded during that time. One Union general said, "In that little period more men fell bleeding as they advanced than in any other like period of time throughout the war."[17] In his memoirs, Grant would call Cold Harbor the only battle he ever regretted fighting: "At Cold Harbor no advantage was gained to compensate for the heavy loss we sustained."[18]

According to Grant:

> Richmond was fortified and entrenched so perfectly that one man inside to defend was more than equal to five outside besieging or assaulting.[19]

But Confederate General Lee didn't want to fight in the trenches around Richmond, but rather he wanted to go on the offensive and destroy Grant's army.

General Grant chose to go around Richmond, just what Lee wanted. Union troops would approach the city from the south, because, Grant said, "a full survey of all the ground satisfies me that it would be impracticable to hold a line northeast of Richmond."[20] But making that move cost the Union army more than five times the losses suffered by the Confederates. Since the Battle of the Wilderness, Grant's losses had totaled more than 55,000 men. It was as many troops as had been lost in the previous three years under McDowell, McClellan, Pope, Burnside, Hooker, and Meade together.[21] No wonder Grant was called "The Butcher." Yet despite the growing losses, the movement of the war was with the North.

Lee's position north of Richmond and the swamps around the Chickahominy River first forced Grant into the Battle of Cold Harbor and later into the final siege of Richmond. "Once on the south side of the James," Grant wrote

Halleck in Washington, "I can cut off all sources of supply to the enemy."[22] Lee, of course, had realized this for most of the war. If the railroads were cut, only the canal along the James River could be used to supply the Confederate capital, and that would never be enough. Grant "determined to make my next left flank move carry the Army of the Potomac south of the James River."[23]

"Old Brains" Halleck had been promoted to the Union army's chief of staff. The correspondence continued between him and the man he once thought of as his rival. Grant at one point admitted "the feeling of the two armies now seems to be that the rebels can protect themselves only by strong entrenchments." Union forces, Grant believed, could "beat and drive the enemy wherever and whenever he can be found" outside the protection of extensive entrenchments; Lee realized that as well, and he dug in. General Grant's move set up the final ten-month siege of Petersburg and Richmond just as he knew it would and just as General Lee feared it might.

In August the Richmond *Whig* claimed the war went well:

> At all points, the enemy are not only held at bay, when not to advance is defeat, but are receiving from time to time severe punishment. . . .

> At Clinton, Petersburg, Atlanta. . . .

> Grant failed to take Petersburg, his campaign was at an end. He had traversed the entire field that bore upon Richmond. . . .

> He. . .attacked and failed, and so ended his campaign against Richmond. What he is doing now is intended for nothing but to postpone the humiliation of acknowledged defeat.[24]

"So far Grant has unquestionably failed in his enterprises against Richmond," John Jones wrote, adding, "Thank God, the prospect of peace is 'bright and brightening,' and a dark cloud is above the horizon in the North."[25]

"The inhabitants of Richmond were very closely confined to the city," Sallie Putnam wrote, "not only be the active duties of benevolence, which absorbed so much of their time, means, and talents, but frequently by the actual impossibility of travel."[26] Only the Richmond-Fredericksburg road was open to the north, and often that was in danger of Yankee attacks. To the south, toward Petersburg, there were "our insecure railroads," Putnam wrote. It was not an easy trip to go that way, and one "accomplished [it] between the roads in which tracks were torn up, burned, and other damage done." "While the war lasted," she added, "most of us were fixtured in Richmond and we ventured outside the city limits only when the skillful maneuvering of our army made it possible to go with a certainty of being able to return when we desired."

The uncertainty of movement pertained, not just to people, but to foodstuffs as well. As the siege continued, goods grew more scarce, and thus, more expensive.

On August 1, 1864, the Commissioners of Appraisement issued a revised schedule of food prices. Prices adopted in May and June were too low to attract sufficient supplies. A new and higher schedule would "stimulate the sale and delivery of small grain, &c. . .now so much needed as to be indispensable."[27] Wheat would be sold at $7.50 per bushel, "and a corresponding advance of 50 percent on all the grades of flour, mill-offal, &c.; and corn we assess at $6 per bushel, and corn meal at $6.30 per bushel." The next day, the Richmond *Whig* claimed that "Every commission merchant's shop is filled with flour, and it is still coming in."[28] Merchants "still ask $250 per barrel," the *Whig* writer claimed, "down from the $450 that they asked for the identical article on the glorious 31 [*sic*] of June." "[W]hen the same old Grant was pestling away at little Petersburg and the Weldon railroad, on the 15th of June," he added, flour sold for $500 per barrel.

The *Whig* article continued: "While on the subject, we will take occasion to ask why is all flour sent to market in barrels?" It was suggested that flour be "put up in bags, small bags, say of fifty pounds." With the price of a barrel of flour so high, "now it is one of the serious concerns of life, a matter only to be decided by a family counsel after a long and grave deliberation." Not one man in 500—"it matters not how fine their raiment"—could afford offhand to buy a full barrel of flour.

Apparently, this obviously simple suggestion had never been brought up before. Why buy hundreds of pounds of flour when smaller portions were all that was needed at the moment? This was a minor point in history, not one to determine the outcome of battles, wars, elections, or coups. Was the modern day five-pound bag of flour invented—out of necessity, out of price—during the siege of Richmond?

On August 2, "every commission merchant's shop" was filled with flour, but by the end of the month, John Jones would again write, "Our agent was heard from today; he has no flour yet, but we still have hopes of getting some."[29] Flour and all other foodstuffs were "sometime" things—and more and more, less and less was available.

Alexander Gustavus Brown was a minister of the gospel, denomination unknown, who lived in Petersburg during part of the siege. Later, he moved to Richmond where his brother resided. While in Petersburg, Reverend Brown often corresponded with his wife, Fannie, whom he'd tucked away in the relative safety of bomb-free Lynchburg. Despite the constant attack on Petersburg ("the shells are falling once again quite fast"), the people of his congregation there were "moving back to their homes."[30] Thanks to gifts from his parishioners, Brown

was able to keep "a goodly house. . . . I have on hand Chickens
& eggs, butter—a plenty of splendid tomatoes—corn occasionally—and nice rich milk three times a day." Thanks to another
gift, a cow. He'd keep the cow so long as the grass held out, but
then would "have her killed and sell the meat to my friends."[31]

Despite the rations J. B. Jones and his son, as war
department clerks, drew from the government, the family often
felt the pinch of hunger. "No news of our wheat and molasses
yet," he wrote in mid-September, "and we have hardly enough
money to live on until the next pay-day."[32] Jones would note
when the war and siege finally ended that he was several
pounds lighter than when he worked at his newspaper office in
Philadelphia. In the 1990s, weight loss might be looked on by
some as a welcome event; in the 1860s, it wasn't seen as good
come from evil.

By October 1864, flour was down to $425 per barrel, and
Jones recorded some salaries then being paid in Richmond:

> At the Tredegar [iron] works, and in the government
> workshops, the detailed soldier, if a *mechanic*, is paid
> in money and in rations (at the current prices) about
> $16 per day, or nearly $6000 per annum.[33]

A member of the Confederate Congress would earn less,
"$5500, a clerk $4000."[34] Fifteen months earlier, the Richmond *Dispatch* wrote that "all persons dependent on salaries
find it exceedingly difficult to make both ends meet, however
economical they may be, and many of them can scarcely live at
all."[35] It added that "$100 will not go so far as $10 would
before the commencement of the war." The Richmond city
government realized the problem and found it necessary to
raise the salaries of its officials and to raise them often.

In August 1862, the city paid its mayor $3,000 per year
and the city auditor received $1,800. In September 1864, they

raised the mayor's salary to $6000 with the auditor's salary increased to $5,000 per year. Three years into the war, the engineer on a Richmond City Fire Department steam engine was paid more than the mayor had earned two years earlier.[36]

One problem not solved, and indeed probably exacerbated by the frequent wage increases, was that of price speculators, a recurring topic for diarists and newspaper accounts. The Confederate government should "wage war against" the speculators, Jones wrote, calling them "enemies as mischievous as the Yankees."[37] He believed "there is abundance of clothing and food held by the extortioners." They drove prices up, withheld goods from the market, hoping for still higher prices until, "if our coat-tails were off, we should, in nine cases out of ten, be voted a nation of *sans culottes*." Richmonders were "already meager and emaciated."

As with others living in Richmond under siege, Jones turned to selling his possessions. He had already sold one valuable possession ("my dear old silver [fishing] reel") for seventy-five dollars to buy cloth to make clothing: "$30 yards of brown cotton, . .at $2.50 per yard." He considered it a bargain; the seller had recently purchased it in North Carolina at that price and sold it to Jones for just about what he'd paid. In Richmond, the same cloth would have cost him five dollars a yard.[38]

Still, lack of goods or high costs never stopped the people from hoping.

An advertisement in the Richmond *Dispatch*: T. W. Royster's of No. 229 Broad Street, T. D. Quarles' Store, received

> 300 ladies' corsets; 20 dozen ladies black kid gloves; 40 dozen Gent's Merino Undershirts and Drawers; 50 pieces of black calicoes; 100 silk Pocket Handkerchiefs, all hemmed; 1,000 silk neckties, for Gents.

In addition, they offered for sale Twenty pieces of "Superior White Shirting [for] only $12."[39]

The same issue of the *Dispatch* that carried these items for sale also carried an ad for 50 reams of fine English letter paper, 200 gross pens and holders; 100 dozen pocket knives, pocket combs, and pocket hooks; and 150 dozen hair brushes and dressing combs. R. R. Roberts offered sundries for sale: "Old Apple and French Brandy, Old Rye Whiskey, Blackberry Wine, Sorghum and New Orleans Molasses."

Schools called for pupils and teachers; information was requested of old friends; farms were offered for sale or rent; and marriages were announced. Druggists were selling "Leonard's Pills." "Two likely young Negro men" would be auctioned off. George Lee wanted to hire a good cook. And Charles G. Talcott, superintendent of the Richmond and Danville Railroad, announced that, beginning August 16, the evening train would be "devoted exclusively to the transportation of sick and wounded soldiers." Another typical day in Richmond under siege.

About this time, Mary Boykin Chesnut wrote of a Richmond friend, Mary Cantey Preston, and her wedding. The bridegroom, apparently a blockade runner, "had brought his wedding uniform with him from England."[40] Obviously, the "wedding uniform" and its wearer were to Chesnut's liking, since the suit "did honor to his perfect figure."

Hour by hour, day by day, life in Richmond went on, and to the editor of the *Sentinel*, "It is remarkable how calm our people have been with the enemy making a desperate effort for the capture of our city." Still, he saw within the city a "few weak-kneed individuals [who] really suppose the enemy would 'this time' take Richmond."[41] No, not this time.

* * *

From letters and newspaper accounts written in Richmond during the fall of 1864:

> September 13, 1864—
> We were formed in line of battle here on last Monday morning to meet the enemy who have been advancing from the direction of Culpeper Courthouse. [The] enemy soon made their appearance.[42]

> October 4—
> The excitement in the city was by no means abated on Saturday, but, on the contrary, the sound of cannonade becoming nearer. The truth was, the cannonading proceeding entirely from our own lines.[43]

> October 7—
> It appears, from the best information at command, that the enemy's position below Richmond is just about four miles and a half from the corporate limits. There is a strange silence about Petersburg.[44]

> October 10—
> Not a circumstance was wanting on yesterday to complete the pleasant illusion of peace as it appeared within the limits of the city. No sound of distant cannon, no thundering of huge wagons, no clatter of hoofs, nor tramp of martial feet, broke upon the cold, still air.[45]

J. B. Jones greeted this "illusion of peace" with hope in his October 13 diary entry:

> If this pause should continue a week or two longer, Gen. Lee would be much strengthened.[46]

But it was just one of several such pauses in the war that never lasted long enough for the Confederacy.

It was during this time, also, that Union General "Beast" Butler began digging a canal below Richmond, trying to cut off the Confederate capital city. The canal didn't worry Richmonders so much as the labor Butler was using. Again, from Jones's diary:

> It appears that Gen. Butler has notified Gen. Lee that he is now retaliating fearfully—making [Confederate prisoners] work in his canal. . .for some alleged harsh treatment of *negro* prisoners in our hands.[47]

It was almost six months to the day since the Rebel army, under General Nathan Bedford Forrest, had attacked the Union-held Fort Pillow along the Mississippi River. The South won, but the Confederates, under Forrest, allegedly massacred most of the Union prisoners, even as they threw down their weapons and held their hands above their heads in submission. Most of those prisoners were black. Forrest denied ordering the massacre.

The War in the West

VII

March to the Sea

General W. T. Sherman ordered Atlanta evacuated, told the surviving 1,600 citizens to pack up their few remaining belongings and to get out of town. Confederate General J. B. Hood, who was already out of town, objected; he sent a message to Sherman: "In the name of God and humanity, I protest!"[1] Sherman ignored the complaint. He was leaving town and wanted nothing at his back that might give him trouble.

"Uncle Billy" Sherman was taking his boys on a "March to the Sea." He checked with Grant; Grant reluctantly approved, and before the approval could be rescinded, Sherman cut the telegraph lines. He wanted no interference.

November 15, 1864: 62,000 Union army men and 13,000 Union army mules and horses rolled through the countryside. Behind them, the city of Atlanta burned. What the Confederates hadn't been able to destroy when they evacuated the city, the Federals finished off.

Between Sherman's mass of men and animals and the Atlantic Ocean, stood only a handful of Georgia militia and Confederate cavalry.

The Federal troops were like a hoard of locusts, cutting a path of devastation 60 miles wide and 300 miles long. Nothing would stop them. Sherman was not out to defeat Southern Armies; he wanted to destroy the Southern spirit. Total war, total devastation.

The march ground on. Looting, burning, stealing. Elias Smith, of the New York *Tribune* marched with Sherman:

> In the rear of each Division followed the foragers, or "bummers," as they are called by the soldiers, constituting a motley group which strongly recalls the memory of [William Shakespeare's] Falstaff's ragged army. . . . Here came men strutting in mimic dignity in. . .old swallow-tailed coat[s], with plug hats, the tops kicked in; there a group in seedy coats and pants of Rebel grey, with arms and legs protruding beyond all semblance of fit or fashion. . . .
>
> The procession of vehicles and animals was of the most grotesque description. There were donkeys large and small, almost smothered, under burdens of turkeys, geese and other kinds of poultry, ox carts, skinny horses pulling in the fills of some parish doctors, old sulkies, farm wagons and buggies. . .all filled with plunder and provisions.
>
> There was bacon, hams, potatoes, flour, pork, sorghum, and freshly slaughtered pigs, sheep, and poultry dangling from saddle tree and wagon, enough, one would suppose, to feed the army for a fortnight.[2]

Sherman didn't object too strongly to the Bummers. He knew the South might withstand the fall of Atlanta, but he wanted more. He wanted the South to howl, and it did.

In late December he captured Savannah. The Richmond *Whig* saw General Hardee's evacuation of the city as

> an event which the military authorities had decided upon some time since. We learn that the evacuation was effected without loss, except of such materials as could not be transported. The last troops of the line crossed the river. . .on Tuesday, the 21st, proceeding into the direction of Charleston. The engineer troops held the bridges until after 6 o'clock, when the bridges were destroyed.[3]

On December 24, Sherman sent Lincoln a telegram:

> I beg to present to you as a Christmas gift, the city of Savannah.[4]

14

Libby and the Biggest Yankee

Early October and rumors circulated once more in Richmond: the enemy was about to make that final push to take the city. The editor of the *Sentinel*, however, denied not only those rumors but denied the panic in the streets Jones and other writers saw.[1] Two days later the same editor even wrote that "the end we seek inspires our confidence." He once more called on God as if the deity were a Southerner: "A firm reliance on a just Providence becomes a people [fighting] for their inalienable rights,"[2] The latter, apparently, was a call on another "god." The editor referred to Thomas Jefferson's words in the U.S. Declaration of Independence, which the South, seemingly, was trying to rewrite in its own cause.

The shelling of Petersburg increased "more so by a great deal than it has ever been," Rev. Alexander Brown wrote at the end of August.[3] It looked "like a flock of fire birds. . .filling the air." Minister of the gospel or not, Brown took no chances with his possessions, and he sent them by train to his wife in Lynchburg, hoping the rail lines were still open. In turn, he received a barrel of molasses that had partially turned to sugar by the time it reached him because the trains were so slow and erratic. But never mind, it will "come in well since I find my supply [of sugar] nearly exhausted."[4]

Reverend Brown's supply of sugar wasn't the only thing near exhaustion. Richmond, too, had reached the bottom of the barrel. The city had been at war for almost four years. Simply surviving had become difficult, not the difficulty of surviving in Atlanta or Vicksburg while they were being bombed, but difficult in other ways. Obtaining food had become expensive at best, nearly impossible at worst.

Richmonders had seen troops march out and the dead and dying brought back in. They had seen the funerals of Stonewall Jackson and Jeb Stuart, and they had mourned those and other heroes of the Confederacy, thousands to be buried in the city's cemeteries or shipped to their boyhood homes. Heroes had become hard to come by lately, what with the growing number of desertions from the battlefield and defeat for those who remained to fight. For Richmonders, life meant just making the best of things and waiting for the end they all knew would come.

A wounded Confederate soldier, serving as hospital guard in Richmond, said "the surgeons and matrons ate rats and said they were as good as squirrels, but having seen the rats running over the bodies of dead soldiers, I had no relish for them."[5] Dining on rats is an old story during hard times. It would gain worldwide repute less than a decade later during the Paris Commune. In both cases, it's likely that legend far outstripped reality, but there's no doubt people frequently had difficulty obtaining food.

Just as obviously, some people did not find obtaining food so difficult as to force them to eat rats "as good as squirrels." Hospital steward Luther Swank, as we've said, was one who readily obtained supplies, but even he had problems. He served a hospital just outside the city limits and made frequent trips to the Richmond markets. He wrote his sister, Katie, and told her of "stimulants in the shape of 'Old Rye'" he had received from their father and the loss of a hand mirror ("I had almost as leif broken my leg").[6]

Swank also told sister Katie "our pickets surprised and captured about 200 [Yankee prisoners]."[7] On October 2, Jones also mentioned the capture of prisoners, "about five-hundred taken near Petersburg and brought to Richmond."[8] The *Daily Enquirer* announced the arrival of "fifteen hundred and fifteen prisoners. . .at Libby Prison on Sunday."[9]

Continuing through the final days of the war, Yankee prisoners continued to be taken into the Rebel city. Some of the new prisoners probably were the ones mentioned earlier by Jones and Swank. Fifty-eight were officers, including one Irishman who "says he has been soldering during the past fifteen years." If we are to believe his own account, the Irishman had served "under Generals Hook, Pender, and R. H. Anderson." Federals taken captive by the Confederates near Richmond were housed at several locations: Libby Prison (if they were officers) or Belle Isle (if they were enlisted men), as well as Castle Thunder and Castle Lightning. All together, there were nearly a dozen others in the Richmond-Petersburg area.

Belle Isle is an island in the middle of the James River. It was intended as a transient camp, prisoners staying there only until they could be moved to more secure camps farther south. But as early as June 1862, after the Seven Days' Battles, as many as 10,000 Union prisoners were kept at Belle Isle. The original precise lines of tents quickly were overrun. Carefully regulated sanitary conditions just as quickly proved inadequate. Food supplies dwindled, trains were too packed with war materials and supplies to carry prisoners of war, the number of inmates grew—nearly 12,000 by the winter of 1863-1864. Disease and dying became commonplace.

Richmond had a large number of military prisons, and like its hospitals, many of the prisons were converted warehouses. For example, the most famous of Richmond's prisons—Libby—was at one time a chandler's warehouse.

Colonel William Powell of Ohio was held in solitary confinement in Libby. During the time, he kept a diary:

> [I have] been in [this] cell four weeks today and still no prospects of getting out. I am so tired of being alone.[10]

Colonel Frederick Bartleston of the 100th Illinois Volunteer Infantry was also held prisoner at Libby. In February of 1864, he wrote his wife, Kate, telling her about a recent escape:

> It was, I think, the most clever performance in that line during the war, and we could see them coming from their subterranean hole and issuing on the street in full view of the guards. Of course, there was great rivalry as to who should go, as all could not. For my part, I could only look on with regret, as it was impossible for me to crawl through or to make the descent, which was through a fireplace to the ground floor, where the tunnel commenced. Some have been brought back, but the rest are safe. . . .
> Now, in regard to the relative treatment of prisoners by respective governments. . . . No man can say that prisoners are as well treated there as they are here. There are two reasons against it; one is, they haven't got the means to treat them as well, and another is, they haven't got the disposition. They are fighting from different motives as us. We are fighting for the

Union, a sentiment. . . . [T]hey are fighting for
independence.[11]

Bartleston added that "the question of exchange looks black,
but perhaps it may clear up one of these days." For Bartleston,
it did clear up; he *was* exchanged, only to die June 27, 1864, at
the Battle of Kennesaw Mountain in Georgia.

Through most of the war, prisoners had been exchanged
or paroled, but in 1863 (thanks in no small part to the General
Forrest-Fort Pillow affair) there was a disagreement, and the
system broke down. At least 194,743 Union soldiers were held
in Confederate prisons; at least 30,218 (15.5 percent) of them
died.

At least 214,865 Confederate soldiers were held in
Union prisons; at least 25,976 (12 percent) of them died.[12]
At the South's most notorious prison, Andersonville, 20 percent
of the prisoners died. The mortality rate in other Confederate
prisons was worse. At Salisbury, North Carolina, for example,
34 percent of the inmates perished.

Richmond's Libby Prison, though not so notorious (nor
so deadly) as Andersonville or Salisbury, was, however, the
largest in the Confederacy, housing over the length of the war
50,000 prisoners by some estimates, 75,000 by others.

Libby Prison was made up of three buildings joined
together, each about 110 by 44 feet, four stories high. They
were built between 1845 and 1852 by a Richmond tobacco
merchant, John Enders. Enders never saw his planned warehouse turned into a prison or even completed; he fell from a
ladder and died while the building was under construction.

A native of Maine, Captain Luther Libby, leased the
western section and put up a sign showing the building's new
name: "L. Libby & Son, Ship Chandlers." When war came in
1861, he was ordered to vacate the property so fast he didn't
have time to remove the sign, and for four years of war—four

years of Richmond under siege—it hung there. After the war, Libby's name was so identified with the prison he had to leave town for a while to escape reprisals by angry Northerners, despite the fact he was Northern-born.

Libby's ground floor was used for offices and guard rooms; the middle floor was the kitchen. Many rooms were given names; the prisoners often referred to "Straight's Room," "Milroy's Room," and the "Chickamauga Room." More dangerous prisoners were housed in the cellar along with spies and slaves.

In the fours years Libby Prison existed, there were many escapes and attempts. Colonel Thomas E. Rose of the 77th Pennsylvania Volunteers led the February 9, 1864 escape about which Colonel Bartleston wrote. Rose and Major A. G. Hamilton of the 12th Kentucky led 107 other officers through a fireplace, down a chimney, and out a tunnel. The tunnel was fifty-three feet long, and the only tools the prisoners had were an old pocket knife, some chisels, bits of rope, and a wooden spittoon. Almost half of the would-be escapees were recaptured—forty-eight of them. Another fifty-nine were able to reach Union lines, and two others drowned trying to make it back home.

Colonel Rose, who led that spectacular escape attempt, didn't get very far; however, he was exchanged for a Confederate prisoner later in the year.

Libby Prison was located at Cary and 20th streets. Not far away lived a woman known variously as "Miss Lizzie," or "Crazy Bet." She was Miss Elizabeth Van Lew, and as a child she attended school in Philadelphia where she became an ardent abolitionist. When her father died in 1860, she freed the family slaves in Richmond.

Miss Lizzie never attempted to hid her Union sympathies, and during General McClellan's 1862 campaign to capture Richmond, she prepared what was described as a

"charming room" in her home for his use when the Union
general took the city. McClellan failed, but Elizabeth Van Lew
continued to call it the "McClellan Room."

    She was a frequent visitor to Libby Prison, taking with
her food and reading materials. According to reports, the
carried away with her information given her by prisoners,
information she passed on to Union agents in the city. She's
believed to have assisted in the February 9 escape, even visiting
one of the escape leaders once he was outside prison walls and
hiding another for a while in her home.[13]

    When she died in 1900, Miss Elizabeth Van Lew's
funeral saw as few mourners as her life had seen friends; she
had been ostracized by Richmond society. It wasn't until years
later that admirers in Boston raised money to place a stone
over her grave in Shockoe Cemetery. The inscription reads:

> She risked everything that is dear to man—friends,
> fortune, comfort, health, life itself—all for the one
> absorbing desire of her heart, that slavery should be
> abolished and the Union preserved.[14]

One of the strangest prisoners incarcerated at Libby was 2nd
Lieutenant David Van Buskirk. He was born near Gosport,
Indiana on November 23, 1826, and in July of 1861 he joined
a company of grenadiers. The unit had one major stipulation:
"They admit no recruits under 5 feet 10 inches, and equally
stout and able bodied."[15] David Buskirk easily fit the bill; in
fact, he overflowed the bill by more than a foot. At a time
when Abraham Lincoln, at a comparatively modest six feet four
inches, was considered tall (remember, the average Civil War
soldier was five feet eight and a-half), David Buskirk stood six
feet ten and a-half inches tall and weighed 380 pounds.

    When the company began drilling, the Indianapolis
Journal took note:

The company is composed of the largest men we have
seen from any section of the state. The second lieutenant (David Van Buskirk) is a "whale," but some of
the others are whales, too, but a trifle smaller.[16]

On May 25, 1862, not long after Luther Libby's warehouse was
pressed into service as a prison, 2nd Lieutenant David Van
Buskirk's unit, the 27th Indiana, was overwhelmed by Confederate troops at Winchester, Virginia. Buskirk was sent to Libby,
and residents of Richmond soon heard about the man referred
to as "The biggest Yankee in the world."

He became so famous that Confederate President
Jefferson Davis (himself, six feet two) paid him a visit. The two
talked about the prisoner's home and family back in Indiana.
The Yankee told the Rebel:

Back in Bloomington, Indiana, I have six sisters.
When they told me good-bye, as I was standing with
my company, they all walked up, leaned down and
kissed me on the top of my head.

Buskirk, it seems, was not averse to telling stories as tall as he
was himself. Certainly, he was a pampered prisoner. Frequently,
he was taken from the prison at night and exhibited in a freak
show in downtown Richmond. At a time when many Richmond
civilians were starving, Libby prisoner David Van Buskirk put
on weight; he took as his percentage of the freak show's
admission fees all he could eat in food. When he was exchanged at Annapolis, Maryland, after three months in Libby
Prison, he tipped the scales at over 400 pounds, a twenty-pound
expansion in ninety days.

Years later, when Buskirk was a civilian, circus owner P.
T. Barnum offered the "biggest Yankee" a job at what apparently was a considerable salary. David Van Buskirk said no;

he'd had enough of freak shows while "suffering" at Libby Prison.

Van Buskirk wasn't the only unusual prisoner of war in Richmond under siege. Take for instance the inmate listed as Lieutenant Harry Buford. Described as just over five feet tall, strikingly handsome, and wearing a Confederate uniform, the young officer drew the suspicion of a military detective, and that led to a prison cell at Castle Thunder. "Lieutenant Buford" was a woman in disguise. She was Loreta Janeta Valesquez, a 24-year-old native of Havana, Cuba. Her husband, a Louisiana planter, joined the Confederate ranks and was killed. His widow wanted to carry on his fight, and Loreta Valesquez raised a company of infantry (the Arkansas Grays), leading it to Virginia where they fought under General Barnard Bee in the First Battle of Manassas.

Even after she was found out, "Lieutenant Buford" insisted on wearing men's clothing, and it wasn't until she agreed to joined the Confederacy's so-called "Secret Corps" of spies that she was released from prison. But Loreta Janeta Valesquez (a.k.a. Lieutenant Buford) persisted in fighting for the Confederate cause. Serving under Lieutenant General Leonidas Polk she was wounded twice before the war ended.

Two other women—sisters Mary and Molly Bell—also were housed at Castle Thunder when it was learned they were posing as men in order to serve in the army. They had fought for two years, Mary rising to the rank of sergeant and Molly to corporal, before the army detected their true sex. After a brief time in Castle Thunder, the sisters were released and sent home.[17]

Both hospitals and prisoners increased the need for additional food in the already starving Richmond. The ever-growing problems of obtaining food undoubtedly led to the willingness of the Confederates to exchange prisoners.

15

With Saddened Mien

Prisoners weren't the only captives in Richmond under siege. There were the large number of slaves. The Richmond *Enquirer* claimed that the "negro question"—a question it claimed had been a major issue in determining secession, "has been transferred to the North. . .and with it [the] great puzzle of 'What to with do with him.'"[1]

The Richmond editor quoted a letter in the New York *Tribune*:

> We furnish them with houses to live in, land to work, tools to work with, seeds to plant, food to live on, and whether they will work or play, they will have the same care without or any self-care upon their part.[2]

Obviously, then as now, racism wasn't confined to the South. The article quotes the New York writer as saying "Negro emancipation is a great thing," but claims the present fighting "is the Southern poor man's war more than the negroes'." The editor of the *Enquirer* was all too happy to say the Northern writer "feels that the negro must be treated as property, for he would take him as we would a 'horse, mule, or other moving power.'"

Although the *Tribune* article undoubtedly shows the presence of racism in at least one writer or editor in at least one Northern newspaper, perhaps more important is that, by copying the article, the *Enquirer* showed the extent of its own bitterness against the North and blacks. African-Americans were asked to serve in both the Union and Confederate armies, to fight for and against the right, as it were, of whites to hold them as slaves. One difference, however, was that in the South, the "offer" of enlistment did not even pretend to include the guarantee of emancipation.

* * *

As a diarist, John Beauchamp Jones recorded everything from the presence or absence of news to the bickering within the Confederate government. He recorded the price of chickens and cabbages and the amount of snow to fall on an April morning. He detailed the death of his daughter's pet cat, although whether the animal died of old age or starvation isn't made clear. Prior to the war, Jones was a journalist and author in Baltimore, Maryland, and Rutherford, New Jersey, the latter just outside Philadelphia. He married Frances Custis, related to the famous Custis family of Virginia, and that made him a "connection," as the Southern saying goes, not only of George Washington through Martha Custis, but of Robert E. Lee. Indirectly, she was F.F.V., one of the First Families of Virginia.

Upon his marriage to Frances, Jones converted to the Southern cause. He was fifty-one when the war began, as one modern author puts it, "comfortably over fighting age."[3] He did, however, serve for a while in the home guard. The Joneses named one son Custis.

John Jones's diary was written with the knowledge, if not the approval, of the secretary of war and of Confederate President Jefferson Davis. It was written at the time of events but edited shortly after the war ended.

For Jones, as for nearly every other resident of besieged Richmond, clothing often was a major problem; it was very difficult for civilians to come by. On November 10, 1864, Jones bought two slightly used undershirts "off a woman who gets her supplies from passing soldiers."[4] His wife washed them and "they bore no evidence of having been worn, except for two small round holes in the body." He paid $15 each for the undershirts, commenting, "the price of new ones, of inferior quality, is $50 a piece." Frances Jones, however, wasn't impressed by the savings and told John it seemed as if she were still washing out blood several days after they were purchased.

Bullet holes or not, they suited Jones well, as did "four yards of dark-gray cloth at $12 per yard" obtained from the Confederate Quartermaster for a full suit. The cloth had been woven for a military uniform. Then, as now, being a government employee had certain advantages. Not only was he kept abreast of the fighting, but he was allowed to buy rations—food and clothing—at government cost. "The merchants ask $125 per yard—a savings of $450," he wrote of his suiting material. He hoped to have it "cut and made by one of the government tailors for about $50, trimmings included."[5] This, at a time when "a civilian tailor asks $350." Jones wasn't the only government worker using his position for personal benefit. A minor scandal broke out when it was learned that members of the quartermaster's family were all well dressed. All well dressed in Confederate gray.

The day he bought the suit cloth, the government increased Jones's salary by $500 a year, but Mrs. Murphy's law (expenses expand to meet income) worked as well then as it does now. The next day, "My landlord gets $400 of the $500 increase."[6]

He wasn't alone, of course. Rent was a worry to many living in Richmond under siege. Quoting one "Artemus Ward" (obviously writing in dialect) the *Daily Dispatch* told the following story:

> I went to Richmond and put up in a leading hotel, where seeing the landlord, I accosted him with: "How d'ye do, Squire." "Fifty cents," was his reply. "Sir?" "Half a dollar. We charge twenty-five cents for looking at the landlord, and fifty cents for speaking to him. If you want supper, a boy will show you the dining room for twenty-five cents. Your bein' in the tenth story, it will cost you a dollar to be shown up there." "How much do you ax a man for breatin' in this equinomikal tavern?" said I. "Ten cents a breath," was his reply.[7]

Throughout the war, several hotels and restaurants continued to operate in Richmond. An ad in the *Examiner* by the Spotswood Hotel—"Notices to Travelers"—offered lodgings of twenty-five dollars per day; single meals were ten dollars for dinner and breakfast; supper was eight dollars. The Spotswood specialized in "good board and comfortable rooms"[8]

Hopeful to the last, the *Examiner* only days before the war's end still included a "Notice to Travelers," advertising "good board and comfortable rooms" to be had "by applying on the corner of Eighth and Main Streets." The price per day for room and board: forty dollars.[9]

* * *

U.S. President Lincoln proclaimed the third Thursday in November a day of thanksgiving, and in the trenches outside Richmond, Union troops dined on chicken and turkey. There were no chickens or turkeys for the Confederates. Still, they chose to honor the Union thanksgiving and didn't fire a shot the entire day.

* * *

From Mary Chesnut's diary:

> Darkest of all Decembers,
>   Ever my life has known,
> Sitting here by the embers,
>   Stunned—helpless—alone.[10]

Virginia and the Confederacy had been at war with the United States for three years and seven months, in terms of human life, the costliest time in the nation's history. The *Whig* tallied the "physical resources" of the South, meaning the number of males eligible for military service. Considering the natural and military rates of death, the "number of youths passing annually from 16 to 17 years of age. . .our net loss is about 12,000 men" a year. That still left "a profuse abundance of the materials of which armies are composed."[11] There would, then, be "material" for years more of fighting.

It was late December, and in Richmond the trees were bare against the wind and snow; the squirrels avoided the cold until midday, curled around nuts reserved against the hardest of days; for people there were fewer and fewer reserves. Acorns began to look good, not to mention squirrels. Outside the city, game birds were not to be found and deer had gone to cover, waiting for the end of winter and the end of war.

As the time of the season approached, the *Dispatch* carried an item titled simply "Christmas." It said "Peace. Peace! Blessed word! What richer gift could Heaven have offered the earth."[12] And the *Daily Examiner* predicted: "We shall have a merry Christmas next year, please God!"[13]

Sallie Brock was then only nineteen and not yet married to Mr. Putnam. As a young lady of some means, she had attended many prewar dinners and dances. Now she missed the "sumptuous banquet, around which we were wont to gather," at Christmas-time; rather, they "sat down to the poverty-stricken board."[14] She "counted again the vacant chairs, and glanced eyes blinded by tears, upon the somber living of woe, that indicated whither had been borne our domestic idols."

* * *

That year of 1864, John and Frances Jones had

> quite a merry Christmas [with] a compact that no unpleasant word [would] be uttered and no *scramble* for anything. The family were baking cakes and pies until late last night, and to-day we shall have *full* rations. I have found enough celery in the little garden for dinner.
>
> A large number of the croaking inhabitants censure the President for our many misfortunes, and openly declare in favor of Lee as Dictator. . . . [Lee's] son, Gen. Custis Lee, alas mortally offended the clerks by putting them in the trenches, and some of them may desert. . . . Many members of Congress have gone home.[15]

Christmas Day 1864 saw once more the Southern custom of firing Christmas guns by young boys, "no doubt pilfering from their fathers' cartridge boxes," Jones wrote.

And it saw families all over Richmond carrying on as best they could after almost four years under siege.

Elisha Hunt Rhodes was in the Union trenches outside Petersburg:

> *Sunday Christmas Dec. 25/64*—This is the birthday of our Saviour, but we have paid very little attention to it in a religious way. Last night a party from the 49th Penn. Vols. came and gave me a serenade. I invited them in and entertained them as best I could. . . . It does not seem much like Sunday or Christmas, for the men are hauling logs to build huts. This is a work of necessity, for the quarters we have been using are not warm enough. This is my fourth Christmas in the Army. I wonder if it will be my last.[16]

"With saddened mien," Sallie and her family "turned our steps toward the sanctuaries of God." Their praise and thanksgiving "were blended with fasting and prayer, with deep humiliation and earnest contrition." On Richmond's fourth Christmas under siege, Sallie and her family must have wondered how the next one would be.

* * *

The winter of 1862-1863 had been one of discontent—victories matched with defeats. The winter of 1863-1864 had been one of hibernation—both sides took time off. But the winter of 1864-1865 was different. Lincoln was reelected; Sherman took Atlanta and Savannah; Union naval forced gathered around the

South's only surviving seaport, Wilmington. And Richmond remained locked under siege.

* * *

From newspaper accounts and diaries:

> December 30—
> Perfect quiet prevails on the Richmond and Petersburg lines. Even the useless cannonade that has been kept up by the army at Petersburg was discontinued.[17]

> December 31—
> There is supposed to be a conspiracy on foot to transfer some of the powers of the Executive to Gen. Lee. It can only be done by revolution, and the overthrow of the Constitution. Nevertheless, it is believed many executive officers, some in high positions, favor the scheme.[18]

> December 31—Scouts report that [Union General Benjamin] Butler made [a] speech at Newbern [N.C.], saying he would eat his Christmas dinner in Wilmington." [19]

Elisha Hunt Rhodes:

> *Trenches before Petersburg, Va., Sunday Jany 1st 1865*—New Years Day and again this is the fourth that I have passed in the U.S. Army. The war drags along, but we feel that we are gaining all the time, and when Petersburg and Richmond fall, as they must soon, the war will end. I am grateful to God for all his mercies toward me and that I am spared in health and

strength to do my share towards restoring the Union.[20]

John B. Jones:

January 1, 1865—The disaffection is intense and widespread among the politicians of 1860, and consternation and despair are expanding among the people. Nearly all desire to see Gen. Lee at the head of affairs, and the President is resolved to yield the position to no man during his term of service. Nor would Gen. Lee take it.[21]

The war raging around the city was but one event in Richmond newspapers' coverage. They continued carrying notices of "Negroes At Auction," "Household Furniture, Shoes, &c For Sale," rooms for rent, and rewards offered for both strayed and stolen mules and horses and runaway slaves. And on the international front, the *Dispatch* told of a "Horrible slaughter in Japan—Six Hundred and Thirty-Five Women and Children murdered in Cold Blood."[22]

* * *

On New Year's Day, 1865, the Federal army detonated a large explosive charge along the James River, south of Richmond. General Butler had tried to clear the final obstacles and complete the Dutch Gap Canal, hoping to eliminate a strange and difficult bend in the river and making it easier to navigate toward the Confederate capital.

When the smoke and noise cleared from the blast, not only was the final obstacle still there in the river, the explosion had refilled much of an earlier excavation. The project was abandoned.

* * *

Mrs. Robert E. Lee wrote her friend, Mrs. William Boswell, at the Boswell's home at the Wilderness in Fluvanna County:

> Genl Lee looks very well but is anxious to have *every man* in the field.
> I hope the soldiers are enjoying their dinner today. It has exhausted the markets here of everything but we are very willing to relinquish in their favor. . . .
> My rheumatism is no better tho' my general health was much improved. . . .
> I hope if you or any of your family visit Richmond you will certainly call & see me. We are on Franklin between 7th & 8th & I am always at home.[23]

Mary Custis Lee was referring to the New Year's dinner for the troops, arranged for by "the Rev. Mr. Dana." But, it didn't quite work out as planned:

> January 3—
> The manager of the *Enquirer* desires to state to his friends in the army that he had nothing to do with the distribution of the New Year's Dinner.[24]

On January 5, the *Examiner* printed its own disclaimer of responsibility, claiming speculators made off with much of the money raised for the meal.

The idea had been fine: raise money to buy the boys in the trenches a good meal to usher in the new year. "The New

Year's dinner had come and gone," a correspondent to the *Dispatch* wrote, and added, "or rather, gone, without coming." Thousands of troops, he said, had been led to expect a good, cheerful meal, "a good treat." For a regiment of 260 men and officers, however, there wasn't much: two barrels that held dinner for all. "Thirty-two ordinary-size loaves of bread," the writer claimed, "two turkeys, one of them a very small diminutive specimen of that species of fowl (some swore that it was a chicken); a quarter of a lamb and a horse-bucketful of apple butter."[25] As the writer sarcastically added: "Of course, this immense weight of provender had to be divided out to the various companies." There were also complaints that some troops of the Virginia line received most of this "good treat," while others—non-Virginians—were lucky to get the leftovers. Leftovers?

Mary Lee saw the dinner for the troops deplete the markets, but the food never reached the Confederate forces, making the reader wonder whether Richmonders themselves hoarded the goods or the purchasers simply absconded with the funds. Perhaps it was just another example of speculators growing rich while the common people grew more desperate. As author Margaret Mitchell's fictional Rhett Butler put it in *Gone With the Wind*, even in war, some people get rich.

Phoebe Yates Pember, of Richmond's Chimborazo Hospital, spent much of the fall of 1864 in Georgia; she returned later in the year and was depressed at what she saw:

> I noticed on my return a great difference in the means
> of living between Virginia and the Gulf States. Even
> in the most wealthy and luxurious house of Rich-
> mond, former everyday comforts had about this time
> become luxuries, and had been dispensed with earlier
> in the war.[26]

Yet, even seeing the difference between Gulf States still able to obtain luxuries, Pember still held out hope:

> There was no doubt. . .as to the ultimate success of the Southern cause.[27]

* * *

But, with or without Pember's missed luxuries, life in Richmond continued. At the New Richmond Theatre, that first week of 1865:

**TRAGEDIES, COMEDIES, PLAYS, DRAMAS,
FARCES, BURLETTAS,
OPERAS, &C, &C.
CHARACTERISTIC AND FANCY
DANCES, SONGS, BALLADS
AND DUETS,**
**All presented in a manner unequalled
in any other Theatre in the Confederacy.[28]**

Outside Richmond, the ring tightened. Inside, people carried on with their lives:

Richmond varieties.
Franklin Street, one door below Exchange Hotel. Mr. James Wells positively will appear tonight in conjunction with Tim Morris, the unequaled Negro Delineator in new Songs, Jokes, Burlesques, &c.

MUSIC, MIRTH AND WIT.
———
FUN FOR THE MILLION.[29]

The same edition carried an essay on slavery and the possibility of gaining foreign support for the Confederacy's war against the North:

> If we are asked whether we would, or would not, purchase the material aid of England and France in our present struggle by abandoning slavery instantly and on the spot, we say again *Yes,* without one moment's hesitation or consideration. That is to say, in other words, we would sacrifice the negro race to ensure our own independence.[30]

* * *

"The New Year," Sallie Putnam wrote, "was ushered in with no better prospects" than was ushered out with the old.[31] "We could," she continued, "at best look forward to an indefinite continuation of the dire evils which had shrouded our land in sorrow and misery." There was no letup: "Day by day our wants and privations increased."

To the south, the Confederacy lost Atlanta and General Sherman's band played "John Brown's Body."

To the west, the South lost Nashville, and the remnants of the Army of Tennessee marched to meet Sherman, singing, to the tune of "Yellow Rose of Texas":

> And now I'm going southward; \ My heart if full of woe.
> I'm going back to Georgia \ To see my uncle Joe.
> You may talk about your Beauregard \ And sing of General Lee,
> But the Gallant Hood of Texas \ Played Hell in Tennessee.[32]

* * *

Richmonders, however, had little to sing about. In the middle of winter, the city raised the price of its gas. No matter that it was gas produced from coal that came from neighboring Chesterfield County. At its first meeting of the year, the city council raised the price to fifty dollars per 1,000 cubic feet of gas. Council members also wanted to know why some of the city's gas-fired street lights didn't burn. "Mr. Compton (the gas works committee chairman) said, because [of] a want of retorts" the lights could not function, the clerk recorded in the council minutes.

The retorts were that part of the gas light in which the fuel was actually heated and burned, producing light. They were made of iron, and the Confederate secretary of war refused to release the needed material to the city.[33] The iron was made in Richmond, but the city couldn't get its hands on it. As a result, as the old retorts broke or became inoperable, nighttime Richmond grew darker.

And, yes, while much coal continued to be dug in Chesterfield County mines, Richmond residents had to pay increasingly higher prices for that same commodity. They couldn't get their hands on Chesterfield coal; they couldn't get their hands on Tredegar Iron Works retorts. Everything was going wrong.

* * *

The *Dispatch* again apologized for the poor New Year's dinner and, on January 5, carried several other interesting items, some advertisements, and some comments. The Virginia Senate passed a resolution authorizing the governor "to issue arms to such civil officers of the Commonwealth as are required to arrest, or to aid in arresting, deserters." Once again, there were several ads listing items for sale ("Bargains, Bargains"), everything from flannel material to linen shirts, from tallow to apple butter, from green tea to molasses. A Richmond resident offered to sell a sewing machine ("in good order") and another notice said "a sum of money had been found by a servant on Eighth Street, between Franklin and Grace Streets."

There are several help wanted notices: wood choppers, washer and ironer, teacher, clerk, and farm manager. Someone had found coupons for registered bonds. This and the "sum of money" found indicate that, at least to some honest citizens, conditions were not at the theft-provoking poverty level. To others, they were that bad or at least that tempting; someone stole the silverware "from the table in my dining room," one writer claimed and offered a $200 reward.

Sheet music was for sale: "You Can Never Win Us Back," "The Moon O'er the Battle Plain," "Hurrah For Our Flag," and "No Surrender" were among the titles. If you wanted, you could even buy an entire hotel, its owners either going broke or deciding to get while the getting was good. The *Dispatch* ran a lengthy story on "How to Prevent Wet Feet."[34]

It's difficult to say what we should infer from the variety of these items, and perhaps we shouldn't infer anything, just take them as facts of life under siege. Perhaps the people of Richmond and therefore the newspaper editors and readers were merely trying to get by as best they could, to make do in the middle of hell, as it were.

The were other items—same newspaper, same day—that give a truer sense that there really was a war going on, and it wasn't very far away. Reports of the fighting in Georgia—the "railroad line from Dalton to Chattanooga is kept constantly cut by our scouts." The Union army once more shelled the

Petersburg railroad—"the fire was promptly and hotly responded to."

Even the editors of the *Dispatch* were feeling the pinch of the siege. Unlike the Vicksburg newspaper while that city was under siege, Richmond newspapers did not have to resort to printing on wallpaper; however, the *Dispatch* ran a request for old rags to make paper for their presses. Richmond, as had Vicksburg before it, was running out of paper on which to print the bad news it reluctantly heard and passed on.

If this is a typical issue of the newspaper—and it appears to be so—then life, neither totally cheerful nor totally cheerless, went on. Except for those items about the war, of course, the reports and advertisements weren't too different from newspapers of, say, five years earlier. Whether by design (to keep the bad news from Richmonders and Northern spies) or by an inability to learn what was going on around them (but this seems doubtful, because travel through Federal and Confederate lines was a daily event), it certainly can be said that newspapers of Richmond under siege didn't depend on the war to sell copies.

War or not, siege or not, at least half a dozen Richmond newspapers continued to publish: the *Dispatch, Examiner, Enquirer, Whig, Times,* and *Sentinel.* At least two religious newspapers were published as was the *Anzeiger,* this last "printed in German [and offering] great advantages as an advertising sheet, being the only German newspaper now published in the Confederacy."[35] Some Richmond newspapers not only offered daily editions but special weekly and semi-weekly editions as well. The quality of newsprint worsened as the siege wore on, perhaps due to the publishers' inability to replace worn type and equipment. Most of these newspapers continued publishing up to the day the city fell, a tribute to the reporters and publishers.

Buying newspapers or anything else for cash grew more and more difficult with time. Fewer members of the general public, not to mention merchants, had faith in Confederate paper money as the war continued. The twentieth century saying, "Save your confederate money, boys" had a different meaning in Richmond under siege. Bartering became necessary and was, as one observer commented, the "best mode of getting supplies."[36] It fluctuated, but generally the value of the Confederate dollar spiraled downward and gold shot up: forty-two dollars on November 22, 1864 (that is, forty-two Confederate dollars for one dollar of gold); fifty dollars two days after Christmas; sixty dollars on January 11, 1865; seventy dollars on January 20; and by February 18, 1865, gold reached one hundred Confederate dollars; for one dollar specie.[37] (A Confederate five-dollar bill, in good condition, might cost you fifteen U.S. dollars in 1995.)

Blockade running, once looked down upon by the gentry, became an accepted major occupation, and not only for providing wedding clothes for Mary Chesnut's friends. Confederate blockade runners reportedly were very successful, "notwithstanding the alleged ceaseless vigilance of the Yankee navy," the *Dispatch* claimed.[38] The government eventually banned imported luxury items such as wine and cigars; more mundane items such as food were needed. Exports continued as well. "Out of 11,796 bales of cotton shipped since the 1st of July," the *Dispatch* claimed, only "1272 were lost—not quite 11 percent." The shipment of cotton through the Yankee blockade brought the Confederates more than 5.25 million dollars in gold. One writer claimed, "It is an easy matter for a good pilot to run a vessel directly out to sea or into port."

On January 31, 1865, General Robert E. Lee was named general in chief of the Confederacy. President Davis's power was slipping away. Promoting Lee to general in chief, however,

staved off an even greater elevation, that to "Dictator" Robert
E. Lee.

* * *

Richmond settled in for its fourth winter under siege. Luther
Swank wrote his "Dear Katie" that along the James River,
Confederate troops cut river ice and filled ice houses "so as to
have a good supply next summer."[39] Obviously, someone
thought the war would continue.

It's about this time that another Richmonder-by-chance
joined the list of diary keepers. Colonel Richard Lancelot
Maury was invalided from the 24th Virginia Infantry and was
serving as a desk-bound officer in Richmond as the war drew
to a close. Writing in two five-by-seven notebooks on lined
foolscap with blue covers (they look like the "blue books" every
college student knows from examination time), Colonel Maury
left an apparently unedited, day-by-day account of his life in
Richmond under siege. "In times such as wherein we now live,"
he began, "daily jotting down of matters of interest cannot. . .
fail in after years to be most interesting."[40]

Richmond became temporary home for Maury as well as
his family. "We went to St. Paul's [Church] with my dear wife,"
Maury wrote in the second week of his diary.[41] At St. Paul's
he heard the Reverend Charles Minnegerode quote Jesus
Christ: "Render unto Caesar the things which are Caesar's and
unto God the things that are God's." To which the good
reverend added his own thoughts: "No good man will take the
Yankee oath."

God, however, may have had His or Her own ideas. The
weather turned bitterly cold, "the coldest night that we have
had yet," and John Jones was faced with the dilemma of not
being able to locate a thermometer to find out just how cold it
was. The Maury family was faced with a major problem: "Gas

meter frozen. No light." It was so cold that the river and canal were closed and "3000 exchange prisoners on their way from City Point [were] delayed by the ice."

Jones agreed on the issue of the weather, the "coldest morning of the winter, [so cold that] my exposure to the cold wind yesterday, when returning from the department, caused an attack of indigestion."[42]

The weather intensified the suffering. "Nothing but the rich speculators and quartermaster and commissary peculators [*sic*] have a supply of food and fuel," Jones recorded.[43] Jefferson Davis issued a proclamation for the observance of March 10 as "a day of fasting, humiliation, and prayer, with thanksgiving," but many Richmonders had already found too much fasting, an overabundance of humiliation in trying to survive, and all too little for which to give thanks.

Many even had trouble holding on to what they had; thefts and robberies increased. "My wood-house was broken into last night," Jones wrote, "and two [of the nine] sticks of wood taken. . . . Wood is selling at $5 a stick this cold morning."[44] The mercury hit zero.

Frank and Mary West also suffered in the bitter cold: "Oh, my dear sister you cannot imagine."[45] Too little fuel due to high prices, too little food due to frequent shortages. But births respect neither war nor cold nor siege; Mary West bore their third child in the final year of the siege, and the baby apparently was affected by his mother's lack of food. "He is remarkably small," little Charlie West's mother wrote.

Despite the cold, Colonel Maury took his family on an outing; "Nothing would do for Susie (his wife) and Jimmie (their son) but they must go aboard the School Ship CSS *Patrick Henry*."[46] The ship (formerly the steamer USS *Yorktown*) was anchored at the Confederate Navy Yard in Manchester, just beyond Gillies Creek on the south side of the James River. It was used, among other things, as a training ship for naval recruits, in effect, the Confederate Naval Academy. There also was a glassworks on board, and the Maury family visited it. "We saw them," the colonel wrote, "making bottles and ink-stands, a pleasant sight." But even this pleasant sight led Maury to realize just how desperate the situation had become for the "poor Confederacy," which, being "unable to obtain the material for the manufacture of glass must buy up all the old glass and melt and blow that up again." Recycling, Civil War Richmond style.

Luckily, there was no shortage of items that could be melted down and recycled into new "bottles and inkstands." Many Richmond residents tried to leave the city before the enemy inevitably arrived, and they sold their possessions at auction. "They have postponed selling until the last moment," according to Jones, "to realize the highest possible prices—and they get them."[47] The red flag used to symbolize the auction-eer was the "blue-light special" of the nineteenth century, and it was seen at almost every corner.

* * *

Another flag was also seen in Richmond. "Yesterday much of the day was consumed by Congress in displaying a new *flag* for the Confederacy," Jones complained in early February. "Idiots," he called the members.[48]

The Confederacy went through a series of flags. Like uniforms, different flags often could be seen side-by-side in the same battle. The first, and unofficial, flag was the Bonnie Blue Flag, a field of blue that, as the song says, "bears a single star" in the middle. The first official flag of the Confederate States of America—the true Stars and Bars—was designed by South-ern educator Nicola Marschall early in 1861 and was raised over the first Confederate capitol on March 4, 1861, in Mont-gomery, Alabama.[49] It had three alternating red and white stripes with a blue canton and bore seven stars, representing the seven states that had seceded when it was adopted. Over time, the number of stars (states) increased to thirteen, even though there were only eleven states in the Confederacy. The extra two stars represented Kentucky and Missouri; the Confederacy thought they would join in secession. They did not, and Missouri and Kentucky were represented on two flags—Union (since they never left it) and Confederate (though they never joined it).

At any rate, the flag was changed on March 31, 1863. It too closely resembled the American banner, the Stars and Stripes (the Confederate flag was so similar, the Rebels even called it a similar name, the Stars and Bars), and was changed because of the confusion it sometimes caused in the heat of battle. Sometimes friendly troops fired on each other, failed to fire on the enemy, and even surrendered to their own side because, with black powder from the guns filling the air, and no breeze stirring the colors, the two flags could easily be mistak-en. Most Confederate military units went over to the battle flag, pretty much as designed by General Beauregard: a square red field, crossed white-backed blue bars—the St. Andrew's cross—with thirteen white stars inset in the blue stripes, usually with a white border or fringe around the flag. The Navy jack was basically the same, only twice as long as it was wide. The Confederate flag for much of the war also was this shape. It placed the battle flag in the canton (the upper, lanyard—side, corner) with the remainder a field of white; it was known as the "Stainless Flag." But as the war (and the Confederacy itself) wore down, there was fear the Stainless Flag might be mistaken for a flag of surrender. Little wind blowing, the flag drooping, all that could be seen was the white. The new standard Jones denounced was the same flag but carried a wide red border opposite the lanyard side. Congress hoped the Yankees would see the red border and realize the South wasn't giving up just yet.

The United States flag also changed during the war. In the beginning, there were only 33 states (stars) in the Union. Then, in 1861 and 1863; respectively, Kentucky and West Virginia were admitted and two more stars were added. Just to add to the confusion, while Congress set down in law just how many stars and how many stripes and where each stripe and the field of blue were to be, it never set a design for the stars. You might see them arranged in concentric circles, rows, or even in a star made up of stars, whatever the flag-maker preferred. It wasn't until the twentieth century that Congress finally got around to setting things straight.

* * *

As for surrendering, the Confederate government might not be ready for it, but some of its troops were, and often they didn't wait for any official proclamation. They simply gave up and went home. On February 15, Richmond newspapers carried "General Lee's Last Appeal." It invoked "all citizens, wherever it is in their power, to place before deserters and absentees from the army the last appeal that Gen. Lee will ever make to them, to return to their duty and resume their place under the flag."[50]

That was General Order No. 2 and asked the public to turn over "all deserters and absentees." General Order No. 3, issued at the same time, offered a pardon to all deserters who would return to duty. If they did not return, they would "suffer the consequences." By mid-March, newspapers carried reports of Southern troops who were being "lodged in the Castle (either prison Castle Thunder or Castle Lightning; both were used to handle deserters and others of doubtful loyalty) yesterday upon the charge of desertion: Benjamin Jenkins, A. Jenkins, Joseph Covington, William Davis."[51] The list would grow longer. Prisons meant for Yankees soon would be used for Rebels—those who preferred to desert in the last days of the Confederacy rather than chance death.

Historian Ella Lonn says that, over the length of the war, 13 percent of the Confederate army deserted. Northern troops deserted at a 9 percent rate.[52] Lonn says that, of 400,000 troops listed on the Confederate rolls at one point, more than half were absent, although many could have been ill. General Beauregard called desertion from the Southern cause "epidemic." In one month, Lee's Army of Northern Virginia saw 8 percent of the troops, as the slang expression of another war would phrase it, "go over the hill." In the final days of Lee's Army of Northern Virginia, it seemed his troops just melted away into the countryside.

Eighty thousand Union deserters were caught and returned at gunpoint to the ranks; 21,000 Confederates were sent back into service in the same manner. At least 147 Yankee deserters were executed; there is no record of the number of Rebels taken before firing squads for desertion.

There were, however, attempts to shoot deserting Rebels. John Jones commented about "the spectacle of men deserting our regiments."[53] As early as 1862, Jones told of letters the war department received from privates in North Carolina regiments demanding they be transferred "or else they would serve no more."[54] "Very reckless," he added.

A year later, in 1863, he told of a man running down Franklin Street in Richmond, apparently a deserter who wore civilian clothing. A uniformed soldier "took deliberate aim with his rifle" and fired. The rifle misfired, however, and both Jones and the deserter stood transfixed as the soldier fired again.

Once more the rifle misfired. All the while, several other passersby watched, curious. "In war," the diarist declared, "the destruction of human life excited no more pity than the slaughter of beeves in peace."[55] A little over a year later he would comment:

> Desertion is the order of the day, on both sides.
> Would that the *men* would take matters in their own
> hands, and end the war. . . . Let every man in both
> armies desert and go home.[56]

It wasn't only the desertion of troops which shocked Sallie Putnam, either. "[I]t was during this session" of the Confederate Congress, she wrote, "that a member of this body attempted to escape to Washington."[57] Yet it wasn't so much in wonder that Richmonders looked on the attempted congressional desertion as in indignation. "Before its adjournment," Putnam added, "the Confederate Congress published an address, which served in a measure to inspirit the despairing, and to confirm the hopeful." It did little good, however; the rate of desertions got worse.

Many on both sides had not wanted to go to war in the first place. When things got bad (and they usually were), and they got the chance, they deserted. Sometimes, it seemed, a commander's attention had to turn more toward catching his own deserters than to fighting the enemy. James Bracy wasn't one of the commanders, just one of the men assigned to catch the deserters:

> [I]t seems hard times when it take one half of the
> men to keep the other half from running away.[58]

In the summer of 1863, J. G. Daniels went home to Georgia on leave. He told, in verse, how he felt. He believed many other

Confederate soldiers shared his feelings regarding both secession and going to war:

> The cesessionists [*sic*] they, did carry the day;
> And often times I have heard them say;
> All the blood spilt, I will drink;
> Now what do you recon, these men does think.
>
> [Their] thoughts I'm sure I do not know;
> But to war, they hate to go;
> And if the blood that's been spilt,
>   they have drinked at all;
> I'm sure their stomachs can never stall.

As in all history, those who declared the Civil War stayed home; those who fought it often had nothing to say about the declaration. Old men declare war; young men fight it.

> The men that was going to drink the blood,
> Are not the men that wades the mud;
> Oh! No they'd rather stay at home;
> And send the inocents [*sic*] to distant
>   lands to roam. . . .
>
> I am here at home today;
> Where I wish I always could stay;
> Where I can get plenty thats good to eat
> And go to see the girls so sweet.[59]

But it was the final year of the war, and soldiers on both sides of the siege line had only a few more months to serve their countries.

16

Rumors of Peace
and Sable Patriots

From John Jones's diary early in the new year:

> January 24, 1865— "What I fear is *starvation*."

> January 26— "This is famine!"

> February 2— "God save us! We seem incapable of saving ourselves."[1]

There was "a great panic" in the streets; there was talk of evacuation. Jones believed Southerners were "incapable of saving ourselves." He told of "information from the United States [that] shows that an effort to obtain 'peace' will certainly be made." Perhaps it was the rumor of peace talks or the talk of evacuation that caused the "great panic"; either might be accurate.

Francis P. Blair, Sr., was in Richmond after visiting President Lincoln in Washington. He was a Missouri politician in 1861 when state officials there wouldn't approve raising troops to aid the Union. In 1865, he represented the United States on a semi-official basis.

Some Confederates hoped Blair brought with him hopes of peace.

The problem was, many Confederate leaders were determined that the only way they'd accept peace was if it came with independence. They expected to gain at the peace table what they had been unable to win in nearly four years of war. The politicians weren't alone in this. Many private citizens— newspaper editors among them—hoped peace talks would result in independence.

The Petersburg *Express* wrote in great detail of one group of Confederate peace negotiators. Under a flag of truce, Confederate Vice President Stevens and the other commissioners entered the Union lines. They spent the night in the company of General Grant and planned to travel by steamer the next day for talks in Washington. "The scene on the lines during the passages of our commissioners was one of lively interest," the *Express* editor wrote, even commenting on the "number of ladies [who] were present. . .some in front of the works, some on top, and many walking and riding the field to the rear."[2] Behind enemy lines, the sight of the commissioners' leave taking was greeted in almost picnic fashion: "It was an impressive scene."

The steamer *River Queen* didn't have to go all the way to Washington. Instead, she lay at anchor in Hampton Roads off Fortress Monroe, and the Southerners were greeted on board by President Lincoln himself. His trip out of Washington made it obvious Lincoln was as anxious for the peace talks to succeed as were many Southerners, but he wasn't about to sell the Union short. He called for an unconditional restoration of the Union; the Confederate commissioners insisted on independence. Neither side gave in, and the talks ended unsuccessfully.

From Colonel Maury's diary: "[T]he Peace Commissioners have come back, having accomplished nothing."[3]

The war continued. Privation continued in Richmond under siege.

* * *

Perhaps because of his inside knowledge and his ties to the Confederate government, J. B. Jones was more realistic than the average citizen of Civil War Richmond. "We have no alternative," he believed, "but to fight on: [we] have no option of ceasing hostilities."[4] He asked, "What Terms may be expected" of any peace talks? And he answered the question himself: "Not independence, unless the United States may be on the eve of embarking in a foreign war, and in that event that government will require all the resources it can command, and they would not be ample if the war continues to be prosecuted against us."

Mexico and its French-run government earlier had trouble with the Washington government, and Paris took offense. Might not France declare war on the United States? Some Confederates hoped so. "Max of Mex [Maximillian of Mexico] has kicked out the U.S. Consul," Colonel Maury wrote, "and closed its ports against their ships." And he added, "Hurra for Max!!!"[5] It wasn't enough, and the war pitting brother against brother continued. Richmond continued to suffer under siege.

General Lee called on his troops "to prepare for the coming struggle," and by mid-February, "the good people of the city are in a great state of alarm and excitement."[6] "Many," according to Colonel Maury, "fear that General Lee is preparing to give up the place. . , that he cannot subsist his army here and therefore he must leave the town and go elsewhere where provisions can be easily obtained."[7] But, he asked, "Where is that place?"

* * *

Confederate troops in the trenches around Richmond and Petersburg felt the coming change. From Lieutenant Luther Rice Mills of the 26th Virginia Infantry, a very sad and almost poetic letter:

> Something is about to happen. I know not what. Nearly everyone who will express an opinion says Gen'l Lee is about to evacuate Petersburg. The authorities are having all the cotton and tobacco moved out of the place as rapidly as possible. . . .
> Unless we are so fortunate as to give the Yankees the slip many of us will be captured. I would regret very much to have to give up this old place.
> The soiled and tattered Colors borne by our skeleton Regiments is sacred and dear to the hearts of every man. No one would exchange it for a new flag. So it is with us. I go down the line, I see the marks of shot and shell, I see where fell my comrades, the Crater, the grave of fifteen hundred Yankees, when I go to the rear I see little mounds of dirt, some with headboards, some with none, some with shoes protruding, some with a small pile of bones on one side near the

end showing where a hand was left uncovered, in fact
everything near shows desperate fighting. . . .
I have just received an order. . .to carry out on picket
tonight a rifle and ten rounds of cartridges to shoot
men when they desert.[8]

* * *

Whatever happened next would cost Richmonders plenty.
Plenty of money, plenty of food, plenty of everything. And
money was running out. The Confederate government, the
Virginia state and the Richmond city governments, the people-
all were going broke. They just couldn't keep up with spiraling
prices.

Most employers tried to keep salaries in line with
expenditures, and wages for nearly every occupation increased
during the siege. By war's end, clergymen were paid upward of
$12,000 per year, according to John Jones, who said, "Dr.
Woodbridge (a local minister) received a Christmas gift from
his people of upwards of $4000, besides seven barrels of flour,
etc."[9] Jones himself was both an employee and an employer.
He had trouble when he tried to negotiate his servant's salary
(he hired another man's slave): "Offered the owner. . .$400 per
annum. He wants $150 and clothing for her. Clothing would
cost perhaps $1000. It remains in abeyance."

Military clothing was equally expensive and equally as
difficult to obtain, but blockade running helped. Jones told of
the Confederate government importing half a million pairs of
shoes in three months, 8 million pounds of bacon, and two
million pounds of saltpeter for gunpowder. It's no wonder the
Confederates were concerned over port facilities. Savannah was
in enemy hands. The port of Charleston was under Northern
control. Norfolk? Portsmouth? The South gave them up early

in the war. Only Wilmington, North Carolina, was still open. Coffee would go up from fifteen to forty-five dollars per pound. Sugar would jump by half again over night.[10] And if Wilmington were lost to the Confederacy, things would become even worse.

* * *

On February 15, the Richmond *Dispatch* called them "sons of Africa," and lectured blacks who would be free that "Cuffee" (as they so often were derogatorily called) must be taught that "the genius of Universal Emancipation has but one boon to bestow upon mankind—'Root, pig, or die.'" One month later, the same newspaper carried an announcement from the Confederate States adjutant general's office:

> You are hearby authorized to raise a Company of
> Companies of Negro soldiers, under the provisions of
> the act of Congress, approved March 13, 1865.[11]

For many in the Confederacy, it was the final means—galling means for many—by which they might achieve their independence: use as soldiers the very people they had pledged to keep in servitude. The *Dispatch* editor added an "Appeal to the People of Virginia":

> It is well known that Gen. Lee has evinced the
> deepest interest in this matter, as vitally important to
> the country.

Lee wasn't the only one. In December 1863, Major General Patrick Ronayne Cleburne had proposed freeing slaves and enlisting them into the army. He made the suggestion during a staff meeting with his commander, Joe Johnston. He argued it

> would, at once, take the wind out of the sails of Northern Abolitionists and cause them to cease the war, for they would no longer have food upon which to keep fanaticism alive.[12]

The idea shocked Johnston's other officers. The Irish-born Cleburne dropped the plan, and it was hushed up by the government in Richmond. More than a year later it was openly proposed in the Confederate Congress, but Cleburne wasn't around to see his idea bear fruit, however bitter it might be. He was killed in the Battle of Franklin after the fall of Atlanta.

Like Johnston's officer corps, much of the Confederate public abhorred the idea of recruiting blacks to save their rebellion. Work, yes; fight, no. They didn't like putting weapons in black hands.

African-Americans already were being used—hired, for the most part from slaveholders—to build fortifications surrounding Richmond, but the decision to recruit them for the Southern army was met by resentment. "It will be a '*bitter pill*,'" Colonel Maury wrote on February 20, his emphasis showing his hatred of the prospect. The next day he wrote in his diary that "This Negro question is the great one of the day," and he added, "Don't free the negroes, though."[13] Sallie Putnam agreed, calling it a "desperate measure [that] was vigorously combated."[14]

Many members of the Confederate armed forces spoke out against the plan. Howell Cobb, formerly president of the Confederate Congress, now a general in the Southern army, didn't like recruiting blacks, saying it would be better to emancipate them at once, conceding to the "demands of England and France."[15]

The Confederate Congress passed the bill 88 to 54 to enlist blacks, albeit at the eleventh hour, as Mrs. Putnam wrote. "Recruiting offices," she reported, "were opened in Richmond and soon a goodly number of sable patriots appeared on the streets, clad in the gray uniform of the Confederate soldier."[16] These latest additions to the Southern cause held dress parades on the capital grounds and "infused a spirit of enthusiasm among those of their own race, that served to increase the numbers of those who were willing to fight."

If the "sable patriots" were, indeed, "clad in the gray uniform of the Confederate soldier," one must wonder where they obtained the uniforms. There are numerous reports of Confederate troops around Richmond being almost naked, even in the coldest weather. (Over the winter of 1864, in fact, North Carolina Governor Gebulon Vance held back 92,000 uniforms from Lee's troops, keeping them for North Carolina's units.[17]) It's difficult to believe the Confederate government would uniform its slaves while allowing its white troops to fight in tattered rags.

* * *

In mid-February, Colonel Maury reported rumors of the Confederate evacuation of Charleston. He found those rumors to be "rather premature," but realized, "it may come to that erelong. Alas!" Three days later, rumor became reality when it was announced to the Richmond public, and on February 20, there was "News of the evacuation of Wilmington!" Maury saw the latter as having many good aspects. "Beauregard," the invalided Rebel predicted, "will now be able to concentrate against Sherman and will no doubt whip him."[18]

The loss of Wilmington, however, posed a major problem for Richmond, one that Maury apparently didn't comprehend. It cut off the last major seaport for Richmond's supplies. The railroads ran—at times, ran around, but ran nonetheless—and as we have seen, the Union blockade wasn't a total success. But with Wilmington closed to the Confederates, the supply situation got worse, and soon John Jones declared, "The markets are now almost abandoned, both by sellers and purchasers."[19]

Yet, obviously, some citizens of Richmond under siege still were able to find food, not only in ample supply but in good quality. On the same day Colonel Maury noted the fall of Wilmington, he confessed:

> Tonight [we went] to a splendid party at Mr. Suttons—oysters, venison, mutton, and all of the delicacies of the season. Best table I have seen in many a long day.[20]

The last seaport supplying Richmond—lost. The rail lines tying the city to the rest of the Southern nation—uncertain. When those ties no longer were intact, the city would die. And so would the Confederacy.

17

The Last Confederate

It was spring again, that soft and gentle time in Richmond, with flowers trying their best, the air fragrant, the James River cool and clear, rushing on. As was the war, rushing on.

Even the most staunch of Confederates realized that Richmond must soon fall. Phoebe Pember of Chimborazo Hospital wrote, in a great understatement, "It began to be felt that all was not as safe as it was supposed to be."[1] There was, she said, the "incessant moving of troops through the city from one point to another [and] the scarcity of rations."

William Murphy Brown, brother to Petersburg Minister Gustavus Brown, wrote to their mother on March 2:

> It seems to be the universal opinion in Richmond that government will be compelled to save the city to feed the army.

Brown admitted he "would not be surprised if the evacuation should take place in a very few days."[2] Colonel Maury saw such evacuation "a disgrace to the South" but confirmed that "fear of evacuation of the city still continues among the craven-hearted."[3]

Spring, and what tall pines that hadn't been burned or used for coffins were soon to stand witness to the destruction of the capital of the Confederacy. It was the spring of a year, the winter of a nation. It was time for the Confederate government to abandon Richmond.

Thomas Cooper DeLeon was President Jefferson Davis's close friend and confidant for most of the Richmond siege. He knew the state of the Confederacy's health, not unlike an asthmatic panting for breath:

> First the archives and papers went, then the heavier stores, machinery and guns, and supplies not in use; then the small reserve of medical stores was sent to Danville or Greensboro. And at last, the already short supplies of commissary stores were lessened by removal—and the people knew their Capital was at last to be given up! Deep gloom-thick darkness that might be felt—settled upon the whole people.[4]

Richmond had less than a month to live as capital of the Confederate States of America. Much of the time was filled with rumor, not news, because as Richard Maury recorded, the newspapers "very prudently forbear to give bad news out."[5]

Spring, and the sweet smell of Richmond's air turned into its own death odor.

President Davis had declared March 10 a day of fasting and thanksgiving; all departments of government, all city shops were closed. As it can be in Richmond, that day was cold and rainy:

The people, not withstanding the bad weather, pretty generally proceeded to the churches, which will be open morning, noon, and night, for it is a solemn occasion.

John Beauchamp Jones:

Thousands will supplicate Almighty God to be pleased to look upon us with compassion, and aid us, in this hour of extremity, to resist the endeavors of our enemies to reduce us to bondage.[6]

Richard Lancelot Maury:

Merciful God. . .forgive us our sins. . . . [S]tand on our side and. . .give us the victory.[7]

The *Examiner* called the day of thanksgiving, "universal." "The rain which fell during part of the day," it reported later, "interfered somewhat with the religious observances, but the churches, nevertheless, were crowded, and excellent discourses were preached."[8] Taverns were empty, "and drunkenness was rare, which was one of the gratifying features of the day."

* * *

Ten days later, on March 20, Richmond City Councilman Richard Frederick Walker brought before that body the problem of widows, orphans, and other abandoned people. The *Examiner* had reported "between five and six thousand women and children whose husbands, fathers, and natural protectors had gone off to the Yankees and left them here as a burden upon the city." Walker apparently believed in "women and children first"—first out the door, apparently. He thought there were other, more deserving poor people, and believed those deserted women and children "should be removed from the City, if possible, and sent north to follow the fortunes of their kindred."[9]

The *Examiner* called Walker's efforts "a step in the right direction," and said "it is absolutely necessary that no mouth remain here to be fed which can be removed and fed elsewhere." Richmond in the spring of 1865 was not the place to be abandoned.

But while the city talked of sending abandoned women and children north, Richmond's population continued to grow. Twenty-four hours after the day of thanksgiving, "some 1500 prisoners, paroled, arrived this morning—making some 10,000 in the last fortnight."[10] Apparently, the North was pushing its unwanted mouths out also.

* * *

March 14:

> The [news]papers contain no news from the armies, near or remote.[11]

While Richmond newspapers were, as both J. B. Jones and Colonel Maury noted, hesitant about carrying information about the nearby war, they did carry notices of another event. April 5, 1865, would be state election day, and the papers were full of political announcements. T. P. August appealed to his fellow citizens and promised, if elected, his "future zeal and fidelity in your service." W. S. Underwood was running for the

Virginia Senate while stationed at Camp Surry, serving in the light artillery. He admitted he was a stranger to most of the voters but pledged "to look to your interests." R. O. Whitehead, running from the Fourth Senatorial District, referred to the "intelligent citizens of my district" and told of the wounds he had suffered at the Second Battle of Manassas. War, it seems, not only does not interfere with politics, it abets the system.

On March 29, the Richmond *Whig* attacked the New York *Tribune*'s claim of "evidence of how near the rebellion, even from the Rebel standpoint, is to its final collapse." The *Whig* denounced the *Herald*'s "diabolical sentiments [that] exceed anything we have ever seen in that most iniquitous of all vile Yankee press."[12]

One problem, the *Whig* editor believed, was that his Northern counterpart was a

> wretch. . .more than seventy years old—standing with one foot in the grave and within a very short distance, according to that course of nature, of that bar before which he must account for all the atrocities of a life of unparalleled infamy.[13]

The *Whig* claimed the *Tribune* editor was a "Southern man" who, while originally espousing Southern independence as the "most holy of all causes," changed colors; "in one night the threats of a mob made him change his oft-repeated sentiments."

Age, like war, depends on which side you stand. The *Dispatch* of March 23, 1865, proudly carried the announcement of the wedding of "Mr. John Pyles, aged seventy-two years. . . to Mrs. Sarah C. Carico, aged fifty." Age might be a deterrent to good newspaper editing, but apparently it was a blessing in marriage.

* * *

In an unsigned letter to the New York *Herald* about a quarter-century later, a visitor to Richmond wrote about those final days of Richmond under siege. A businessman, he traveled often to the city, "and I could always tell quite accurately how the war was going on by the countenance and demeanor of its inhabitants."

"Whenever victory perched upon the Confederate banner," he wrote twenty-six years later, "the faces of [the city's] inhabitants would beam with joy; each one would move with an elastic step and renewed animation."[14] In the end, Richmond had changed dramatically:

> As soon [as] I stepped from the train. . .I knew that something was wrong; there seemed to be a death-like calamity.

A visit to a banker increased that feeling. He was told:

> If you have any paper money, put it into specie at once. "Is it as bad as that?" I replied. "Yes, and much worse; another week and you'll get nothing" for Confederate paper money.[15]

It was obvious to most Richmonders that the city was in grave danger. Money—and the conversion of paper to gold—wasn't the only problem. As usual, food was a major concern:

> The fear of utter famine is now assuming form. Those who have the means are laying up stores for the day of siege—I mean a closer and more rigorous siege.[16]

That visiting businessman found many Richmonders were preparing themselves for the worst:

At the house of a friend with whom I was staying, I asked the question, "How do you think the war will terminate?" The host simply took me to his bed-room, and raising the coverlet, showed me several barrels of flour, sacks of coffee, sugar, and other groceries snugly stowed away. "This," he said, "I would find to be the case in nearly every household in the city."[17]

Food stores might be empty, but auction houses were full. Everywhere there were sales:

We will offer at auction on Wednesday next. . . .

Will be sold at auction at my store. . . .

Valuable household and kitchen furnishings. . . .

On Tuesday. . . .

On Monday.[18]

Among the household items up for sale were the goods of President and Mrs. Jefferson Davis. The head of the Confederate government was about to abandon his capital city, and it can be imagined the panic the knowledge of this must have carried; if your president is about to leave town, you'd better think of getting out yourself.

Varina Davis's old gowns, her silks, feathers, and gloves had been offered for sale weeks earlier. Now, it was time for their household items: paintings, silver, and furnishings—"bric-a-brac" as she described them—from the Confederate White House. When it was all knocked down by the auctioneer, the Davises were sent a check for $28,400. But that was in Confederate funds. In gold, it was worth only $500. In reality, as Davis found out, it was worthless; no one would cash the check.[19] Confederate President Jefferson Davis was broke.

He gave Varina most of the gold coins they possessed and she and their four children boarded a train headed for North Carolina. For his own use, Davis kept just one five-dollar gold coin.

He also gave Varina a pistol, and later she recalled her husband showing "how to load, aim, and fire it." The Confederate President "was very apprehensive of our falling into the hands of the disorganized bands of troops roving about the country and said, 'You can at least, if reduced to that last extremity, force your assailants to kill you.'"[20]

In her postwar letter, Mary Andrews West told her sister that she, too, had been selling off the family goods and even clothing from the very start of the war, trying to have enough money on which to live. "First one article of jewelry and another," she wrote, and "handsome dresses, plain dresses, underclothing until at last. . . . I was reduced to two dresses, which were barely passable to wear."[21] Still, more had to go: "I was trying in my mind to decide which of those two I would give up."

The number of auctions, the sale of personal items, force us to draw two conclusions. One, the situation was widespread and desperate. Two, someone had money with which to buy the items. Obviously, not everyone was hurting.

* * *

The recruiting of black Confederates went ahead. March 24, 1865, the Richmond *Sentinel*:

[Q]uite a number [of black soldiers] have been enlisted, all of them, be it remembered, *volunteers.*[22]

Colonel Maury confirmed the report: "Negro recruiting goes on
bravely." He met some of the new recruits

> walking on the streets with their uniforms. Quite
> military, I say, but ah! how funny. . . .
> I hate the idea of having to buy Cuffee and Sambo
> into the ring very much.[23]

The *Enquirer* did not exactly endorse the Confederate troops,
but proposed "the ladies of Richmond. . .present the negro
battalion with a flag."

* * *

With or without a flag, the black Confederate troops never got
into battle. On March 25, General Lee tried to break out of
Grant's siege of Fort Steadman near Petersburg. The Southern
forces were badly beaten. Colonel Maury, by now no longer
trying to return to the fighting, remained hopeful for the cause.
Lee's action was "only a feeler," he felt, "to see where the
enemy was."[24]

There's an old saying: Be careful what you look for; you
may find it. Lee found Grant.

From the war department, J. B. Jones wrote that, "After
all, I fear Lee's attempt on the enemy's lines yesterday was a
failure." He called the effort "premature."[25] With Lee's "premature" efforts unsuccessful, Grant quickly tried to break the
South's lines, moving toward the South Side Railroad.

* * *

While Grant and Lee skirmished outside Richmond, inside the
city Colonel Maury worried about his next meal. He "determined today that I would make an expedition to the Rappahannock [River] fishing shores—providing I could get somebody
who would go shares with me, furnishing wagon & mule."[26]
Even as an invalided soldier on government rations, Maury
found it almost impossible to feed his family. "My stock of
provisions," he wrote, "have really gotten so low that I am
obliged to do something by which I can get something to eat."

* * *

In that spring of 1865, as they had for four previous springs, the
Confederacy and the Union seemed to agree that Richmond
was the central target. The South's hope for independence and
the existence of the Confederacy itself, depended on Richmond's survival. So long as that city-state (as it had become)
survived, the Southern cause would endure. It wouldn't be long.
    On March 29, 1865, G. A. Magruder of the 13th Infantry
Battalion of General Early's division, wrote his cousin:

> What do you think of our prospects? I think it is one
> of the darkest days of our young Confederacy. I
> believe that in a few months the stars and stripes will
> wave from the frontiers of Va. to the Gulf. I can
> almost say that it makes very little difference with me
> for in the first place I never expected to see the end
> of this war and if I should, I have nothing to live for
> in the future. I could face death of the cannon's

mouth with as much indifference as I can eat my beef
and bread.[27]

Magruder's estimate of "a few months" was grossly inaccurate.
The New York *Tribune*, quoted by the Richmond *Whig*, was
closer to reality with what it purported to be

> positive evidence of how near [the] Rebellion, even
> from the Rebel stand-point, is to its final collapse.[28]

The *Daily Examiner* of Thursday, March 30, 1865,
agreed:

> It is evident that the month of April will witness a
> decisive turn, given one way or another, to Grant's
> converging army.

From that same issue, several small and interesting items tell of
a city trying to live even as it knows it is dying:

> If the dog-catchers don't soon get after the canines of
> high and low degree that swarm the city, they will
> outnumber the human population. . . .

> The bakers, with flour at twelve hundred dollars per
> barrel, after a nice arithmetical calculation, are now
> issuing loaves of three sizes, which are sold at one,
> two and three dollars. The first is only visible by
> micoscopiek [sic] aid. . . .

> In the case of John T. Froman. . .he proved his age to
> be over fifty years and was discharged from military
> service. . . .

> The "Old Dominion Saloon" has been removed from
> No. 126 Main Street to No. 202 where I will be
> pleased to see my old friends and patrons. . . .

> On Saturday night, the Soup House in Metropolitan
> Hall, Franklin Street, was broken into and about one
> thousand dollars worth of bacon stolen.[29]

During that previously mentioned anonymous businessman's
final Civil War visit to Richmond he was "accosted by a friend"
who exclaimed, "Sir, I have just heard that the Petersburg and
Weldon railroad would be cut by the Yankees in a few days."[30]
The friend's daughter was in North Carolina, and the gentleman would "give all I have to get her home!" The businessman
wasn't about to give up his place on the train out of town but
agreed to retrieve the girl himself. And so, with "pockets full of
Confederate notes" and a haversack filled with "rations for a
few days. . .I left next morning for Petersburg." The railroad
ran only at night "for fear of the Yankee batteries which are
alarmingly near." Waiting for darkness, he walked through
Petersburg, "viewing the marks of shot and shell on every side,
hearing now and then the heavy, sullen boom of the enemy's
guns, seeing on every hand the presence of war."

The trip to North Carolina was made, the friend's
daughter retrieved, and the return was accomplished. Once
more the train stopped during the daylight hours. It was
apparent the rail lines were still open, and while they were,
Richmond would survive another day.

Colonel Richard Lancelot Maury:

> March 30th—Calliminous [sic] news today from
> Petersburg—Grant attacked Gordon's line last night
> from 11 o'clock until day—making repeated charges.
> The night was very dark and the scene is described by
> eyewitnesses as being a most beautiful one, lit up as

it was by the flashes from the cannon and the regular
line of fire from the musketry.[31]

It is the final entry in Maury's diary, although more than a
dozen empty pages remain in the small blue notebook.

It rained on March 31, a cold mid-spring rain. "The
reports of terrific fighting near Petersburg on Wednesday
evening have not been confirmed," Jones wrote.

Sallie Brock Putnam, now 20 years old, "slept, as it were,
over the heaving crater of a volcano."[32]

April 1, and Jones wrote of a rumor that "a battle will
probably occur" near the South Side Railroad. There were
"vague and incoherent accounts" of fighting there, and rumors
of 60,000 Virginia troops deserting.

The Richmond City Council met that day and appropri-
ated $5,000 to keep "the Soup House open for the relief of
those who had heretofore participated in its benefits."[33] A
proposal to take down a dangerous brick wall was referred to
committee. And the keeper of the Shockoe Hill Burying
Ground was accused of "failing to clothe some of the hired
Negroes and withholding from them money drawn by him from
the City Treasurer."

* * *

April 1, 1865, was a Saturday. The *Whig* still carried the motto
"The Constitution—State Rights" on its masthead. The editor
wrote that "pride goest before a fall."

The *Dispatch* told of a long list of letters remaining in
the Richmond Post Office, waiting for receivers. Waiting.

The *Dispatch* also detailed the bombardment of Petersburg the night before but claimed "all continues, and seems likely to continue, quiet on the north side of the James River."

The Petersburg *Express*, from the south side of the James, sensed the city's death:

> The bloody work of battle has only begun, but it is progressing in earnest on the right. Grant's long contemplated and long anticipated movement to extend his left. . .has come to pass.[34]

Confederate Lieutenant Colonel R. T. W. Duke took time off from the war and "went down on a small steamer to 'Wilton,'" the home of a friend, Colonel W. C. Knight. "All was quiet in the neighborhood," he remembered years later.[35]

In hindsight, Sallie Putnam wrote, "We dreamed not . . .of the sad morrow in reserve for us."[36]

* * *

The Confederacy still controlled one rail link into Richmond and one into Petersburg. From a junction fifty miles southwest of the capital city, the lines led either farther south or to the Tennessee border. These two lines were all that remained to supply both the Army of Northern Virginia and the city of Richmond.

Lee sent Major General George Pickett with five brigades to reinforce Five Forks, an area southwest of Petersburg. Sheridan briefly moved back to Dinwiddie Courthouse, then pushed his powerful column on to Five Forks; it was 4:00 A.M.

Lee's order to Pickett was to "Hold Five Forks at all hazards," an order that, by its nature and Pickett's own (not to mention his enmity toward Lee since Gettysburg), did not please the ringlet-wearing general. Further, Pickett was told to "Protect [the] road to Ford's Depot and prevent Union forces from Striking the South Side Railroad." To Pickett, the order seemed tinged with unnecessary panic. He did not believe the Yankees would attack, and so General Pickett accepted an offer to attend a fish fry hosted by Major General Thomas Rosser, fried shad under the towering pines north of a creek called Hatchers Run. It was well behind the front lines. With him went Robert E. Lee's nephew, Fitzhugh Lee (not to be confused with the army commander's son, William Henry Fitzhugh "Rooney" Lee).

Pickett later said he never heard the fighting, although it wasn't far from where he and Fitz Lee dined *alfresco*. Neither officer had told his subordinates where he was going, and while the presumably succulent shad were consumed, Sheridan attacked Pickett's troops. It was a rout. By the time Pickett returned to his lines, the Union army had taken 5,000 Confederate prisoners. The remainder of the Southern army had streamed away, far from any point at which they could be rallied by their general's return.

After the rout of Pickett's troops, Robert E. Lee drew three brigades from his center, and that, clearly, stretched his forces too thinly. That's when Grant ordered the Federal attack. Union Major General Horatio Wright of Ohio led a charge that cost the Federals 2,000 men. It was a wild and confusing charge, but in the end, the North won. Won it all.

Federal troops advanced toward the James River. The Rebels struggled but fell back. Confederate General A. P. Hill died in the action, shot and killed by a band of Union stragglers as he tried to rally his troops along the Boydton Plank Road at Petersburg.[37]

Sheridan's troops firmly controlled the South Side Railroad. The Confederacy's last link between its capital city and the rest of the rebelling country had been broken.

April 2, 1865, was a Sunday. The siege of Richmond was over.

18

The Yankees Are Coming

The day "dawned brightly over the capital of the southern Confederacy," Jones recorded; "A soft haze rested over the city [and] no sound disturbed the stillness of the Sabbath morn."

It was a pleasant day, especially after a long, hard winter. Sap flowed in the trees, seeds had begun to sprout, and trees everywhere were beginning to bud. Gently, spring came to Richmond.

In the Confederate war department, John Jones heard nothing about what might be going on around Petersburg, and that worried him. "A decisive struggle," he wrote, "is probably at hand—and may possibly be in progress while I write."[1] He was correct.

President Jefferson Davis of the Confederate States of America was in pew number sixty-three at St. Paul's Episcopal Church, wearing his now-famous gray trousers and vest along

with a Prince Albert coat. He sat stiffly upright, Secretary of
the Navy Mallory noted, and wore a "cold, stern expression."
Reverend Minnegerode had just intoned in his thick, thunder-
ing German accent, "The Lord is in His Holy temple: let all the
earth keep silence before Him." He paused as the church
sexton passed a telegram to Davis. It was from General Lee:

> I advise that all preparations be made for leaving
> Richmond tonight.[2]

Another churchgoer saw "a sort of gray pallor creep over
[Davis's] face." At once, the president arose and left the
church; he walked down Ninth Street to his office at the war
department. An "ominous fear fell upon all hearts," and then
other church-goers were summoned to leave.[3] Finally, Reverend Minnegerode himself was called to the vestry room. The
city was to be evacuated, he was told. When the priest returned
to the chancel, he found the congregation had beaten him to
the door; they were on their way out. He tried stopping them
but had little success. Some returned to take communion, but
Reverend Minnegerode could no more stop his congregation
from leaving St. Paul's than General Lee could stop the Union
forces from pushing through his lines.

By Sunday afternoon, Richmond's banks were opened,
and their customers retrieved their valuables, hoping to keep
them out of Yankee hands. They didn't bother to retrieve their
Confederate money and bonds.

As the Confederate government evacuated Richmond,
the city government met in special session. The two city
regiments, the 19th and the 1st, would be retained to protect
Richmond from the panic the council was sure would come.
They were right. When Confederate forces left the city, the
destruction began. Those refugees and deserters, spies and
criminals, gamblers and speculators—all who had only recently

strayed into the city—poured now into the abandoned city's streets. Customers and residents of cheap hotels and saloons, of gambling dens and brothels, all joined the melee. The guards at the state penitentiary ran off, and the prisoners broke lose to roam and steal.

A city that, just four years earlier, was home to just 39,910 souls, Richmond now counted more than 100,000, possibly as many as 200,000. Regular citizens, refugees, soldiers, and prisoners of war. Now, it seemed, the whole city was running around confused, not knowing whether to evacuate, to put up a defense, to give up, to plunder, the burn, or to hide. They did some of each.

Under city council orders, a committee was set up in each ward. The city's forces would destroy as much of the liquor stock as possible. Barrels and bottles of alcoholic beverages were broken; casks of the finest southern bourbon opened, their contents allowed to run through the gutters, and the whiskey flowed like water. Women and children dipped out what they could; they used rags tied to sticks to dip up the whiskey. Some even knelt down to drink.[4]

It was Sunday, and Richmond was lost.

The South's capital city had been the unclaimed prize of several long, hard-fought battles. Occasionally, it had been bombed but never leveled, often attacked but never conquered.

Now it was all over.

At his friend's home, Lieutenant Colonel Duke learned that Richmond was to be evacuated, the Confederate government was moving to Danville. Duke was given a small piece of ham bone by his hostess, the only food he would taste for three days. "As I was passing over [Mayo's] Bridge," he wrote, "a few cavalry videttes passed me."[5] He was, he believed, "the last Confederate who crossed the bridge."

Seeing a flag of truce on the southern bank of the James River, Duke surrendered his sword. He wrote down the name of the Union officer to whom he surrendered and years later recovered his sword after first paying a twenty-five dollar reward.

The scene inside Richmond was, as the council had feared, one of panic; the Confederate government had abandoned the people of Richmond; the people were tearing the city apart. John Jones observed "quite a number of men—some in uniform, and some of them officers—hurrying away with their trunks."[6] Officials at the war department told him clerks such as he with families must remain in the city. All others tried to pile onto the last train out.

Varina Davis tried to leave the Confederate White House, but someone (possibly one of Elizabeth "Crazy Bet" Van Lew's spies) had stolen her horse and saddle. When she tried to board a train, rail officials refused to load her carriage on board.

Some residents of Richmond, including Robert E. Lee's ailing wife, declined to leave the city. Many locked themselves inside their homes. Meanwhile, Jones reported, "the negroes stand about mostly silent, as if wondering what will be their fate." The *Whig* reported the evacuation as commencing "in earnest Sunday night [and ending] at daylight on Monday morning with a conflagration."[7]

The crowd was more of a mob. The pandemonium of daylight became chaos at night. Hundreds, thousands, were drunk, stealing anything they could. Plundering stores, homes, shops, and offices.

Earlier it was decided that, should Richmond be in danger of being lost, her stocks of tobacco should be destroyed to prevent their falling into enemy hands. Over the protest of Mayor Mayo, Confederate General Richard S. Ewell went ahead with the plans (years later, General Ewell denied the charge, claiming in a postwar report to Robert E. Lee that it was the rioters and arsonists, but not his men, who set fire to

Richmond). Torches were laid to the Shockoe warehouse and others where 10,000 hogsheads of tobacco were stored. A strong wind sprang up, and sparks and burning fragments of tobacco blew toward the city's business district—to the Franklin Paper Mills and the Gallego Flour mills, ten stories high. The *Whig* reported the next day, "The fire spread rapidly [and] by noon the flames had transformed into a desert that portion of the city bounded by 7th and 15th Streets, from Main Street to the James River." A Confederate officer said, "The old war-scarred city seemed to prefer annihilation to conquest."[8]

Mrs. Lee left her Franklin Street home briefly when it was touched with fire, but she soon returned. Almost all day, fire hoses were trained on the house to prevent its destruction.

Confederate warships were anchored in the James, including the still uncompleted CSS *Virginia II* and several other ironclads. Fifty of the sixty cadets at the Confederate Naval Academy were assigned to escort the government's archives to safety. The remaining ten set fire to their academy, the steamer *Patrick Henry*. Sparks touched other ships, and their loaded powder magazines blew. To the north, the army's arsenal also exploded, taking with it the lives of several young Virginia Military Institute cadets stationed there. It was their only touch with the war. Shells flew high into the smoke-filled air; red-hot metal rained down and started more fires.

Stragglers and scavengers roamed the city, pillaging and sacking stores and homes. They carried their spoils with them from pillaged store to plundered home—paintings, chairs, household goods. An elderly woman rolled a horsehair-covered sofa along the street on its castors.[9] Down Broad Street the looters went, to Central Station, but the last train had left them behind.

The last remnants of Confederate General Joseph B. Kershaw's brigade had been guarding the lines east of Richmond, but now they clattered through the city and headed

south to join Lee on the road to Appomattox. They fought
through streaming crowds trying to leave the burning city and
finally reached Mayo's Bridge. The rear guard galloped over
the bridge, and General Martin W. Gary shouted, "All over,
good-bye; blow her to hell." Tar-fill barrels had been placed
under the bridge, and following General Gary's orders Colonel
Clement Sulivane signaled his men. Engineers put those tar-fill
barrels to the torch; flames reached for the already rose-red
skies, and flames from the two railroad bridges burned high
into the night.[10]

J. Webster Stebbins was a first sergeant with Company
I, 9th Vermont Volunteer Infantry. He was just outside Richmond when he wrote:

> The city has fallen and the black clouds of smoke
> from its burning ruins are rising to the heavens. . . .
> The enemy evacuated last night, and I have heard no
> fighting at all today this side of the river. The rebels
> fired the arsenal Co. and the bridge across the James
> River also. We heard the shell in the arsenal bursting
> for half an hour.
> The country is a fine looking one; some fine residenc-
> es. So far as I have seen, the citizens are glad to see
> the Union soldiers coming. . . .
> It was just five minutes of five this morning when we
> halted in this fort and planted our colors on the para-
> pet, giving three cheers for the *fall of* Richmond.[11]

The night sky had first been warm pink, then red hot. The
morning was hazy-gray with smoke from the overnight fires.
When a crowd gathered at the government commissary at 14th
and Cary Streets, government clerks began handing out supplies
to any and all who wanted them, all the items the people of
Richmond had missed for so long. First, it was an orderly
distribution, but order turned to chaos. The drunken crowd

from the whiskey barrel destruction rushed for the stored food—hams, bacon, flour and sugar, molasses, rice, coffee and tea—all thrown out the warehouse windows to waiting crowds below.

From the official minutes of the Richmond City Council, April 3, 1865:

> The City was, on this day, occupied by the United States forces, and the Council did not, therefore, meet.[12]

From Chimborazo Hospital, Matron Phoebe Yates Pember:

> [I] sat all the weary Sunday of the evacuation, watching the turmoil, and bidding friends adieu, for even till noon many had been unconscious of the events that were transpiring, and now when they had all departed, as night set in, I wrapped my blanket-shawl around me, and watched. . . .
> Then I walked through my wards and found them comparatively empty. Every man who could crawl had tried to escape a Northern prison. Beds in which paralyzed, rheumatic, and helpless patients had laid for months were empty. The miracles of the New Testament had been re-enacted. The lame, the halt, and the blind had been cured.[13]

Colonel Elisha Hunt Rhodes, Company D, 2nd Rhode Island Volunteers, was outside Petersburg:

> *Monday April 3rd 1865*— We heard today that Richmond has been evacuated and is in flames. Well, let it burn, we do not want it. We are after Lee, and we are going to have him.[14]

The sounds of war were over, replaced by dread and hope and fear. Carriage wheels moaned over cobblestones as Mayor Joseph Carington Mayo, at age sixty-nine, rode through the streets of Richmond, looking for Union forces to whom he could surrender his city. For a while, he was unsuccessful.

After four years under siege, there was no one to whom he could quit. Finally, he found a small party of Federal cavalry three miles south of the city, at the junction of the Osbourne Turnpike and the New Market Road.

The mayor handed the troops' leader, U.S. Major Atherton H. Stevens, Jr., 4th Regiment, Massachusetts Cavalry, a note:

Richmond Monday, April 3, 1865

To the General Commanding the
    United States Army in front of Richmond:

General,

The Army of the Confederate States Government having abandoned the City of Richmond, I respectfully request that you take possession of it with an organized force, to preserve order and protect women and children and property.

Respectfully,
Joseph Mayo, Mayor[15]

Later that morning, Major Stevens raised the flag of the United States of America over the Virginia statehouse. They didn't have a regular flag, so they used one of two guidons carried by his cavalry unit. For almost four years, the Virginia capitol had been the home of the Confederate Congress; once more the building was part of the Union.

As the Confederates left the city, the Union race was on to occupy it—cavalry units, infantry, all hoping to be the first to take control of the once proud city. Some black units were among the first Federal troops to enter Richmond, and the now-freed slaves of the Confederacy rushed out, knelt down, and cried, "Glory to God! Glory to God!"[16] "Floods of tears poured down their faces," Edward H. Ripley, a Union officer remembered.

Blue-clad horsemen rode into town, the Yankee cavalry riding such horseflesh as hadn't been seen in horse-loving Richmond in many long months. With them, their band, playing "The Girl I Left Behind Me," and even "Dixie."[17]

J. B. Jones "walked down Broad Street to the Capitol Square." Everywhere he looked, desolation. And Union soldiers. "The street was filled with *negro troops*," he said, "cavalry and infantry, and were cheered by hundreds of negroes at the corners."[18]

On April 3, 1865, the Richmond *Whig* was the only one of the city's newspapers to publish, and the banner no longer carried the motto "Constitution—State Rights." It tried to describe the devastation to the city:

> We can form no estimate at this moment of the number of houses destroyed, but public and private it will certainly number 600 or 800. . . .
> The Bank of Richmond, the Traders' Bank, the Bank of the Commonwealth, and the Bank of Virginia all were destroyed.

The American Hotel was leveled, as was the Columbian Hotel. The Confederate Post Office, with all those uncollected letters, was no more. The State Court House was gone from Capital Square. J. B. Jones's war department, the former Mechanics' Institute, was destroyed.[19]

"As the sun rose on Richmond," Sallie Putnam remembered, "such a spectacle was presented as can never be forgotten by those who witnessed it."[20] "The roaring, the hissing, and the crackling of the flames," she wrote, "were heard above the shouting and confusion."

Piles of salvaged furniture (some of it obviously stolen) were scattered wherever the destroyed buildings allowed—beds, paintings, silverware, family heirlooms, the treasures that until now had been carefully hoarded and preserved. The grass around the Jefferson-designed state capitol, Jones recorded, was "covered with parcels of goods snatched from the raging conflagration, and each parcel [was] guarded by a Federal soldier."[21] Parading in front of the massive white columns of the capitol were Union troops, pausing now and then to look at what they had conquered, what was left of what they had conquered.

On the 4th, Jones

> walked around the burnt district this morning. Some seven hundred houses, from Main Street to the canal, comprising the most valuable stores, and the best business establishments, were consumed. All the bridges across the James were destroyed. . . .
> The War Department [where Jones had been employed] was burned. . . . [T]he flames were arrested, mainly by the efforts of the Federal troops.[22]

"At last the Federals have reached the haven of their hopes," Mary Andrews West wrote nine days later. There "arose the cry of 'The Yankees are coming,'" she added. But the Yankees were already there:

> Richmond has been given up and General Lee has surrendered! Thank God there is to be no more bloodshed in our dear state! Sincerely do I hope dear

Clara never to witness such a scene as that presented to us on the morning of the arrival of federal troops.[23]

"The bell rang amidst shouts of 'fire, fire,'" Mary continued, and the occupying Union forces put out the fires. Southerners had been told the Yankees were "desperadoes, thieves, I may say devils;" they were not. "How agreeably have all been disappointed," Mary told Clara now that the war was over.

"[T]he day after the evacuation," Phoebe Pember remembered, "the first blue coats appeared at [Chimborazo Hospital]—three surgeons inspecting the hospital." The three Union surgeons along with one Confederate physician walked through the wards nearly emptied by newly "cured" patients, and she added:

> One of our divisions was required for use by the new-comers, cleared out for them, and their patients laid by the side of our own sick so that we shared [our food] with them, as my own commissary stores were still well supplied.[24]

By the end of the week, the Confederate patients were transferred to the hospital at Camp Jackson, leaving Chimborazo Hospital to the Union army.

Julia Grant was visiting her husband outside Richmond when the final push began. While Ulysses went off chasing Lee, Julia visited the city he had defeated:

> When we arrived at the landing, we took a carriage and directed the coachman to drive through the principle streets and past the public buildings. I only saw that the city was deserted; not a single inhabitant visible. Only now and then we would meet one or two carriages with visitors from the North, coming like

ourselves to see this sad city, and occasionally an old
colored servant would pass alone, looking on us as
intruders as we all felt we were.[25]

And soon another visitor arrived in Richmond: Abraham
Lincoln. It was Tuesday, April 4, 1865. Three Union ships
sailed up the James River from City Point. Two, the *Bat* and
the *River Queen*, ran aground; the third, the *Malvern*, tried to
avoid sunken Confederate ships until it too touched bottom. A
barge pulled alongside; President Lincoln and his son Tad
transferred to it. The president's party, accompanied by a small
guard, docked at Rocketts Landing. "Thank God," Lincoln said,
"I have lived to see this."[26] He added: "It seems to me that I
have been dreaming a horrid dream for four years, and now the
nightmare is gone. I want to see Richmond." As crowds
watched—some hostile, some grateful—he strolled toward the
scene of his four-year nightmare. He walked through Jefferson
Davis's capitol, sat in Davis's chair in the Confederate White
House, and everywhere he went conqueror and conquered
wondered at him. The Emancipation Proclamation that he had
signed January 1, 1863, now could be enforced in Richmond,
and the newly freed slaves crowded around him and cheered.

"The cheers that greeted President Lincoln," John Jones
wrote

> were mostly from the negroes and Federals compris-
> ing the great mass of humanity. The white citizens [of
> Richmond] felt annoyed that the city should be held
> mostly by negro troops. If this measure were unavoid-
> able, it was impolitic if conciliation be the purpose.[27]

On April 7, back at City Point, Virginia, Lincoln used military
stationery to write General Grant:

Head Quarters Armies of the United States

Lient. Gen. Grant,

Gen. Sheridan says "If the thing is pressed I think that Lee will surrender." Let the thing be pressed.

A. Lincoln[28]

In Richmond, the conquerors and conquered—Union troops and Richmond citizens—who had watched President Lincoln walk the streets now plundered the wreckage of the former Confederate capital until Union officers posted guards. Federal forces even set a guard to watch over Mrs. Robert E. Lee, who had remained behind because of her crippling illness. The Lees reciprocated. "I saw a Federal guard promenading in front of the [Lees'] door," Jones wrote, "his breakfast being just sent him from within."[29]

Everywhere were ashes. They covered the old burned bricks and newborn flowers. They settled on pink and white petals of flowering dogwoods. They drifted into the air as troops of both armies shuffled in and out, in and out.

Red clay to the west, black earth to the east, all gray now with settled ashes. Cobblestones and crumbled homes, covered with ashes.

They were the gray ashes of a city nearly destroyed, of a nation ended before it began. But like other ashes of other fires, they would lead to rebirth and growth if given the chance.

* * *

Pictures of a city. Victorious Federal troops gather at Libby Prison; they'd heard so much about it. Some had even been housed there for a while.

Wagonload after wagonload rolls down Main Street, and the citizens of Richmond look on, stand and watch as Mathew Brady and others photograph their lost cause.

Union troops stand at attention on the state capitol. Look, Ma! Look at me. We won. We won. We won. Thank God it's over.

Ghostlike, women of Richmond, dressed in black, skirt past destruction. For whom do they mourn? City or friend or loved one?

Richmond men and boys stand side by side with Union troops, with newly freed slaves.

Oh, what shall we do? Forty acres and a mule? What shall any of us do?

Freed Southern troops under guard.

Freed Southern blacks.

Freed Southern city.

Dust and ruin slowly disappear.

* * *

In the days after Jefferson Davis's government evacuated Richmond and headed for the Carolinas, General Robert E. Lee found his Army of Northern Virginia starving in the rolling hills around Appomattox Courthouse. In the confusion of abandoning Richmond, the Confederate war department had issued conflicting orders about supplying Lee's army.

Near the small stream called Sayler's Creek, Federal troops captured 6,000 Confederates. And General Lee exclaimed, "My God! Has the army been dissolved?"[30]

The Confederates stumbled; the Federals surrounded them. It was April 7.

Under a flag of truce, Grant sent Lee a note calling for the surrender of the Army of Northern Virginia. Lee responded:

> I reciprocate your desire to avoid useless effusions of blood, and therefore, before considering your proposition, ask the terms you will offer on condition of its surrender.[31]

The same, he was told, as at Vicksburg—parole until exchanged. It was April 8.

Lee responded again:

> I received at a late hour your note of to-day. In mine of yesterday I did not intend to propose the surrender of the Army of Northern Virginia, but to ask the terms of your proposition. To be frank, I do not think the emergency has arisen to call for the surrender of this army, but, as the restoration of peace should be the sole object of all, I desired to know whether your proposals would lead to that end. . . .
> [A]s far as your proposal may affect the Confederate States forces under my command. . .I should be pleased to meet you at 10 a.m. to-morrow on the old stage road to Richmond, between the picket-lines of the two armies.

Grant had a headache; Meade was nauseated. Lee wanted to discuss a "restoration of peace." Grant said no; that was a political subject, and he had no authority to negotiate such matters.

April 9 was Palm Sunday, and the final Rebel yell screamed in the Civil War was heard over the hills of Virginia;

two Union infantry corps had gotten behind the Southerners. General Sheridan had marched all night, had drawn a solid line across the road to the west. Sheridan in front of him, Meade behind him, General Lee said, "there is nothing left for me to do but go and see General Grant, and I would rather die a thousand deaths."[32]

Grant's headache vanished: "The pain in my head seemed to leave me the moment I got Lee's letter."[33]

The two leaders finally agreed to meet in the parlor of Wilmer McLean's home. In 1861, Wilmer McLean had left his home near Manassas, Virginia, to avoid the war he saw begin in his front yard; now he saw it end in his front parlor in Appomattox Court House.

April 9, and Confederate General Robert E. Lee, taller at five feet eleven than his average trooper, sat waiting, wearing a new full-dress uniform complete with sash and jeweled sword, the tops of his brightly polished black boots stitched in red.

April 9, and U.S. General Ulysses S. Grant, shorter at five feet seven than his average trooper, stood stoop-shouldered and wearing a private's blouse and muddy boots. He walked up to Lee, and they shook hands.

They remembered meeting once during the Mexican War. And then they spoke of surrender terms. They were, Lee said, about what he had expected. The Southern general asked that those terms be put in writing, and Grant agreed, began writing in a manifold order book.

Grant sat as a marble-topped table. Lee sat at a smaller one made all of wood, one of two matching tables in the room. Lee read the hand-written terms of surrender, noted an omitted word, and it was corrected. Grant looked at Lee's sword (he carried none himself), but Lee didn't offer to turn his over to the man who had beaten him. Grant didn't ask for his defeated opponent's sword; the time was past for such formalities.

It was over.

Afterwards, the two generals saluted each other. Somberly, they parted.

* * *

Elisha Hunt Rhodes, who had enlisted as a private in Co. D., 2nd Rhode Island Volunteers and rose to colonel, who participated in every campaign of the Army of the Potomac, who had seen Bull Run and the Wilderness, was at Appomattox:

> *Sunday April 9/65, Near Appomattox Court House, Va.*—Glory to God in the highest. Peace on earth, good will to men! Thank God Lee has surrendered, and the war will soon end. How can I record the events of this day? . . .Some time in the afternoon we heard loud cheering at the front, and soon Major General Meade commanding the Army of the Potomac rode like mad down the road with hat off shouting: "The war is over, and we are going home!" Such a scene only happens once in centuries. . . .
> The Rebels are half starved, and our men have divided their rations with them. The 2nd R.I. had three days' rations and after dividing their rations with the Rebels will have to make a day and a half's rations last for three days. But we did it cheerfully. Well, I have seen the end of the Rebellion. I was in the first battle fought by the dear old Army of the Potomac, and I was in the last. I thank God for all his blessings to me and that my life has been spared to see this glorious day. Hurrah, Hurrah, Hurrah![34]

James Coburn was a corporal with the 141st Pennsylvania Volunteer Infantry:

Dear ones at home:
Hip! Hip! Hurrah! General Lee surrendered. . . . It
was the greatest day that I ever saw.
We have had one of the hardest campaigns that I ever
saw—night and day—but the results how glorious!
The papers will tell you more than I can about what
we have done and are doing. "There's a good time
coming." My health is good and spirits never better.
Love to all, more anon.[35]

On April 10, Lee dictated a farewell order. He made only a few
revisions before sending it to his men:

GENERAL ORDERS NO. 9 HD. QRS. ARMY OF N. VA.
APRIL 10, 1865

After four years of arduous service marked by unsur-
passed courage and fortitude, the Army of Northern
Virginia has been compelled to yield to overwhelming
numbers and resources.
I need not tell the brave survivors of so many hard
fought battles, who have remained steadfast to the
last, that I have consented to this result from no
distrust of them; but feeling that valor and devotion
could accomplish nothing that could compensate for
the loss that must have attended the continuance of
the contest, I determined to avoid the useless sacrifice
of those whose past services have endeared them to
their countrymen. . . .
With an unceasing admiration of your constancy and
devotion to your Country, and a grateful remembrance of your kind and generous consideration for
myself, I bid you all an affectionate farewell.

R. E. Lee
Genl.

On April 12, the Confederates—many of them barefoot—marched in formal parade at Appomattox Courthouse, surrendering their arms and flags. The Union officer given the honor of receiving the formal surrender was Brigadier General Joshua Chamberlain, the man who had led the Federals to victory at Little Round Top at Gettysburg. The Rebels marched by. By instinct, perhaps in admiration and sympathy, Chamberlain ordered his men to salute the Confederates. Not a sound, no drum roll, no cheer, not a word was spoken. The Confederates returned the salute.

The Army of Northern Virginia had marched its final march; its men broke ranks forever.

U.S. General Grant didn't wait for the surrender march; he rode off to Washington.

Confederate General Lee also hadn't waited; he rode straight to Richmond to see his wife and family.

April 13, and outside Richmond "a small group of horsemen appeared at the far side of the [James River] pontoon [bridge]." It was Lee, his son Rooney, Colonel Walter Taylor, and three other aides. It was raining steadily, and water dripped from Lee's already sodden hat and cape:

> It became known that General Lee was amongst them, and a crowd gathered along the way, silent and bare headed. There was no excitement—no cheering, yet as the great chief passed, a deep, loving murmur ...rose from the very hearts of the crowd. Taking off his hat and merely bowing his head, the man passed silently.[36]

Robert E. Lee rode on, through the city he had protected for four years. It was war worn, dilapidated, burned, and nearly destroyed. It was also at peace.

* * *

On the morning of April 14, 1865, Major General Robert
Anderson raised the American flag over Fort Sumter. It was
the same flag he had hauled down exactly four years before.

On the afternoon of April 14, 1865, President Abraham
Lincoln met with his cabinet. General Grant was there and they
discussed ways to return conditions in the country, including the
South, to a state approaching normalcy.

And that night, the President and Mrs. Lincoln attended
a performance of *Our American Cousin* at Ford's Theatre in
Washington. General and Mrs. Grant were to attend, but
declined an invitation to join the presidential party at the
theatre. (Unexpectedly, the Grants had decided to leave town
for Burlington, New Jersey.) The evening had been planned as
a gala affair—announcements made, invitations sent out—so,
even though he "felt inclined to give up the whole thing," the
president agreed to his wife's request and went.[37] Instead of
the Grants, a young military aid to the president, and the aid's
wife, were made part of the soon to become historic party.

In the middle of the third act, a shot was fired, a man
jumped from the box where the president sat. John Wilkes
Booth caught a spur in the bunting draped around the box and
broke his ankle. He brandished a knife and shouted *"Sic semper
tyrannis!"* ("Thus Always to Tyrants" or "The South shall be
free!" Or both. He slowly, then, deliberately, limped across the
stage and out a back door where a horse stood waiting for him.

Inside the theatre, Mrs. Lincoln stood shrieking that the
president had been murdered.

He was slumped unconscious in the rocking chair where
he'd been sitting. He'd been shot in the base of the neck and
the bullet was lodged there.

19

Damnyankees and Damnrebels

"Richmond," the ever hopeful Sallie Putnam wrote, was "still fair and beautiful." The city had a destiny it must fulfill, she believed, and "There is life in the old land yet."[1] She was correct.

The city's years of glory have been many; its years of fear, all things considered, were few. The city has recovered and so have its people. Many of the battlefields in the Richmond-Petersburg area are now attractive sites for tourists and historians. At other sites, suburban homeowners carefully tend their lawns and every now and then they dig up a spent minié ball. In 1991, the bodies of three unknown Confederate soldiers, victims of the siege and fighting, were found; they were buried with full honors. Similar events happen regularly throughout the old Confederacy—sometimes the dead are Confederates, sometimes Union. All are reinterred with honors.

The Franklin Street home rented by Robert E. Lee and lived in by Mrs. Lee and their daughters during the siege still stands, now recognized only by those few who know where to look. A plaque on the Lee home commemorates its Civil War tenants. Look closely and you may see signs of fire on an outer wall. Nearby houses also burned while the ailing Mrs. Lee sat, rocking and knitting, refusing to leave. Most of those houses are gone now. The alley behind the house carries an unusual street sign: "Traveller's Lane," in honor of Marse Robert's big gray stallion. He often stood waiting in that alley while his owner visited friends and family.

Many public buildings were destroyed during the April 2, 1865, fire, and others have fallen to what the twentieth century calls "progress." Some have gone on to bigger and, perhaps, better things—parking lots and pizza restaurants.

Libby Prison has a history unto itself. The building was a chandler's warehouse before the war, then a prison for the four years Richmond was under siege, then was torn down. The prison was reassembled in Chicago during the Columbian Exposition where it stood for ten years. That once-feared, once-hated brick and wood warehouse was rebuilt as a museum of atrocities and opened to the public. Here was the infamous, the hated, the soul of the rebellious South.

A decade later, when the public lost interest in the museum, the reborn Libby Prison was torn down once more. Parts of it were given by the museum owner to the Chicago Historical Society. In 1991, the society opened a permanent display of "A House Divided" using portions of Libby Prison" one door, a wall built of slave-made bricks, items carved by prisoners—a pin cushion, a cross, a napkin ring—all made from animal bones, an eagle and an eleven-and-a-half-foot chain, the chain carved from a single piece of wood. Several inmates apparently took parts of the prison home with them. The Chicago Historical Society also has three gavels made of the wood from Libby Prison, gavels with minié balls still in place where they'd been shot into the walls. (The Society also has the marble-topped table where Ulysses S. Grant sat during the surrender at Appomattox as well as the bed where Abraham Lincoln died. Another table, one of the two matching wooden ones in the McLain House, is in a private collection in Chicago.)

Not all of Libby ended up in Chicago. Much of the old prison was to be taken on a nationwide tour, to be viewed by any who cared to spend a dime, one thin dime, a tenth part of a dollar; step right up to see the house of horrors where more than 75,000 of our brave boys were incarcerated. A traveling museum of outrage, so to speak.

Its floors would be walked again by those once held prisoner, memories once more would be evoked, tales once more would be told, lies once more lied, and tears once more shed. The disassembled warehouse-turned-prison headed east, but as the train traveled through the Indiana countryside, near Route 30, there was an accident, and the train derailed. Whether by sale or by theft, the boxcars carrying the numbered and counted planks and rafters of Libby Prison were opened. Libby Prison, some said, was put to better use. It was used to build stalls in a barn, and there it stood for more than half a century, near the little town of Hamlet, on the border between LaPorte and Starke Counties. During the centennial of the Civil War, the barn attracted a lot of attention, too much attention for its owner. He tore down the prison-turned-barn and sold the used lumber. Souvenir hunters walked the barnyard, looking for stray nails from Libby.

And that's when remnants of the prison finally made it back down south, more or less. Rafters and beams, some still carrying names of Yankee prisoners—handcarved during the late unpleasantness—were bought by a realtor in Spencer, Indiana. And if you draw the old Mason-Dixon line far enough east, Spencer just about makes it "way down yonder, in the land of cotton." Once again, Libby Prison is part of a barn, this time a steel barn surrounded by mobile homes. Timbers from the former prison are now locked inside, now rotting away to history.

Spencer is not far from Gosport, Indiana, the home of the "Biggest Yankee," Lieutenant David Van Buskirk, who spent some months in the original Libby Prison.

Phoebe Yates Pember's Chimborazo Hospital has long since been torn down; it, too, was mainly built of wood. The site is now a public park, drawing most of its patrons from nearby slum districts. Black districts. Few who go to the park on spring afternoons know who or what Chimborazo was. Or care.

Shockoe Slip now is an "in" spot for young Richmonders looking for restaurants, shops, and nightlife. Many of those who work there are black. Most of those who shop and play there are white. There is some—often reluctant—mixing of the races.

The Brockenbrough House still stands, renamed at the time the White House of the Confederacy. Abraham Lincoln visited there on that April morning he strolled into Richmond accompanied by only a small guard, cheered by former slaves. Lincoln wanted to see where and how Jefferson Davis lived. You might say Lincoln was the first postwar tourist to Richmond. He certainly wasn't the last. Furniture that stood in the house while it was home to Jefferson Davis and his family was spread around the country by nineteenth century souvenir hunters—Federal soldiers.

The White House of the Confederacy stands next to the Museum of the Confederacy, and the Museum keeps so busy it recently had to expand. Its visitors mostly are white, drawn from the middle class of a heritage-loving South; they're the ones who proclaim "Forget, Hell."

Sharing the same parking ramp with the Museum of the Confederacy and White House is the Medical College of Virginia. Its patients mostly are black, drawn from Richmond's poorer society; they also say they won't forget, but for a different reason.

The physical Richmond recovered.

The emotional Richmond, however, frequently still seems to live in the past. The suffering during the siege is well remembered, but the real cause of that suffering has been shifted.

There is no doubt the North did not want to destroy Richmond; otherwise, the city would have been shelled long and often as were Petersburg, Vicksburg, and Atlanta. Still, the people of Richmond suffered greatly. To a large extent, this suffering was at the hands of fellow Southerners.

Although the siege certainly hampered the supplying of the city, hoarders, farmers, and speculators—J. B. Jones and Sallie Putnam were among the many who complained of such speculators—all withheld food, trying and succeeding in driving prices up. Just as obviously, there was food to be had if one could and would pay the increasingly higher prices. Colonel Richard Maury, it may be remembered, dined on February 20, 1865, on "oysters, venison, mutton and all of the delicacies of the season."

That anonymous last-minute visitor to Richmond reported hoarded "barrels of flour, sacks of coffee, sugar and other groceries." After quelling the Bread Riot, the Confederate government handed out rice; obviously, it had the rice on hand before the riot. As that same government fled the city, it opened its commissary to the people of Richmond. Even pouring out barrels and bottles of whiskey indicates supplies were available.

J. B. Jones was able to buy, at cost, clothing material from Confederate supplies, an indication that clothing, if not available to all (Mary Andrews West had to sell all but two of her dresses), was there if you knew the right people.

Knew the right people. Were the right people. Paid the right price.

The North Carolina governor's preference for keeping for his own troops thousands of much-needed uniforms is reminiscent of a conversation the author had with a Southern governor during the oil and gas crisis of the 1970s. Many natural gas wells in his state, wells capable of producing that much-needed fuel, were capped and would not be uncapped, he said, until prices rose. And then, he added, the supplies would go first to his own state. To hell with everybody else, apparently, was his attitude.

These examples, surely, are not the only ones found in private letters and diaries; remember the "starvation parties." It is all too clear that Richmonders suffered far more during the siege than there was any need to.

The near destruction of the city during evacuation need not have occurred. The fires—started by the Confederates themselves—burned the stores of tobacco to keep them out of the hands of the Union army.

Yet, during the war, there was frequent trade, not just among individuals, but between the two armies in general; tobacco was traded for beef with the foreknowledge and approval of the commanders. When one shipment of Confederate tobacco, scheduled to be traded for Union cattle, was inadvertently burned by Union troops in Fredericksburg, cigar-smoking Ulysses S. Grant ordered that the cattle be shipped to the South without obligation. After all, he reasoned, it was the Union that reneged and burned the tobacco.

The North, then, had access to tobacco; Richmond's supplies of the weed would only have added to what they had on hand. Why not trade it? Burning it not only harmed the owners of the tobacco, for it was privately held, but the resulting fires nearly destroyed Richmond.

And the Rebels rode off, leaving the Yankees to put out the Confederate-started fires in the South's capital city.

Not infrequently, not always jokingly, Southerners still refer to those Damnyankees—one word, not two, spun together into a single epithet. Considering that Richmond under siege suffered more at the hands of its own than the enemy's people, perhaps there should be a more critical look taken at Jefferson Davis's government and the speculators that kept the South half-starved and ragged.

Perhaps Richmonders should refer to them as Damn-rebels.

Epilogue

A Personal Afterthought

Robert E. Lee symbolizes the Confederacy. He is that most-Southern of all Southern gentlemen. Perhaps never before and never since has one individual looked so much like a general should—straight out of Hollywood's "Central Casting." Acted and performed so much like a general should. He was everything his state and chosen country wanted him to be.

Unlike many others who fought in the war, Robert E. Lee refused to write his memoirs. In his words, "I should be trading on the blood of my men."

Unlike many others in the South, he took the view that the preamble to the U.S. Constitution ("We the People") meant just that, people, not "We the States." He followed Light Horse Harry Lee's belief that "The expression was introduced. . .with great propriety. The system is to be submitted to the people for their consideration."

Robert E. Lee worried long and hard over what to do if his native Virginia seceded. He knew if the Old Dominion did leave the Union, he would also. But he preferred to remain a civilian. In writing to his son Custis in January of 1861, Lee said:

> As an American, I take great pride in my country, her prosperity and institutions, and would defend any State if her rights were invaded. But I can anticipate no greater calamity for the country than a dissolution of the Union. . . . Secession is nothing but revolution. The framers of our Constitution [would] never [have] exhausted so much labor, wisdom and forbearance in its formation, and surrounded it with so many guards and securities, if it was intended to be broken by every member of the Confederacy at will. It was intended for "perpetual union" so expressed in the preamble, and for the establishment of government, not a compact, which can only be dissolved by revolution or the consent of all the people in convention assembled. It is idle to talk of secession. Anarchy would have been established, and not a government by Washington, Hamilton, Jefferson, Madison, and the other patriots of the Revolution. . . . [A] Union that can only be maintained by swords and bayonets, and in which strife and civil war are to take the place of brotherly love and kindness, has no charm for me. I shall mourn for my country and for the welfare and progress of mankind.[1]

In February, Robert E. Lee received a telegram from President Lincoln. When Lincoln offered him command of all Union forces, Lee-the-Virginian declined and resigned his commission in a letter to Lieutenant General Winfield Scott on April 22, 1861.

Virginia Governor John Letcher invited Lee to Richmond to talk about the Confederacy. Riding to Richmond from his home at Arlington, Lee wore, not a military uniform, but

civilian clothes; it could be argued that at that moment he
wanted to be nothing more than that, a civilian.

But, at Letcher's plea, Lee accepted a position in the
Virginia militia, only transferring to the Confederate states'
army when President Jefferson Davis made him his military
advisor. He took to the field in 1862 after General Joseph E.
Johnston was wounded at the Battle of Seven Pines. "Granny"
Lee his men joked at first. And they derided him for digging
in—the "King of Spades," he was called for a while—not
fighting the war as many thought it should be fought.

A point now for consideration: Was Robert E. Lee the
best thing to happen to the South or the worst? Obviously, his
was a brilliant military mind. Obviously, he led the South
through perilous times and hard-fought battles. Without Lee,
we can argue, the Confederacy would have succumbed much
faster. And that is just the point. Perhaps Lee's very greatness,
that talent, which kept the Confederacy a contender for so long,
actually harmed the South in the long run.

What, for instance, would have been the fate of the
South if, say, Lee had lost the Seven Days' Battles along the
Virginia peninsular—Mechanicsville, Gaines' Mill, Savage's
Station, Malvern Hill? What if he had surrendered to McClel-
lan at Malvern Hill on July 1, 1862, instead of to Grant at
Appomattox Court House on April 9, 1865?

Might not the war have ended then? True, the Confederacy still had a sizable army in the western theatre, much larger
than it had in 1865. But Lee's surrender, whether in 1862 or
1865, would see Richmond fall to the Union. Richmond was
always the key to the Confederacy. As Richmond went, so went
the Confederate States of America.

Surrender at Malvern Hill *might* have saved the South
(and the North) nearly three years of conflict and death. No
Second Manassas, with 25,251 casualties. No Antietam, with
26,134 casualties. No Chancellorsville, with 30,099 casualties.

No Gettysburg, with 51,112 casualties. No Chickamauga, no Stones River, Wilderness, or Spotsylvania, with a total of 112,084 casualties. No burning of Richmond, no bombardment of Vicksburg and Atlanta. No "march to the sea" by Sherman. Perhaps no assassination of Abraham Lincoln and with his death the enforcement of a more severe, more damaging, more devastating Reconstruction than ever he would have permitted if alive to fight a vindictive Congress.

What if, what if?

To ask again: Was Robert E. Lee the best thing to happen to the South or the worst?

Notes

Chapter 1: Prologue of Spring

1. Robert E. Lee, a letter written to his son in January 1861, quoted in Chuck Lawliss, *The Civil War Sourcebook: A Traveler's Guide* (New York: Harmony Books, 1991), 56.

2. Frank Moore, ed., *Rebellion Record: A Diary of American Events*, Vol. 1 (New York: Ayer, 1976), 315.

3. Emory M. Thomas, *The Confederate Nation, 1861-1865* (New York: Harper Torchbooks, 1979), 307.

4. *Ibid.*, 37-64.

5. As quoted in William A. Swanberg, *First Blood: The Story of Fort Sumter* (New York: Charles Scribner's Sons, 1857), 108.

6. Robert Young Conrad to unknown, February 27, 1861, Robert Young Conrad papers, Virginia Historical Society, Richmond.

7. Robert Young Conrad to unknown, March 2, 1861, Conrad papers, *op cit.*

8. Robert Young Conrad to unknown, March 13, 1861, Conrad papers, *op cit.*

9. Roy C. Basler, ed., *The Collected Works of Abraham Lincoln*, (New Brunswick, N.J.: Rutgers University Press, 1952-55), Vol. 4, 323.

10. Robert Young Conrad to unknown, April 14, 1861, Conrad papers, *op cit.*

11. Robert Young Conrad to his son, Powell Conrad, April 18, 1861, Conrad papers, *op cit.*

12. Robert Young Conrad to his wife, Elizabeth Whiting (Powell) Conrad, April 20, 1861, Conrad papers, *op cit.*

13. *Ibid.*

Chapter 2: Revolution or Rebellion?

1. New York *Tribune*, April 12, 1855.

2. *Congressional Globe*, 36 Congress, session 2, 11.

3. Quoted in James M. McPherson, *Battle Cry of Freedom: The Civil War Era* (New York: Oxford University Press, 1988), 181, emphasis added.

4. Richmond *Enquirer*, November 1, 1812, hereafter REQ.

5. Albert Fishlow, "The Common School Revival: Fact of Fancy?" in Henry Rosovsky, ed., *Industrialization in Two Systems* (New York: G. P. Putnam's Sons, 1966), 40-67.

6. *Journal of the Congress of the Confederate States of America, 1861-1865*, Vol. 1 (Washington, D.C.: Government Printing Office, 1904-1905), 100.

7. John Beauchamp Jones, *A Rebel War Clerk's Diary at the Confederate States Capital* (New York: J. B. Lippincott, 1866), entry for June 28, 1861.

Chapter 3: Every House a House of Mourning

1. Bruce Catton, *The Centennial History of the Civil War: Never Call Retreat*, 3 vols.,(New York: Doubleday, 1965), vol.1, 205 Emory M. Thomas, *The Confederate Nation; 1861-1865* (New York: Harper Torchbooks, 1979), 191f; Shelby Foote, *The Civil War: A Narrative*, 3 vols. (New York: Random House, 1954-1978), Vol. 2, 55.

2. Sallie A. Brock Putnam, *A Lady of Richmond: Richmond During the War: Four Years of Personal Observations* (New York: G.W. Warleton, 1867), 46. Sallie Brock was sixteen when the war began. After the war, at about the time of her book's publication, she was married. Throughout this book, she is referred to as Mrs. Putnam or Sallie.

3. *Ibid.*

4. *Ibid.*, 40-41.

5. Col. Robert E. Lee to his wife, Mary Custis Lee, written January 23, 1861 at Fort Mason, Texas. Quoted in Mark McKenna, "Lee's Last U.S. Army Post," *Blue & Gray Magazine*, April 1992.

6. John Esten Cooke to Lt. J. E. B. Stuart, U.S. Army, April 14, 1861, Cooke family letters, Virginia Historical Society, Rich-

mond. Cooke was Stuart's friend and relative; after the war, he wrote about both Stuart and Gen. R. E. Lee.

7. Arthur M. Schlesinger, Jr., ed., *The Almanac of American History* (New York: G. P. Putnam's Sons, 1983), 278.

8. Richmond *Dispatch*, January 7, 1861, hereafter RD.

9. Quoted in Schlesinger, *op cit.*, 286.

10. Hunter Holmes McGuire to his father, Hugh Holmes McGuire, July 24, 1861, Hunter Holmes McGuire papers, Virginia Historical Society, Richmond, emphasis his.

11. Eugene Blackford to his father, July 24, 1861, Lewis Leigh Collection, Department of the Army, U.S. Army Military History Institute, Carlisle Barracks, PA.

12. Quoted in Bruce Catton, *Glory Roads: The Bloody Route From Fredericksburg to Gettysburg* (Garden City, NY: Doubleday & Co., 1952), 57.

13. Putnam, *op cit.*, 60.

14. Jones, *op cit.*, October 9, 1861.

15. Putnam, *op cit.*, 63.

16. Jones, *op cit.*, October 9, 1861, emphasis his.

War in the West I: Fort Donelson

1. U. S. Grant, John Y. Simon, ed., *Personal Memoirs of U.S. Grant*, 2 vols. (New York: Charles Webster, 1885-1886), Vol. 1, 37-38.

2. For a good account, see William S. McFeely, *Grant: A Biography* (New York: W.W. Norton & Co., 1981).

3. Harry Hansen, *The Civil War: A History* (New York: Mentor, 1961), 103.

4. McPherson, *op cit.*, 393.

5. *War of the Rebellion: Official Record of the Union and Confederate Armies*, Ser. 1, Vol. 7, pt. 2, (Washington, D.C.: Government Printing Office, 1894-1922), 125, hereafter OR.

6. Curt Johnson & Mark McLaughlin, *Civil War Battles* (New York: Crown Publishers, 1977), 46.

7. Maj. Gen. Lewis Wallace, "It was not possible for brave men to endure more," in *Battles and Leaders of the Civil War*, Ned Bradford, ed. (New York: E. P. Dutton, 1956), 63. This is the edited version; Robert U. Johnson and Clarence C. Buel edited a four-volume version published in 1887 and 1888 by The Century Company of New York City. Both works will be cited in this work.

8. Hansen, *op cit.*, 38.

9. Bruce Catton, *The Centennial History of the Civil War*, *op cit.*, Vol. 2, 38.

10. Grant, *op cit.*, 101.

11. Catton, *The Centennial History of the Civil War, op cit.*, vol. 2., 156-157.

12. Maj. Gen. Lewis Wallace, "It was not possible for brave men to endure more," in Bradford, *op cit.*, 72-75.

13. Grant, *op cit.*, 1, 312-313.

14. REQ, February 18, 1862; Richmond *Examiner*, February 19, 1862, hereafter RE.

15. C. Vann Woodward, *Mary Chesnut's Civil War* (New Haven, CT: Yale University Press, 1981), 293.

16. Samuel R. Curtis to his brother, dated February 25, 1862, in the Samuel Ryan Curtis Letters, Huntington, WV Library.

17. Thomas B. Allen, *The Blue and the Gray* (Washington, D.C.: National Geographic Society, 1992), 166-167; Steven L. Walker & Matti P. Majorin, *Civil War Parks: The Battlefields of Freedom* (Scottsdale, AZ: Camelback/Elan, 1991), 20.

18. David Ash, written March 11, 1862 to Eliza (no last name known), Collection of the Department of the Army, U.S. Army Military History Institute, Carlisle Barracks, PA.

19. Samuel R. Curtis, to his brother, dated March 13, 1862, *op cit.*

Chapter 4: Prince John and the Little Napoleon

1. Douglas Southall Freeman, *Lee's Lieutenants* (New York: Charles Scribner's Sons, 1942), Vol. 1, 19.

2. RD, July 4, 1861.

3. Quoted in Warren W. Hassler, Jr., *General George B. McClellan: Shield of the Union* (Baton Rouge: Louisiana State University Press, 1957), xv.

4. OR, Ser. 3, Vol. 1, 389-388.

5. Gen. George B. McClellan, quoted in John Bartlett, Justin Kaplan, gen. ed., *Bartlett's Familiar Quotations* (Boston: Little, Brown & Co., 1992), 16th edition, 507. Later, Ethelind Beers wrote a poem using this phrase and it, in turn, became a song often sung by Union troops.

6. George B. McClellan, written July 27, 30, Aug. 9, Oct. 31, 1861, to his wife Ellen Marcy McClellan, McClellan Papers, Library of Congress. Originals of these letters no longer exist; rather, these are extracts copied by McClellan himself after the war. Just how much, if any, editing he did is unknown. Before the war, Ellen Marcy was widely courted. A.P. Hill once proposed marriage to her, but she rejected him in favor of his West Point roommate, George McClellan. Hill, of course, went on to become a lieutenant general in the Confederate army; several times McClellan and Hill faced each other across the battle lines.

7. Attributed in Bartlett, *op cit.*, 449.

8. James I. Robertson, Jr., *Civil War Sites in Virginia: A Tour Guide* (Charlottesville: University of Virginia Press, 1982), 67.

9. Maj. Gen. George B. McClellan to his wife, Ellen Marcy McClellan, April 8, 1862, McClellan papers, *op cit.*

10. Rod Gragg, *Civil War Quiz and Fact Book* (New York: Harper & Row, 1985), 16.

11. Pvt. Edward M. Burruss to his father, written April 16, 1862 outside Richmond, Burruss Papers, Hill Library, Louisiana State University, Baton Rouge.

12. Thomas Cooper deLeon, *Four Years in Rebel Capitals* (New York: Crowell, Collier, 1962 [reprint], 220.

13. Putnam, *op cit*, 119-120.

14. Quoted by Geoffrey C. Ward in his foreword to Robert Hunt Rhodes, ed., *All For the Union: The Civil War Diary and Letters of Elisha Hunt Rhodes* (Lincoln, RI, A. Mowbray, 1985), *vii.*

15. Johnston to Robert E. Lee, written April 22, 1862. OR, Ser. 1, Vol. 11, pt. 3, 456.

16. For an exceptional account of McClellan's Peninsula Campaign, see Stephen W. Sears' *To the Gates of Richmond: The Peninsula Campaign* (New York: Tichnor & Fields, 1992).

17. Rhodes, *op cit.*, 61-62, 64. The *Teazer* was later captured by Union forces while it sailed a balloon, one of the Confederacy's few, to spy on Federal positions.

18. McPherson, *op cit.*, 462-463.

19. Joseph P. Cullem, *Richmond Battlefields* (Washington, D.C.: National Park Service Handbook, Government Printing Office, 1961), 5.

20. Cullen, *Richmond Battlefields, op cit.*, 6.

21. OR, Ser. 1., Vol. 4, 570-573.

22. Rhodes, *op cit.*, 67-68

23. Quoted in Bartlett, *op cit.*, 431.

War in the West II: Shiloh, Bloody Shiloh

1. Henry W. Halleck to U.S. Grant, OR, March 4, 1862, 319n. See also, U.S. Grant in "Regiments broke at the first fire," in Bradford, *op cit.*, 84.

2. Grant, ibid.

3. McFeely, *op cit.*, 104.

4. Quoted in T. Harry Williams, *Lincoln and His Generals* (New York: Alfred A. Knopf, 1952), 225-226. As entertaining and as often repeated as this statement is, as a quote it cannot be verified. One historian even claims it originated with Britain's King George III, speaking about General Wolfe.

5. U.S. Grant, in Bradford, *op cit.*, 85.

6. Quoted by Ephraim C. Dawses in *The Battle of Shiloh*, papers of the Military Historical Society of Massachusetts, Vol. 7, 115-116.

7. Quoted in John K. Duke, *History of the 53rd Ohio Volunteer Infantry* (Portsmouth, OH, 1900), 41.

8. Albert Sidney Johnston to soldiers of the Army of Mississippi, quoted in Shelby Foote, *The Civil War: A Narrative*, 3 vols. (New York: Random House, 1954-1978), Vol. 1, 327.

9. OR, Ser. 1, Vol. 1, pt. 1, 396-397.

10. Gragg, *op cit.*, 116.

11. Grant to Halleck, April 5, 1862, OR, Ser. 1, Vol. 10, pt. 1, 89.

12. *Ibid.*

13. OR, Ser. 1, Vol. 10, pt. 1, 397.

14. John St. John, written to his father on April 14, 1862; Bela St. John Papers, Library of Congress, Washington, D.C. The author is reminded of one early edition of a Charleston, S.C., cookbook which listed ingredients for a special punch. In addition to varieties of whiskey, club soda, and fruit drinks, the recipe called for "1 pound gunpowder." It was a typographical error corrected in a later edition; it was supposed to have read "1 pound gunpowder tea." I have often wondered whether anyone followed the original recipe, and, if so, what were the results?

15. Gragg, *op cit.*, 63. There are other candidates for the sobriquet "Johnny Shiloh," but John Clem of the 22nd Michigan seems to have the best credentials.

16. Hansen, *op cit.*, 135.

17. William Preston Johnston, *The Life of General Albert Sidney Johnston* (New York, 1878), 613-615, as quoted in Bruce

Catton, *The Centennial History of the Civil War*, vol. 2, *op cit.*, 235.

18. Hansen, *op cit.*

19. Bruce Catton, *Grant Moves South* (Garden City, N.Y.: Doubleday, 1960), 241

20. Robert S. Henry, *First with the Most: Nathan Bedford Forrest* (Indianapolis, Bobbs-Merrill, 1944), 79.

21. Andrew Devilbliss to Mary (last name unknown), written April 16, 1862; in the Civil War Miscellaneous Series, Tulane University, New Orleans. LA.

22. Oliver Wendell Holmes, Jr., *Touched with Fire: Civil War Letters and Diary of Oliver Wendell Holmes, Jr., 1861-1864*, ed. Mark DeWolfe Howe (Cambridge: Harvard University Press, 1946), 45.

Chapter 5: Phenomenally Mismanaged

1. Jones, *op cit.*, May 23, 1862.

2. Mary Andrews West to "Clara," last name unknown but probably her sister, April 12, 1865, West letterbook, Virginia Historical Society, Richmond.

3. Quoted in Bill, *op cit.*, 95.

4. Jones, *op cit.*, May 26, 1861.

5. *Ibid.*, May 29, 1862.

6. Edward P. Alexander quoted in Clifford Dowdey, *The Seven Days: The Emergence of Robert E. Lee* (New York: Alfred Knopf, 1964), 4.

7. Constance Cary Harrison, "The Vast Pity of It," in Bradford, *op cit.*, 274. Constance and her cousin, Hetty, were among the most popular of all Richmond young ladies during the siege. In 1867, she married Burton Norvell Harrison, not of the Virginia Harrisons (as in Benjamin and William Henry) but from New Orleans. He'd been an assistant professor at the University of Mississippi and replaced Robert Josselyn as Jefferson Davis's private secretary in 1861. After the war, Constance wrote more than a dozen books, including, in 1911, a memoir of the war years, *Recollections Grave and Gay*. Cousin Hetty had had to move to Richmond from Baltimore after waving a Confederate flag at Union troops.

8. David A. Weisiger to his wife, June 2, 1862, Weisiger family letterbook, Virginia Historical Society, Richmond.

9. Jones, *op cit.*, June 15, 1862.

10. Quoted in Greene and Gallagher, *National Geographic Guide to the Civil War Battlefield Parks* (Washington, D.C: The National Geographic Society, 1992), 129.

11. *Ibid.*, 130

12. Quoted in Sears, *op cit.*, 314.

13. Quoted in Greene & Gallagher, *op cit.*, 130-131.

14. D. H. Hill, in Johnson & Buel, *op cit.*, Vol. 2, 394. Malvern Hill is just one of many Civil War sites under attack once more, in this case by a sand and gravel company given permission by

the Henrico County, VA, Board of Zoning Appeals to mine the area adjacent to the Richmond National Battlefield Park.

15. Catton, *The Centennial History of the Civil War, op cit.*, Vol 2, 326.

16. Roy C. Basler, ed., *The Collected Works of Abraham Lincoln, op cit.*, Vol. 5, 336-337.

17. *Ibid.*, 388-389.

18. Johnson & McLaughlin, *op cit.*, 64; Gragg, *op cit.*, 21; John Gibbon, *Personal Recollections of the Civil War*, quoted in McPherson, *op cit.*, 537.

19. Thomas M. Anderson, in Johnson & Buel, *Battles and Leaders*, Vol. 2, 656n. Anderson's comment is in the original four-volume set of the reminiscences but is not included in Bradford's one-volume edited version published in 1956.

20. Quoted in McPherson, *op cit.*, 348.

Chapter 6: Somebody's Darling

1. Gragg, *op cit.*, 80.

2. Jones, *op cit.*, June 24, 1862.

3. Quoted in Putnam, *op cit.*, 153-154.

4. *Ibid.*, 150.

5. *Ibid.*, 151.

6. Constance Cary Harrison, in Bradford, *op cit.*, 276.

7. Quoted in Woodward, *op cit.*, 601.

8. *Ibid.*, 602.

9. Putnam, *op cit.*, 146.

10. Jones, *op cit.*, June 26, 1862.

War in the West III: Stones River

1. McPherson, *op cit.*, 420.

2. Woodward, *op cit.*, 329-332, emphasis hers.

3. *Ibid*, 419.

4. Gragg, *op cit.*, 138.

5. McPherson, *op cit.*, 419.

6. Hansen, *op cit.*, 163.

7. McPherson, *op cit.*, 552.

8. Allen, *op cit.*, 191.

9. Quoted in Johnson & McLaughlin, *op cit.*, 46.

10. McFeely, *op cit.*, 128-129.

11. Hansen, *op cit.*, 233-235.

12. Reid Mitchell, *Civil War Soldiers: Their Expectations and Their Experiences* New York: Viking Press, 1988), 109, reprinted Harper Touchstone Books, 1989; McPherson, *op cit.*, 579.

13. Gragg, *op cit.*, 29.; McPherson, *op cit.*, 580.

14. McPherson, *op cit.*, 580; John MacDonald, *Great Battles of the Civil War* (New York: Macmillan, 1988), 184.

15. Quoted in Greene and Gallagher, *op cit.*, 108.

16. Quoted in Foot, *Civil War, op cit.*, Vol 2, 87.

17. Edward Wood to his brother, Will, written January 12, 1863; Lewis Leigh Collection, Department of the Army, U.S. Army Military Institute, Carlisle Barracks, PA.

18. McPherson, *op cit.*, 580.

19. Gragg, *op cit.*, 42.

20. McPherson, *op cit.*, 580.

21. Quoted in W. J. Worsham, *The Old Nineteenth Tennessee C.S.A.* (Knoxville, TN: Press of the Paragon Printing Co., 1902), 100. Worsham was chief musician of his regiment.

22, McPherson, *op cit.*, 582.

23. Mrs. L. D. Whitson, *Gilbert St. Maurice* (Nashville: Tavel, Eastman and Howell, 1874), p. 117, quoted in Bob Womack , *Call Forth the Mighty Men* (Bessemer, AL: Colonial Press, 1987), 216.

Chapter 7: A Thief and Harlot Riot

1. Quoted in Hansen, *op cit.*, 278.

2. Quoted by James Longstreet in "The Battle of Fredericksburg," Johnson & Buel, *op cit.*, Vol. 3, 79.

3. Quoted by Douglas Southall Freeman, *R. E. Lee: A Biography*, 4 vols. (New York: Charles Scribner's Sons, 1934-1935), Vol. 2, 462.

4. Jones, *op cit.*, January 1, 1863.

5. Johnson & Buel, *op cit.*, Vol. 6, 28-30.

6. See Reid Mitchell, *Civil War Soldiers: Their Expectations and Their Experiences* (New York: Touchstone, 1989 [reprint], 126-127.

7. Quoted in Hansen, *op cit.*, 294.

8. Quoted in T. Harry Williams, *Lincoln and His Generals* (New York: Alfred A. Knopf, 1952), 232.

9. OR, Ser. 1, Vol. 25, pt. 1, 171.

10. Gen. Darius Couch, "The Chancellorsville Campaign," Johnson & Buel, *op cit.*, Vol. 3, 161.

11. Quoted in Hansen, *op cit.*, 308.

12. As reported by Jackson's aide, Lieutenant Joseph F.

Morrison, quoted in Douglas Southall Freeman, Lee's Lieutenants, *op cit.*, Vol. 2, 567.

13. Quoted in Hansen, *op cit.*, 310.

14. Constance Cary Harrison, *Recollections Grave and Gay* (New York: Charles Scribner's Sons, 1911), 141.

15. Bill, *op cit.*, 173-174. Note: The Richmond *Dispatch* and the Richmond *Daily Dispatch* were printed separately. In 1861, the newspaper's masthead read, "The Daily Dispatch is served to subscribers at six and a quarter cents per week. . . . The Semi-Weekly Dispatch is issued every Tuesday and Friday. . . . The Weekly Dispatch is issued every Friday." All are justly called The "Dispatch," and, as used here, the terms daily, weekly, semi-weekly, or even simply The "Dispatch," are meant solely to clarify which issue is mentioned, in as much as on some days (Fridays, for example) three separate issues would be printed.

16. RD, January 1, 1861; Jones *op cit.*, November 10, 1864; R*E*, October 30, 1864.

17. Jones, *op cit.*, October 30, 1864.

18. REQ, January 28, 1864.

19. Richmond *Sentinel*, March 12, 1863, hereafter RS.

20. RD, December 30, 1888.

21. Jones, *op cit.*, April 1, 1863.

22. Putnam, *op cit.*, 208.

23. Sara Agnes Pryor (Mrs. Roger Pryor), *Reminiscences of Peace and War* (New York: Macmillan & Co., 1905), 238. Roger Pryor was a U.S. congressman but resigned in 1861 to enter the Confederate army. He led the 3rd Virginia Infantry at the Battle of Williamsburg, in the Seven Days, at Second Manassas, and at Antietam (Sharpsburg). He was captured in November 1864 and held at Fort Lafayette. After the war, Sara recounted their experiences.

24. *Ibid.*

25. Jones, *op cit.*, April 2, 1863.

26. Quoted in Hudson Strode, *Jefferson Davis: Confederate President* (New York: Harcourt, Brace & World, 1904-1905), 381.

27. Putnam, *op cit.*, 209.

28. RD, December 3, 1888.

29. RE, April 3, 1863.

30. Putnam, *op cit.*, 208.

31. For a good report on the Richmond Bread Riot, see Michael B. Chessum in the *Virginia Magazine of History and Biography*, Vol. 92, No. 2, April 1984, 131-175. Bruce Catton offers an opposing view in *The Centennial History of the Civil War*, Vol. 2, *op cit.*, 100-101.

32. Catton, *The Centennial History of the Civil War*, *op cit.*, Vol.2, 100.

33. Quoted in Eric Foner, "The South's Inner Civil War," *American Heritage*, March 1989, 52.

34. Jones, *op cit.*, April 3, 1863.

35. RD, April 3, 1863.

36. RE, April 4, 1863.

37. Putnam, *op cit.*, 210.

38. Quoted in Chessum, *op cit.*, 210.

39. RD, December 30, 1888.

40. Jones, *op cit.*, April 2, 1863.

Chapter 8: The Greatest Extortioners

1. Putnam, *op cit.*, 210-211.

2. RD, June 16, 1864.

3. Alfred Hoyt Bill, *The Beleaguered City: Richmond, 1861-1865* (New York: Alfred A. Knopf, 1946), 14-15.

4. Jones, *op cit.*, December 22, 1863.

5. Putnam, *op cit.*, 251, 345.

6. Jones, *op cit.*, December 22, 1863.

7. West, *op cit.*, April 12, 1865.

8. Edward Alfriend, *Southern Historical Society Papers* (Richmond: Southern Historical Society, 1891), Vol. 19, 380.

9. Jones, *op cit.*, November 14, 1863; Diary of Richard Lancelot Maury, March 8, 1865, in the Virginia Historical Society Library, Richmond.

10. Putnam, *op cit.*, 303.

11. Bill, *op cit.*, 187.

12. Alfriend, *op cit.*, 380-386.

13. Bill, *op cit., 188.*

14. Putnam, *op cit.*, 303.

15. Jones, *op cit.*, August 17, 1863.

16. *Ibid.*

17. Jones, *op cit.*, February 22, 1865.

18. Jones, *op cit.*, April 2, 1864.

19. Jones, *op cit.*, October 6, 1862.

20. Jones, *op cit.*, August 4, 1863; August 6, 1863; October 22, 1863; May 22, 1865.

21. Alfriend, *op cit.*, 381.

22. Jones, *op cit.*, May 24, 1864.

23. Robert B. Goodyear, written at a U.S. convalescent camp in Virginia, May 30, 1863, Collection of the Department of the Army, U.S. Army Military History Institute, Carlisle Barracks, PA.

24. Henry B. McClellan, *The Life, Character and Campaigns of Major-Gen. J. E. B. Stuart*, An address before the Virginia Division of the Army of Northern Virginia in Richmond, 1880.

25. Quoted in Bruce Catton, *Lee's Lieutenants, op cit.*, Vol. 3, 8-9.

26. W. W. Blackford, unpublished memoirs, Reminiscences of the War, 1861-1865, in the possession of the Blackford family, Richmond, VA.

27. RE, June 12, 1863.

28. RS, June 21, 1863; June 25, 1863.

29. William Miller Owen, *In Camp and Battle with the Washington Artillery of New Orleans* (Boston: 1885), 240.

Chapter 9: Butchers, Quacks, and Claude Minié

1. Quoted in Peter Parish, *The American Civil War* (New York: 1975), 147.

2. *Ibid.*

3. Quoted in Samuel Eliot Morison, *The Oxford History of the American People* (New York: Oxford University Press, 1965), 624, emphasis added.

4. Council, 508f.

5. *National Parks Service Bulletin* (Washington, D.C.: Government Printing Office), ND, NP.

6. Phoebe Yates Pember & Bell Irwin Wiley, ed., *A Southern Woman's Story: Life in Confederate Richmond* (Jackson, TN: McCowat-Mercer Press, 1959), 15, reprint, first published in 1879.

7. Told in Robert W. Waitt, Jr., *Confederate Military Hospitals in Richmond* (Richmond: Civil War Centennial Commission, Official Publication No. 22, 1964), 10.

8. *Ibid.*,14.

9. Catton, *The Civil War* (New York: The Fairfax Press, 1980), 164, reprint from *The American Heritage*. Also, see editor Bell Wiley's comment in Phoebe Yates Pember's *A Southern Woman's Story: Life In Confederate Richmond*. He quotes reports filed in the National Archives of officers of the day at Richmond's Chimborazo Hospital No. 2, from October 17, 1864-March 28, 1865.

10. John Pierson to his wife, written June 10 (year unknown), in the John Pierson Letters, Schoff Collection, Clements Library, University of Michigan, Ann Arbor.

11. See Woodrow Borah and Sherburne F. Cook, "Conquest and Population: A Demographic approach to Mexican History," *American Philosophical Society, Proceedings* (Philadelphia, PA: American Philosophical Society, 1969), 182. For the southeastern and northeastern portions of the United States see John R. Swanton, "The Indians of the Southeastern United States," *Smithsonian Institution, Bureau of American Ethnology,*

Bulletin (Washington, D.C.: Government Printing Office, 1946), #137, 11; and James B. Griffin, "The Northeast Woodlands Area," in Jesse D. Jennings and Edward Norbeck, eds., *Prehistoric Man in the New World* (Chicago: University of Chicago Press, 1964), 256.

12. Council, 241n.

13. Paul E. Steiner, *Disease in the Civil War* (Philadelphia, PA: Whitmore Publishing, 1968), 10-11.

14. Luther L. Swank to his sister Katie, August 25, 1864, Swank family papers, Virginia State Library, Richmond.

15. *Ibid.*, October 11, 1864.

16. Pember & Wiley, *op cit.*, 59.

War in the West IV: Vicksburg

1. McPherson, *op cit.*, 629.

2. McFeely, *op cit.*, 130-131; Thomas B. Allen, *op cit.*, 195.

3. Quoted in Bruce Catton, *Grant Moves South* (Garden City, NY: Doubleday & Co., 1960), 438, emphasis added.

4. Allen, *op cit.*, 206n.

5. *Ibid.*, 195.

6. *Ibid.*

7. Numa Barned, written December 27, 1862 to Annie Barned, Numa Barned Letters, Schoff Collection, Clements Library, University of Michigan, Ann Arbor.

8. James K. Newton, in *A Wisconsin Boy in Dixie: The Selected Letters of James K. Newton*, Stephen E. Ambrose, ed. (Madison: University of Wisconsin, 1961), 72.

9. Numa Barned, *op cit.*

10. Allen, *op cit.*

11. *Ibid.*

12. Quoted in Johnson & McLaughlin, *op cit.*, 120.

13. Quoted in McPherson, *op cit.*, 636.

14. Gragg, *op cit.*, 116.

Chapter 10: The Saddest Day

1. RE, July 7, 1863.

2. Lt. John Townsend Ketchem, written at Frederick, Maryland., July 8, 1863, to his mother, quoted by A. J. H. Dugann, ed., *Fighting Quakers: A True Story of the War For Our Union*, (Philadelphia: J. P. Robens, 1866), 186.

3. Quoted in Johnson & McLaughlin, *op cit.*, 87.

4. New York *Times*, July 6, 1863.

5. Quoted in Hansen, *op cit.*, 382.

6. Quoted in Hansen, *op cit.*, 387.

7. "Annals of the War, Written by Leading Participants North and South" in the Philadelphia *Weekly*, written in 1878. There now exist reprints from these articles in the Princeton University Library. See also Buel & Johnson, *op cit.*, Vol. 3, 343, for a slightly different version of Longstreet's claimed conversation with Lee.

8. Quoted in "Pickett's Division Swept Out of the Wood," in Bradford, *op cit.*, 393.

9. *Ibid.*, 395.

10. *Ibid.*

11. Quoted in Hansen, *op cit.*, 395.

12. Lt. Col. A. J. L. Fremantle, *Three Months in the Southern States, April-June, 1863* (New York: J. Brandon, 1864), 265-266, reprinted 1991, University of Nebraska Press.

13. Fremantle, *op cit.*, 266.

14. Quoted in Lawless, *op cit.*, 231. In 1870, shortly before Lee's death, Pickett and Col. John S. Mosby (the Gray Ghost who replaced Stuart) visited Robert E. Lee in Richmond. After the three spoke, Pickett and Mosby left Lee and, outside, Pickett said, "That old man. . .had my troops massacred at Gettysburg." Mosby reminded Pickett, "Well, it made you famous." Famous or not, Pickett ended his life as an insurance salesman in Norfolk.

15. Quoted in Foote, *op cit.*, Vol. 2, 167-168; see also Fremantle, *op cit.*, 269.

16. Fremantle, *op cit.*, 271.

17. Freeman Cleaves, *Meade of Gettysburg* (Norman, OK: The University of Oklahoma Press, 1960), 172.

18. Rhodes, *op cit.*, 117.

19. *Ibid.*

20. Florence McCarthy, written in Williamsport, MD, July 10, 1863, to his sister. McCarthy Family Papers, Virginia Historical Society, Richmond.

War in the West V: Chickamauga and Chattanooga

1. Robert Self Henry, *op cit.*, 100.

2. See Peter Andrews, "The Rock of Chickamauga" in Stephen W. Sears, ed., *The Civil War: The Best of American Heritage* (New York: American Heritage Books, 1991), 206-221.

3. *Ibid.*; Joseph S. Fullerton's "The Army of the Cumberland at Chattanooga," in Buell & Johnson, *op cit.*, Vol. 3, 725; and James A. Connolly, & Paul M. Angle, ed., *Three Years in the Army of the Cumberland* (Bloomington: University of Indiana Press, 1959), 158.

4. Gen. Gordon Granger, quoted in Hansen, *op cit.*, 474.

5. OR, Ser. 1, Vol. 31, pt. 2, 666.

6. *Ibid.*

7. See *The Lincolnian*, Vol. 10, No. 3, January-February 1992. Lincoln scholar Lloyd Ostendorf says the sixth copy has been tested by several handwriting experts and other analysts and that it appears to be the draft of the Gettysburg Address Lincoln sent to his host at the dedication ceremonies, Judge David Wills.

Chapter 11: Inflation, Croakers, and Tunnels

1. Woodward, *op cit.*, 493.

2. *Southern Punch*, Richmond, VA, November 14, 1863.

3. Richard J. Sommers, *Richmond Redeemed: The Siege of Petersburg* (New York: Doubleday, 1981).

4. RD, June 17, 1864.

5. Levi E. Kent Diary, February 14, 1862, in the Schoff Collection, Clements Library, University of Michigan.

6. Gragg, *op cit.*, 71.

7. Henry Pleasants, Jr., *The Tragedy of the Crater* (Boston: Christopher Publishing House, 1938), 32.

8. Maj. William H. Powell, "All In the Crater Who Could Hang On," in Bradford, *op cit.*, 562.

9. OR, Vol. 40, pt. 1, 753.

10. Petersburg *Dispatch*, July 31, 1864.

11. RW, August 2, 1864.

12. Pember & Wiley, *op cit.*, 105-106.

War in the West VI: Atlanta

1. Quoted in Johnson & McLaughlin, *op cit.*, 120.

2. Quoted in McPherson, *op cit.*, 755.

3. Quoted in Hansen, *op cit.*, 440.

4. Woodward, *op cit.*, 642.

5. *Ibid.*, 648.

6. Jones, *op cit.*, September 3, 1864.

7. *Ibid.*

Chapter 12: Rusty, Dilapidated, and War Worn

1. Robert Beverley Munford, Jr., *Richmond Homes and Memories* (Richmond: Garrett & Massie, 1936), 220.

2. George C. Eggleston, *A Rebel's Recollections* (Bloomington: Indiana University Press, 1959), 220-222.

3. Putnam, *op cit.*, 270.

4. REQ, December 4, 1863; November 4, 1864.

5. *Ibid.*, February 5, 1864.

6. Putnam, *op cit.*, 314-315.

7. *Ibid.*

8. *Ibid.*, 350.

9. *U.S. Census Report, 1860* (Washington, D.C.: Government Printing Office, 1860), NP.

10. RD, July 9, 1864.

11. Louis H. Manarin & Robert W. Waitt, Jr., eds., *Richmond At War: The Minutes of the City Council 1861-1865* (Chapel Hill: Univ. of N. C. Press, 1966), 508*f*, hereafter Council.

12. Putnam, *op cit.*, 360.

Chapter 13: Oh, Lord, How Long, How Long?

1. Henry Morrison, written near Spotsylvania, Virginia, to his aunt, May 5, 1864, Collection of the Department of the Army, U.S. Army Military History Institute, Carlisle Barracks, PA.

2. Horace Porter, *Campaigning With Grant* (New York: The Century Co., 1897), 69-70.

3. Quoted in Foote, *op cit.*, Vol. 3, 186.

4. See Foote, *op cit.*, 146-251, for a more complete accounting of the Battle of the Wilderness.

5. Philip H. Powers to his wife, written from Spotsylvania, May 15, 1864, Leigh Collection, Virginia Historical Society, Richmond.

6. *Southern Historical Society Papers*, 49 vols. (Richmond: 1876-1944), Vol. 7, 108.

7. Bill, *op cit.*, 216.

8. Henry B. McClellan, *The Life and Campaigns of Maj.-Gen. J. E. B. Stuart* (Richmond: 1882), 416. McClellan had never seen the flag before, but after Stuart's death he found it in his dead leader's hat "stained with the sweat of his brow."

9. McClellan, *op cit.*, 416-417. The spurs were passed on to Lee's grandson, William Fizhugh Lee Simpson, who died in France in 1917 while serving under Gen. John J. "Blackjack" Pershing. They were since lost. The sword, is a different matter. In 1973, a sword turned up in a Deland, Florida antique shop with the inscription: "J. E. B. Stuart From A. S. Brown." Historians agree this sword was owned by Stuart but aren't certain if it is *the* sword in question. See George H. Tucker, "Up To Its Hilt In History," from one of his newspaper columns, "Tidewater Landfalls," Norfolk *Virginian-Pilot*, January 10, 1973.

10. Jones, *op cit.*, May 12, 1864.

11. Putnam, *op cit.*, 263.

12. Quoted in Joseph P. Cullen *Where a Hundred Thousand Fell: The Battles of Fredericksburg, Chancellorsville, the Wilderness, and Spotsylvania Court House* (Washington, D.C.: National Parks Service Historical Handbook, Government Printing Office, 1966), 52-53.

13. Eugene Blackford, written to his sister, "in the line of battle near Spotsylvania C.H., Va, 14th May, 1864," in the Lewis Leigh Collection, Department of the Army, U.S. Army Military History Institute, Carlisle Barracks, PA.

14. Jones, *op cit.*, May 21, 1864; May 22, 1864.

15. Quoted in A. A. and Mary Hoehling, *The Day Richmond Died* (San Diego, Ca.: A. S. Barned, 1981), 48.

16. OR, Ser. 1, Vol. 36, pt. 3, 206.

17. Quoted in Joseph P. Cullen, *Richmond Battlefields* (Washington, D.C.: National Park Service Historical Handbook, Government Printing Office, 1961), Series 33, 34.

18. U. S. Grant and E. B. Long, eds., *Personal Memoirs of U. S. Grant* (New York: DeCapo, 1982), 444-445.

19. Cullen, *Richmond Battlefields, op cit.*, 30.

20. Grant & Long, *op cit.*, 445.

21. Foote, *op cit.*, 295.

22. Grant & Long, *op cit.*, 446.

23. *Ibid.*, 447n.

24. RW, August 4, 1864.

25. Jones, *op cit.*, August 21, 1864.

26. Putnam, *op cit.*, 319.

27. RW, August 3, 1864.

28. *Ibid.*, August 2, 1864.

29. Jones, *op cit.*, August 31, 1864.

30. Alexander Gustavus Brown to his wife, Fannie A. Cooksey Brown, written at Petersburg, August 29, 1864, Brown Family Papers, Virginia Historical Society Library, Richmond.

31. *Ibid.*, September 6, 1864.

32. Jones, *op cit.*, September 14, 1864

33. *Ibid.*, October 8, 1864, emphasis his.

34. *Ibid.*, October 4, 1864.

35. RD, July 22, 1863.

36. Council, 201, 506-507.

37. Jones, *op cit.*, September 11, 1864.

38. *Ibid.*, September 12, 1864.

39. RD, October 15, 1864.

40. Woodward, *op cit.*, 648.

41. RS, October 1, 1864.

42. G. S. Magruder to his sister, Eva Magruder DeJarnett, written at Hamilton's Crossing, September 18, 1864, Magruder Family Letters, Virginia State Library, Richmond.

43. RE, October 4, 1864.

44. *Ibid.*, October 7, 1864.

45. *Ibid.*, October 10, 1864.

46. Jones, *op cit.*, October 13, 1864.

47. *Ibid.*, October 15, 1864, emphasis his.

War in the West VII: March to the Sea

1. Gragg, *op cit.*, 116.

2. New York *Tribune*, November 22, 1864.

3. RW, December 26, 1864. The same issue carried a notice for "Large Sale of Slaves." Fifty slaves would be sold on January 4; obviously, Lincoln's Emancipation Proclamation was having no effect in Richmond.

4. Johnson & McLaughlin, *op cit.*, 124.

Chapter 14: Libby and the Biggest Yankee

1. RS, October 1, 1864.

2. *Ibid.*, October 3, 1864.

3. Alexander Brown to Fannie, August 31, 1864, Brown Family papers, *op. cit.*

4. *Ibid.*, September 6, 1864.

5. Quoted in Burke Davis, *The Long Surrender* (New York: Random House, 1985), 5-6.

6. Luther Swank to his sister, Katie, October 22, 1864, Swank Family Papers, *op cit.*

7. *Ibid.*, November 19, 1864.

8. Jones, *op cit.*, October 2, 1864.

9. REQ, October 3, 1864.

10. Col. William Powell, written in Libby Prison, Richmond, in 1863; letter in collection of the Chicago Historical Society, Chicago.

11. Col. Frederick Bartleston, written in Libby Prison, Richmond; to his wife, Kate, February 26, 1864, in Margaret W. Peelle, ed., *Letters from Libby Prison* (New York: Greenwich Book Publishers, 1956), 186-187.

12. McPherson, *op cit.*, 802.

13. Richard M. Lee, *General Lee's City* (McLean, VA: EPM Publications, 1987), 99-100.

14. Katherine M. Jones, *Ladies of Richmond-Confederate Capital* (New York: Bobbs-Merrill Co., 1962), 221.

15. Bloomington (Indiana) *Republican*, July 13, 1861.

16. Indianapolis *Journal*, August 16, 1861.

17. Lee, *op cit.*, 109.

Chapter 15: With Saddened Mien

1. REQ, October 4, 1864.

2. *Ibid.*

3. Hoehling and Hoehling, *op cit.*, 16.

4. Jones, *op cit.*, November 10, 1864.

5. *Ibid.*, December 1, 1864.

6. *Ibid.*, December 2, 1864.

7. RD, October 15, 1864.

8. RE, January 3, 1865.

9. RE, March 29, 1865.

10. Woodward, *op cit.*, 695.

11. RW, December 22, 1864.

12. RD, December 24, 1864.

13. RE, December 24, 1864.

14. Putnam, *op cit.*, 341.

15. Jones, *op cit.*, December 25, 1864.

16. Rhodes, *op cit.*, 202-203.

17. RD, December 31, 1864.

18. Jones, *op cit.*, December 31, 1864.

19. RD, December 31, 1864.

20. Rhodes, *op cit.*, 205.

21. *Ibid.*, January 1, 1865.

22. RD, December 31, 1864.

23. Mrs. Robert E. Lee to Mrs. William (M. E.) Boswell, January 2, 1865, written at Richmond, to The Wilderness, Columbia, Fluvanna County; Robert Young Conrad papers, Virginia Historical Society, *op cit.*

24. RQ, January 3, 1865.

25. RD, January 6, 1865.

26. Pember & Wiley, *op cit.*, 87.

27. *Ibid.*

28. Copy of the broadside in possession of the Museum of the Confederacy, Richmond, VA.

29. RE, January 2, 1865.

30. *Ibid.*

31. Putnam, *op cit.*, 341.

32. Quoted in Thomas, *op cit.*, 282.

33. Council, 543n.

34. RD, January 5, 1865.

35. RW, December 29, 1864.

36. *National Parks Service Bulletin* (Washington, D.C.: Government Printing Office, 1981), ND, NP.

37. Jones, *op cit.*, November 22, 1864; December 22, 1864; January 11, 1865; January 20, 1865; February 18, 1865.

38. RD, January 3, 1865.

39. Swank Family Papers, *op cit.*, January 29, 1865.

40. Col. Richard Lancelot Maury's diary, February 5, 1865, in the Virginia Historical Society Library, Richmond.

41. *Ibid.*, February 12, 1865.

42. Jones, *op cit.*, February 13, 1865.

43. *Ibid.*, January 27, 1865.

44. *Ibid.*

45. West letter, *op cit.*, April 12, 1865.

46. Maury diary, *op cit.*, February 9, 1865.

47. Jones, *op cit.*, March 21, 1865.

48. *Ibid.*, February 4, 1865, emphasis his.

49. Gragg, *op cit.*, 8.

50. RD, February 15, 1865.

51. RE, March 13, 1865.

52. Ella Lonn, *Desertion in the Civil War* (New York: The Century Co., 1928), 28.

53. Jones, op cit., October 12, 1864.

54. *Ibid.*, September 9, 1862.

55. *Ibid.*, September 23, 1863.

56. *Ibid.*, October 16, 1864, emphasis his.

57. Putnam, *op cit.*, 355.

58. James Bracy to Mary Bracy, written May 11, 1863; in the Confederate States of America Archives, Army-Miscellany, Officers and Soldiers Letters, Duke University, Durham, NC.

59. A song written by J. G. Daniel, Co. E., 30th Regiment, Georgia Volunteers, June 29, 1864; Daniel papers in the Emory University Library, Atlanta.

Chapter 16: Rumors of Peace and Sable Soldiers

1. Jones, *op cit.*, January 24, 1865, emphasis his; January 26, 1865; February 2, 1865.

2. Petersburg *Express*, February 4, 1865.

3. Maury diary, *op cit.*, February 5, 1865.

4. Jones, *op cit.*, January 29, 1865.

5. Maury diary, *op cit.*, March 8, 1865.

6. *Ibid.*, February 13, 1865.

7. *Ibid.*, February 25, 1865.

8. 2nd Lt. Luther Rice Mills to John Mills, written March 2, 1865, in the North Carolina Division of Archives and History, published in the *North Carolina Historical Review*, July 1927.

9. Jones, *op cit.*, January 2, 1865.

10. *Ibid.*, January 3, 1865.

11. RD, February 15, 1865; March 13, 1865.

12. Quoted in Mitchell, *op cit.*, 190.

13. Maury diary, *op cit.*, February 20, 1865, emphasis his; February 21, 1865.

14. Putnam, *op cit.*, 351.

15. Quoted in Jones, *op cit.*, January 20, 1865.

16. Putnam, *op cit.*, 351.

17. Lonn, *op cit.*, 30.

18. Maury diary, *op cit.*, February 16, 1865; February 20, 1865, emphasis his.

19. Jones, *op cit.*, February 24, 1865.

20. Maury diary, *op cit.*, February 20, 1865.

Chapter 17: The Last Confederate

1. Pember and Wiley, *op cit.*, 150.

2. William Murphy Brown to Ann Murphy Brown, March 2, 1865, Brown Family Papers, Virginia Historical Society, Richmond.

3. Maury diary, *op cit.*, March 4, 1865.

4. DeLeon, *op cit.*, 348.

5. Maury diary, *op cit.*, March 4, 1865.

6. Jones, *op cit.*, March 10, 1865.

7. Maury diary, *op cit.*, March 10, 1865.

8. RE, March 13, 1863.

9. Council, March 2, 1865.

10. Jones, *op cit.*, March 10, 1865.

11. *Ibid.*, March 14, 1865.

12. RW, March 29, 1865.

13. *Ibid.*

14. New York *Herald*, March 13, 1891.

15. *Ibid.*

16. Jones, *op cit.*, March 24, 1865.

17. *Ibid.*

18. RD, March 20, 1865.

19. Varina Howell Davis, *Jefferson Davis: A Memoir By His Wife* (New York: Balford, Co., 1890), 228.

20. *Ibid.*

21. West letter, *op cit.*

22. RS, March 24, 1865, emphasis theirs.

23. Maury diary, *op cit.*, March 23, 1865.

24. *Ibid.*, March 27, 1865.

25. Jones, *op cit.*, March 26, 1865; March 27, 1865.

26. Maury diary, *op cit.*, March 29, 1865.

27. G. A. Magruder, written March 29, 1865, at Hamilton's Crossing, to an unidentified cousin; Magruder Family Letters, *op cit.*

28. RW, March 29, 1865.

29. RE, March 30, 1865.

30. New York *Herald*, March 13, 1891.

31. Maury diary, *op cit.*, March 30, 1865.

32. Putnam, *op cit.*, 362.

33. Council, April 1, 1865.

34. Petersburg *Express*, March 31, 1865.

35. RD, December 3, 1888, a letter by R. T. W. Duke, dated April 25, 1887.

36. Putnam, *op cit.*, 362.

37. Gragg, *op cit.*, 96.

Chapter 18: The Yankees Are Coming

1. Jones, *op cit.*, April 2, 1865.

2. Quoted in Cullen, *Richmond Battlefields, op cit.*, 40.

3. Katherine M. Jones, *Ladies of Richmond-Confederate Capital* (New York: Bobs-Merrill, Co., 1962), 270.

4. Council, April 2, 1865.

5. RD, December 3, 1888; R. T. W. Duke letter written, April 25, 1887.

6. Jones, *op cit.*, April 2, 1865.

7. RW, April 3, 1865.

8. Quoted in Catton, *Grant Moves South, op cit.*, 279.

9. Bill, *op cit.*, 275.

10. Cullen, *Richmond Battlefields, op cit.*, 42.

11. J. W. Stebbins, written to his mother, April 3, 1865, outside Richmond, Lewis Leigh Collection of the Department of the Army, U.S. Army Military History Institute, Carlisle Barracks, PA, emphasis his.

12. Council, April 3, 1865.

13. Pember & Wiley, *op cit.*, 98.

14. Rhodes, *op cit.*, 227.

15. Council, April 3, 1865.

16. Quoted in Edward H. Ripley, "The Occupation of Richmond," in Military Order of the United States, New York Commandry, *Personal Recollections of the War of the Rebellion*, 3rd Series (New York: G. P. Putnam's Sons, 1907), 467.

17. Bill, *op cit., 275.*

18. Jones, *op cit.*, April 3, 1865.

19. RW, April 3, 1865.

20. Putnam, *op cit.*, 365.

21. Jones, *op cit.*, *April 3, 1865*

22. Jones, *op cit.*, April 4, 1865.

23. West letter, *op cit.*, April 12, 1865.

24. Pember & Wiley, *op cit.*, 98.

25. Julia D. Grant (Mrs. U. S. Grant) and John Y. Simon, ed., *Personal Memoirs of Julia Dent Grant* (New York: G. P. Putnam's Sons, 1975), 150.

26. Burke Davis, *To Appomattox—Nine Days in April 1865* (New York: Rinehart & Co., 1959), 183.

27. Jones, *op cit.*, April 5, 1865.

28. Abraham Lincoln to U. S. Grant, written April 7, 1865, at City Point, Chicago Historical Society, Chicago.

29. Jones, *op cit.*, April 4, 1865.

30. Douglas Southall Freeman, *R. L. Lee: A Biography* (New York: Charles Scribner's Sons, 1934-1935) Vol. 4, 84.

31. As recorded by Brevet Brig. Gen. Horace Porter in "Lee . . .facing Grant" in Bradford, *op cit.*, 603-610.

32. Freeman, Lee, *op cit.*, 120-123.

33. Porter, *op cit., 606.*

34. Rhodes, *op cit.*, 229-230.

35. James Coburn, written "on the road to Lynchburg, Virginia, April 10, 1865," in the Collection of the Department of the Army, U.S. Army Military History Institute, Carlisle Barracks, PA.

36. DeLeon, *op cit.*, 404.

37. Quoted in Noah Brooks, Herbert Mitgang, ed., *Washington, D.C. in Lincoln's Time: A Memoir of the Civil War Era by the Newspaperman Who Knew Lincoln Best* (Athens, GA: University of Georgia Press, 1958), 229.

Chapter 19: Damnyankees and Damnrebels

1. Putnam, *op cit.*, 388-389.

Epilogue: A Personal Afterthought

1. Quoted by McKenna, *op cit.*

Selected Bibliography

There is so much literature (good, bad, indifferent) on the Civil War that I doubt anyone could or perhaps should read it all. Most histories, however, virtually bypass Richmond. Certainly, there is little written about the people of Richmond during the war years, which is strange considering how much the people of Richmond wrote about themselves at the time.

Alfred Hoyt Bill's *The Beleaguered City: Richmond, 1861-1865* was written in 1946, and much has been learned about the city in the intervening fifty years; it still remains a worthy, if somewhat dry, account of the city's war time life. A. A. and Mary Hoehling's *The Day Richmond Died* is what is sometimes disparagingly called "popular history." Now, what's wrong with being popular? Theirs is a good report on the final days before Richmond surrendered. Its greatest fault is weak documentation. Burke Davis's *The Long Surrender* is another popular history, a readable account of Jefferson Davis's attempt to escape capture. It goes into some depth about Davis's efforts to have Robert E. Lee send his Army of Northern Virginia into the hills to fight a guerrilla war, efforts that Lee refused.

There are several good diaries and personal narratives written by full- or part-time residents of Richmond during the war. Mary Boykin Chesnut's is the best-known Civil War diary, having gone through several editions, versions, variations, and explanations. Her husband John was an aide to Jefferson Davis and Mary was a confidant of Varina Davis, but for those interested in Richmond at war's end, Chesnut's diary has little to offer; she wasn't there at the time.

Chesnut's counterpart as confidant was Thomas Cooper DeLeon, a long time friend of Jefferson Davis, but his *Four Years in Rebel Capitals* is virtually an apology for his friend.

Davis's wife Varina told her own story, or rather her husband's, but it was written twenty-five years after the war ended, and that raises questions of memory and editing. Naturally, Varina Davis is biased toward her husband.

Phoebe Yates Pember, in her *A Southern Woman's Story* as edited by Bell I. Wiley, gives much firsthand information on the hospital situation in Richmond, as well as the treatment of the wounded; both, by modern standards, were sad situations indeed. As a young and widowed Southern belle, Phoebe Pember adds information about the social life of Richmond as well.

Sallie A. Brock Putnam was just sixteen when the war began and when, we presume, she began gathering material for *Richmond During the War: Four Years of Personal Observations*. The first edition was published anonymously, crediting "A Richmond Lady" as the author. The reader is left to wonder if someone a bit older with more experience in living would have seen events during the siege with eyes not so innocent.

John Beauchamp Jones *was* older, but I still get the feeling of innocence (and, regretfully, antisemitism and racism) in his *A Rebel War Clerk's Diary At the Confederate States Capital*. Like Putnam's book, it saw a bit of postwar editing. In Jones' case, the author even edited in mistakes, in one instance dating a battle before it had occurred. However, there is no doubt that Jones was knowledgeable about the war, and as an author and former journalist, he was able to weed out much extraneous material. His diary (like Chesnut's, it comes in several versions) remains the fullest insofar as war time Richmond is concerned. Jones was born in Baltimore on March 6, 1810, and, with his parents, lived in Maryland, Kentucky, and Missouri. Very little is known about his early childhood or education. In 1840, he married Frances T. Custis, a distant relative of the Custis family, which, through his "connections" as Virginians say, made him kin to the Lees as well. John and Frances had two sons and two daughters. His career centered around the written word: newspaper editor and author (his *Wild West Scenes* was considered a classic western of its day). He also wrote an anti-secession novel entitled *Wild Southern Scenes*. Because of ties to the Whig party (he was editor of the *Madisonian*, the official party newspaper), he once held the consulate in Naples, Italy. When war became imminent, Jones volunteered for duty with the Confederate government. He served under Confederate Secretary of War Leroy Pope Walker and was in charge of passports. He volunteered in February 1862 to raise a local company for defense of Richmond and saw duty of about a month in a battery near the capital city, retiring as captain on April 23, 1863; he was later conscripted but never called to active duty. J. B. Jones died on February 4, 1866, of unknown causes, in Burlington, New Jersey. At the time, his book was just going to press.

There were several small, unpublished diaries written while Richmond was under siege. Colonel Richard Lancelot Maury's diary, now in the Virginia Historical Society in Richmond, is interesting, although it begins only a few months before the war's end. For any would-be historian, I might suggest research into Maury's life.

The Journal of the Congress of the Confederate States of America is a day-by-day account of the official business of a nation that almost was. The reader sees, albeit with 130-year hindsight, the problems the Confederacy faced or failed to face.

On a more local side, *Richmond At War: The Minutes of the City Council, 1861-1865* shows the researcher how the city government tried first to cope with being part of a rebelling nation and second with being that nation's capital. Richmond was the capital of Virginia for eighty-four years before the state seceded from the United States. It had experience with a major government but never had known problems such as it faced during four years under siege. For example, in 1850, the city's population was 27,570; by the end of the war, that number had grown to approximately 200,000, not many fewer than it is today. How do you cope with such a population rise?

Although it's doubtful a full edition of any Richmond wartime newspaper is extant, there are many microfilm-/microfisch partial editions available in various libraries. Another worthwhile project would be compiling, in one location, a complete edition of these newspapers. Even though those newspapers often neglected or chose not to report the nearby fighting, they remain a valuable historical source and interesting reading as well. For instance, in one 1864 newspaper, I ran across an ad for a home for rent on Franklin Street in the Fan District. It's hard to certain, but it seems to be the same location where I had an apartment in 1960. I hope the 1864 residents had better luck getting heat from the owners than did its 1960 tenants.

Manuscripts and Other Unpublished Material

Brown Family Papers, Virginia Historical Society, Richmond. These consist of several letters, most from Alexander Gustavus Brown to his wife Fannie. Others are from Alexander's brother, William Murphy Brown, to their mother. Alexander was a minister in Petersburg. William lived in Richmond.

Hunter Holmes McGuire Papers, Virginia Historical Society, Richmond. There are forty-four items, not all pertaining to the Civil War. McGuire was a Winchester, Virginia, physician at the beginning of the war and enlisted as a private. In May 1861, he was appointed chief surgeon to the post of Harper's Ferry under then Colonel Thomas J. Jackson. In a letter written after the war, as part of a recommendation for McGuire as professor of Richmond Medical College, Professor D. L. Dabney of the Union Theological Seminary at Richmond says of McGuire, "as his patron [Jackson] rose, he rose with him. . . . He has served through the war with zeal and devotion few ever show and now leaves it to earn his living by his own labors." McGuire amputated Stonewall Jackson's arm after Chancellorsville and was with Jackson when the general died. McGuire later became president of the American Medical Society, and McGuire Hospital in modern Richmond is named for him.

Magruder Family Letters, Virginia State Library, Richmond. These consist of three letters, the most interesting of which is dated March 29, 1865, from near Hamilton's Crossing, Virginia. It was written by G. S. Magruder (attached to the 13th Infantry Battalion of General Early's division) to his otherwise unidentified cousin. It tells of military operations and of a time he calls "one of the darkest days of our young Confederacy." An earlier letter from Magruder's sister Eva to their brother John Bankhead Magruder (who successfully stalled General McClellan's cautious push to capture Richmond) is of interest only in that, even in 1863, the primary topic was the high cost of living in Richmond. Another tells more of the food price situation.

Swank Family Papers, Virginia State Library, Richmond. Luther L. Swank was a hospital steward stationed near Chester, Virginia, just outside Richmond, attached to General Pickett's division. His letters to his sister ("Dear Katie," "Dear *Little sister Kate*,") quote prices in Richmond. Those prices were high, but in Swank's case, not so high as to prevent his eating well enough to put on weight during the siege.

West Letterbook, Virginia Historical Society Library, Richmond. Although this consists of only one letter, and that written after the fall of Richmond, it is extremely valuable. In it, Mary Andrews West details to her sister Clara the opposite side of the coin. It is the story of Mary and her husband Frank, both of whom opposed the war yet remained in Richmond. The letter, of course, is handwritten, and, because of the changes in color of ink, appears to have been written over a period of time, the writer not waiting until the final day to write and mail the letter. This, of course, is only speculation. Of the West family, perhaps the one who suffered most was the one who knew least about it, their newborn son Charlie. He was born small, stayed small and frail, a fact that modern nutritionists might easily claim was caused by a lack of adequate food in Richmond under siege.

Final Comment

This book was inspired by two sayings: "Like Grant took Richmond" and "Like Grant going through Richmond." I heard them so often I began the research that is here concluded. For the record, I can find no evidence that Ulysses S. Grant ever stepped foot in Richmond, much less "took" it in the truest sense of war. It was and remains Robert E. Lee's city.

Mike Wright   Chicago

Index